Heart Renovation

A Construction Guide
to Godly Character

Compiled by Katy Kauffman

Lighthouse Bible Studies

Heart Renovation

A Construction Guide
to Godly Character

Dedication

To the Faculty and Conferees of the
Blue Ridge Mountains Christian Writers Conference,
Thank you for your contributions
to our writing, our ministries, and our joy.

~ Katy

Contents

Weeks 1-2 Repairing the Hidden Problems of Character

Weeks 3-4 Constructing Character that Overcomes Life Issues

Week 5 Blueprints of Character: People in the Bible

Week 6 Christ: The Model of Godly Character

Weeks 7-8 Construction Zone: Helping Our Children to Grow in Godly Character

Weeks 9-10 Craftsman at Work: The Fruit of the Spirit

Weeks 11-12 Building in Blessing: The Beatitudes

Acknowledgements

A lot of love and hard work went into this project, and I would like to thank every author who contributed to it. We tackled a new adventure—our first Bible study compilation. Your insights and stories have made this book a resource rich in encouragement, wisdom, strategies, and personality. Thank you for being a part of the journey.

I would also like to thank my fellow editor and raider of midnight snacks, Beebe Kauffman. Every project is better and more enjoyable because I have you.

Most of all, I would like to thank our ultimate Project Manager. Not just for this book, but for character renovation. Thank You, God, for faithfully working in our hearts and never giving up on making us more like Your Son. And thank You for bringing together this "reno" team.

~Katy Kauffman

Introduction:
Renovation Needed

Introduction: Renovation Needed

The home had once been stunning.

Its winding staircase was a work of art that drew the eyes of visitors up to a second story stained glass window at its crest. Tall windows flooded rooms with light for family gatherings, neighborhood socials, and church functions. Travelers kept showing up on the inviting front porch, asking if they could see the house or take photographs of the gardens that surrounded it.

Decline happened gradually. The toll that neglect took was slight at first. Then disease struck one of the homeowners, and time, attention, and resources were focused elsewhere. The gardens withered, paint peeled, and wallpaper sagged. Storms blew debris against the tall windows and cracked or broke them. Rotting floorboards went unrepaired. Finally the expense to repair such a mansion became so great that the surviving owner abandoned it. It sat dark and desolate, forlorn and forgotten, with no hope of renewal or restoration.

As a last resort, the house was donated to the city. A young man worked there who had grown up nearby when the house was in its heyday. He loved the old house and knew its potential. He undertook a renovation of it to draw visitors to the city. He organized the work of taking out what was old and decaying and replacing it with what was beautiful and functional. He was a very dedicated project manager.

When our weary and sin-battered souls need a heart renovation, God can make them stunning. He can fashion our character into a work of art that blesses the people around us and draws their attention up to Him. He can flood the "rooms" of our hearts with spiritual light that heals them and makes them spiritually sound, in the likeness of His own character. He can conform us to the truth so that we walk in faith and love in every area of our lives. God can teach us how to share the good news of Jesus Christ and the truth of His word with friends and strangers so that it is inviting and welcoming.

God can reverse the ravages of sin, worldly temptations, and the neglect of spiritual disciplines. He can repair the parts of our thinking and living that were cracked or broken. He knows how to pinpoint what is wrong on the inside and set it right. When we make this renovation project more difficult with our neglect, apathy, or rebellion, God's goodness and love keep Him motivated and dedicated to continue on with the work until it is completed.

> God's goodness and love keep Him motivated and dedicated to continue on with the work.

This renovation is a cooperative effort between God and each believer. The more we say yes to God's work in our hearts, the more we will be conformed to Jesus' likeness. When we refuse what hurts godly character and choose what builds it up, our hearts and characters become more beautiful to God and more useful to His plan. As we cooperate with His work, love will fill every room of our souls and truth will be established as the framework of our lives. We will discover more and more how to mirror God's heart in daily life and how to show this world the greatness of His love.

The Bible studies in this book are a construction guide for building godly character in our hearts. Thirty authors have contributed stories, strategies, and insights that help us to identify the hidden problems of character and to know how to cooperate with God as He renovates our hearts to be like His own. It's our prayer that they will prove to be a great blessing to you.

So grab your hard hat and tool belt, and get ready for an adventure. When our hearts are renovated by the Master Builder, we can be certain that the results will be stunning.

He who has begun a good work in you will complete it
until the day of Jesus Christ.
Philippians 1:6 NKJV

Prayer:

Dear God,
Thank You for being a very dedicated Project Manager. Help us in this study to learn more about Your construction methods and Your plans for our hearts. Help us to cooperate with the building process so that the result is stunning for You and Your kingdom. In Jesus' name, Amen.

Questions:

1. Have you ever been involved in a house renovation?
    a. Which part was the most enjoyable?
    b. Which part was the most challenging?
    c. Was the end result worth the process?

2. How do you think growing in godly character is like a heart renovation?

3. What do you think is the most challenging thing about growing up spiritually?

4. Who has the hardest work in a heart renovation—God or us? Why?

5. Why is it worth it?

Repairing the Hidden Problems of Character

Weeks 1-2

Open the Walls of My Heart, Lord

by Penny Cooke

Renovations are meant to make something new and more beautiful, but they aren't always without challenges. One warm fall day, I arrived on the jobsite to find my contractor husband pacing. He had the phone to his ear with one hand and waved the job list in the air with the other. His tone was tense. He glanced at me and shook his head.

It was demolition day for our client's master suite renovation, whose bathroom was larger than my whole bedroom. The lengthy proposal had been agreed upon, and the client was to move out for several weeks while the renovation took place. As the decorator, I had chosen coordinating colors, patterns, and textures. Workers and tools were on the job, and we were ready and excited to see this stunning suite come to life.

As my husband finished the call, he lifted his cap and ran his hand over his head with a sigh. He explained as he dropped the papers on the counter, "The walls are full of mold."

Torn-down walls in the bathroom had exposed old, cracked, slowly leaking pipes, which resulted in mold. Mold is a serious issue and causes varied health problems, so it must be removed. The job would now take more time and be more costly to complete. This is especially frustrating for my husband who makes it a priority to finish jobs in the projected time frame.

For contractors, demolition often uncovers hidden problems behind walls—old faulty wiring and leaking pipes, poor workmanship not done to code, and sometimes termites. For decorators, even reupholstering jobs can reveal rotting or stained foam, split frames, or bugs. You just never know until you get inside.

It can be the same with a heart renovation. What might God find hidden inside the walls of our hearts? What is necessary for a heart renovation? Are there special tools needed? Will we decide it's too difficult, costly, or time-consuming?

No worries, friends. God is in the renovation business, too. He is the Master Renovator. Making things new and beautiful is His expertise (Revelation 21:5, Ecclesiastes 3:11). He has all the right tools for the job, and if we allow Him, He'll work with us for the best heart renovation you've ever seen.

The first thing needed for heart renovation is God's Toolbox.

God's Word is like a toolbox filled with essential tools. Let's take a look inside where we'll find some fascinating ones. In the Ephesians 6:13-17 section of His toolbox, we find truth, righteousness, peace, faith, and salvation. They are necessary tools when we are faced with the enemy's lies, anxiety, fear, or doubt in our hearts. They can even protect us on the hazardous construction site of life. But unless we open God's toolbox, we won't be able to access them.

God's toolbox includes everything needed for every heart renovation job. In 2 Timothy 3:16-17 (NKJV), we're told His tools are "profitable for doctrine, for reproof, for correction, for instruction in righteousness, that the man of God may be complete, *thoroughly equipped for every good work*" (emphasis mine).

Hebrews 4:12 describes His tools as "living and powerful, and sharper than any two-edged sword, piercing even to the division of soul and spirit, and of joints and marrow, and is a discerner of *the thoughts and intents of the heart*" (emphasis mine). God's words are tools that are able to get inside our hearts and transform them.

The second thing needed for heart renovation is God's power tool.

We discover another tool in Ephesians 6:18, "praying always." Prayer is God's power tool. James 5:16 encourages us that as we pray fervently, our prayers are effective.

"Fervent," meaning with fervor, earnest.

"Effective," meaning energized, powerful.

When we pray fervently, God's power is at work like a live electrical current flowing through a wire to energize a power tool. However, in order for the power tool to work, we have to turn on the power. Prayer is like an on/off switch to God's power (as long as the plug is connected to the outlet—His Spirit).

John 15:7 instructs us, "If you abide in Me, and My words abide in you, you will ask what you desire, and it shall be done for you." Prayer and the Word are how we abide, or stay connected, in Him. John 15:4 (NIV) instructs us to "remain" in Him. First Thessalonians 5:17 directs us to "pray without ceasing." In other words, keep your prayer power tool plugged in and ready to be turned on.

Prayer keeps us abiding with Him and gives us strength and power. Prayer produces help and guidance, comfort and healing. We receive answers in the form of wisdom, revelation, and changed circumstances. And we are granted forgiveness as we confess our sins to Him (1 John 1:9).

Prayer, like a live electrical current, releases God's power into our hearts and situations.

But, when our Contractor gets inside the walls of our hearts, will He find we haven't been using our tools for regular maintenance?

- Might He uncover pride short-circuiting our worship? (Psalm 51:17)

- Might He reveal desires smoldering that are not wired properly with His will? (James 4:3)

- Might He expose unconfessed sin decaying and keeping our prayers from being answered (Psalm 66:18), or unforgiveness towards others keeping relationships from being rebuilt (Mathew 6:15)?

Sin can hide in our hearts like mold and be toxic to our spiritual health and relationships. But it's not a problem for our Contractor. Before you know it, He'll have everything fresh and new.

However, just as our client had to allow us access to their home for as long as the job would take, we must allow God access to our hearts to show us what needs renovating and make the necessary heart changes to make them new again.

Fortunately, our client cooperated and my husband was able to remedy the problem and complete the job only a few weeks later than scheduled. They love their sprawling marble counter with his-and-hers sinks and the Coastal Green paint covering their now mold-free walls. It coordinates perfectly with the backdrop of sea glass tile behind the claw foot tub. My favorite is the chandelier hanging from the coffered ceiling.

So, just as my husband wouldn't show up to a job without his tools, let's not show up for our day without our tools—God's Word and prayer.

Note: Continual upkeep is needed so there won't be any surprises when the Contractor gets inside. Do not allow renovations to become long overdue. Regular prayer and confession and being in God's Word will eliminate unforeseen problems and an unnecessarily long length of time to complete the job. You cannot have real heart renovation without them, and what beautiful things He will do with them!

Prayer:

Dear Lord,
You have been so good and gracious to us. You provide everything we need for life and godliness, but so often I am too distracted and busy to keep my heart with all diligence. I don't mean to. Forgive me. I need Your help. I ask today that You take my heart and make it new and beautiful. Come in and do the necessary renovations to make me more like You. See if there is any wicked way in me and lead me to Your everlasting ways so I can radiate Your love and life to those around me. Our world needs more of You. Let them see You in me. In Jesus' mighty name, Amen.

Questions:

1. Ephesians 6:17 and Hebrews 4:12 (above) call the Word of God a "sword." How is it a sword? How can we sharpen our sword?

2. Take another look at 2 Timothy 3:16-17 above. What "good work" do you think God has for you and how can you be more "thoroughly equipped?"

3. Read John 14:15 and 23. What would be the result if a contractor only knew a little about his or her trade? Why is it so important to keep up with regular heart maintenance by knowing His word better? How can you practice this more this week?

4. If you haven't already, look up the verses referenced in the bulleted text above and consider the questions with them. Now read 1 John 1:9 and Proverbs 28:13. Is there anything hiding in your heart that might hinder God's blessing in your life? Why not confess it now? He is faithful and ready to forgive.

5. Reflect on John 15:7 above, then look up John 14:13-14. What are we invited to do? What will be the result? (Consider what "abide in Me" and "in His name" have to do with confession of sin.)

6. James 4:2 informs us, "You do not have because you do not ask." What might you ask God which you have not yet asked? Why not ask Him now?

*All Scripture verses are taken from the NKJV unless otherwise indicated.

The Hidden Cost of Character Renovation
by Karen Griffin

In 2003, my husband and I moved into a home built in the 1970s. Every area in our home needed to be renovated, from the orange, brown, and yellow indoor-outdoor carpet to the walls of dark brown paneling. Thirteen years later, we had renovated almost every room in our home. Doing the work ourselves has been rewarding but costly. Each project had hidden cost that we had to pay if we wanted to live in an updated home.

Building godly character also involves hidden costs. As we carry out a character renovation, we can use the following four steps to help us deal with these costs.

1. To gain the benefits of renovation, be willing to pay its costs.

> Suppose one of you wants to build a tower. Won't you first sit down and estimate the cost to see if you have enough money to complete it? For if you lay the foundation and are not able to finish it, everyone who sees it will ridicule you, saying, "This person began to build and wasn't able to finish." (Luke 14:28-30 NIV*)

In the planning stages of any house renovation, we price the materials and tools that will be needed. It would be very unwise to begin a project not knowing whether we have the funds to complete it. In fact, if we do so we may be ridiculed.

Likewise, when we begin a character renovation, we are wise to sit down and count the cost. God's word warns us of many of the costs we will face. "Whoever wants to be my disciple must deny themselves and take up their cross daily and follow me" (Luke 9:23).

The first cost we must pay is denying ourselves. This does not mean that we do away with our personalities. It means we no longer demand our rights. We live to please God by focusing on what He wants, which is to grow in godly character. To learn to be more like Jesus, we must learn to treat others with kindness even if they mistreat us. We may need to say nothing during an argument and let the other person have their way. As we learn to walk in Christlikeness by denying ourselves, we will be showing Jesus to the world and pleasing our heavenly Father who has called us to be like Him.

Second, we must take up our cross daily. The cross is a place of sacrifice. As we follow Jesus, we must be willing to give up anything He asks us to. God may lead us to spend less so that we can give more. He may ask us to give up certain hobbies so that we have more time to serve Him. We may be convicted to stop participating in an activity that might cause our brother to stumble. We must want His plan for our lives so much so that we are willing to pay any cost He requires.

Finally, we are to follow Jesus by striving to respond to situations as He would. We do this by studying the Bible and living accordingly. God calls us to reject the norms of society and live according to His standards. This may involve giving up old friends who want us to live the way they do. We may be ostracized at work because we refuse to participate in break room gossip. We may even lose a promotion or our jobs by refusing to engage in unethical practices. Each choice we make to live by His standards causes us to be more like Christ. This is what character renovation is all about: "being transformed into his image" (2 Corinthians 3:18).

God has given us everything we need to complete our character renovation. His Word is our blueprint for the project. His Holy Spirit is our own personal contractor that teaches us to read and apply the plans. We have the phone line of prayer to contact the Project Manager anytime we need help. God Himself "works in you to will and to act in order to fulfill his good purpose" (Philippians 2:13). When we use the tools He has provided, our project will be possible.

2.   Have a plan to deal with unexpected cost.

Almost every renovation will have unexpected costs. We are wise to prepare for them by setting aside extra funds. The same is true when we undergo a character renovation. As we become more Christlike in one area, we will discover other areas of our lives that need renovation.

How can we plan for these unexpected costs that will occur? First, we should determine in advance that we are willing to deal with every area that God shows us that needs renovation. What good does it do to focus on one area, while God is trying to transform another? God is the Project Manager. He determines the specific project and assigns the daily tasks that need to be done. Second, we need to plan ahead by memorizing and meditating on Scripture. We must know the blueprints if we are to follow them. Our contractor, the Holy Spirit, will use the Scriptures we have learned to tear out ungodly character and build new.

3.   Be willing to spend what is needed to complete the job.

The man in the parable of Luke 14 did not have the funds he needed to complete his tower. We, on the other hand, have all that we need. God in His "divine power has given us everything we need for a godly life" (2 Peter 1:3). We can never say, "I didn't have what I needed to complete the job."

If our character renovation becomes stalled, it may be because we are not willing to spend what is necessary. We must spend the time it takes to renovate. If we are willing to keep working until the job is done, we will have renewed character. We must also be willing to spend the energy. Nothing is more tiring than tearing out old construction and building new. This is also true for character construction. Are you willing to expel energy to transform your character?

4. Be encouraged by envisioning the completed project.

There is a great sense of accomplishment when remodeling is complete. Imagining the completed job will help you persevere when the work gets difficult. When we are working to renew our character, we can look to Jesus to give us inspiration. He is our example of godly character. Ephesians 5:1-2 (NASB) tells us to "be imitators of God, as beloved children, and walk in love, just as Christ also loved you."

Character transformation should be a joyful experience. Hebrews 12:2 tells us that Jesus faced His mission of dying on the cross by looking to the joy set before Him. As we strive to become more like Jesus, we can look to the joy that is ahead of us. Think about how Jesus lived, treated others, and responded to temptation. Imagine yourself responding as He did. Let this inspire you to persevere in the work until your character renovation is complete.

Prayer:

Dear Lord Jesus,
I place my life in Your hands to be used as You desire. I know that there are areas of my character that need to be renewed. Show me the area in which You are working. Transform me in every area to make me more like You. Fill me with Your Spirit. Lead me to the Scriptures that will teach me, and help me memorize and apply them. It is my uttermost desire to be like You in every way. In Your name, Amen.

Questions:

1. What area of your character do you sense God wants to renew?

2. List the cost you anticipate.

3. What other areas of your character might be affected?

4. Write a brief commitment to deal with any areas God shows you.

5. Find a Scripture that will help in this renovation. Record it below; begin memorizing it.

6. Describe what you imagine your character will look like when it is complete.

*All Scripture verses are taken from the NIV unless otherwise indicated.

What Lurks Beneath

by Dawn Owens

Through each building renovation I've participated in, I felt God speaking to my heart, "I bring dead things to life, and now you will, too." Once a year over the last five years, I have been in the process of renovating a building.

It started when my ministry exchanged renovation of a neglected building for payment of rent. A preschool formerly occupied the space, which meant it had bright purple, red, blue, and yellow walls and the water pipes resembled LEGOs®. Because the building lay vacant for years, the stale, sour smell stung our nostrils.

A year later, I renovated my home. The wood paneling on the exterior was rotting, and the windows were too thin to withhold the weather.

More recently, our ministry partnered with a local church to renovate their *old* building. Allow me to emphasize the word *old*. It was early 1900s old, and in 2016, it had been vacant for a few years. The prior tenants only did what was necessary for its upkeep. The wall colors wavered between nineties black-youth-room to seventies peach from wall to ceiling. And who ever thought rugs on the front of counters was a good idea, I will never know, but they too were found in this gem of a building.

Renovations Aren't Surface-Deep

When God told me that He makes dead things come to life and I had a part in it, the hair on my arms stood up, and a chill ran down my spine as I considered the power in that message. Not only for the buildings but for people's hearts. For someone who leads a ministry to the poor focused on life transformation, those words were mind-altering.

God renovates our hearts much like the way we renovate buildings. However, with every renovation I undertook, I realized not everything was as it seemed.

There were always internal issues lurking behind walls or in the flooring. Like the creatures living in the walls and basement at the first building, or the intense amount of damage that termites burrowing into our walls had done to our home, or the electrical and plumbing issues we found at the last building. There were always more flaws than what we could physically see.

And so it is with our hearts.

When it comes to God renovating our hearts, there is always more at work than what appears on the surface.

If the contractors slapped siding on top of the wood paneling of my home, but never located the deeper issue of termites, we would still have an infestation that could have destroyed it. The only way to rid ourselves of these insects was to have an exterminator spray the inside walls. So it is with the way we respond to our character flaws. It is easier sometimes to mask the problem by prettying up our outsides, but on the inside our walls or foundations are decaying.

Identifying the Real Cause of the Problem

Recently my husband and I had yet another "heated" discussion about expectations, his and mine. I reported a catalog of all the chores I completed, and demanded for him to share his. I knew his list was not as extensive as mine, but the disparity was leverage to deflect why I was not meeting all of *his* expectations.

Sometime later, I was reading in Jonah when a passage hit me like never before. God had just relented from judging the Ninevites, and much to Jonah's dismay, the Ninevite king decreed the entire city to repent and turn to God. In God's grace and mercy, He saved them.

Jonah fumed. He said to the LORD:

Isn't this what I said, LORD, when I was still at home? That is what I tried to forestall by fleeing to Tarshish. I knew that you are a gracious and compassionate God, slow to anger and abounding in love, a God who relents from sending calamity. Now, LORD, take away my life, for it is better for me to die than to live. (Jonah 4:2-3 NIV)

I can almost hear the whine in his voice. God reacted to Jonah in a way I never would have expected. God said, "Is it right for you to be angry?" (Jonah 4:4 NIV).

Was it right for Jonah to be angry? Really?! God just let a bunch of murderous heathens go. For Jonah, it was a punch in the gut. For me as I read the passage that day, it did much the same.

Both Jonah and I were angry, but what we were angry about was only the character flaw visible on the surface. Kind of like the rotting wood on my house. Our anger rose because we were screaming "Justice!" but in its place God granted mercy. The same mercy we each would have desired, had the roles been reversed. Underneath our angry exteriors, destruction was happening, an outward emotion of an internal character defect. For both of us, we had a sin problem needing a permanent solution.

I came to realize my addiction to approval was causing more strife in my marriage than I grasped. I used my anger, control strategies, and even manipulation to placate the fact I felt unloved, unapproved, and undervalued.

However, now that I have learned who I am in Christ, I no longer put lofty expectations on my husband, but rather rest in the fact I have all the approval, love, and value I need in God. I cannot control or manipulate my husband into doing the things I want him to do. I am responsible for me, and that is all I have the ability to control. I had no right to be angry.

Searching Within

In your own life, are you seeing attitudes surfacing like anger, gossip, vanity, or greed? Could there be a hidden problem lurking beneath the surface that is causing these attitudes? Seek the LORD, the God who is gracious and compassionate, "slow to anger and abounding in love, a God who relents from sending calamity" to find what lurks below. The renovation and mending process will be worth every ounce of energy spent to become more godly from the inside out.

> The renovation and mending process will be worth every ounce of energy spent to become more godly from the inside out.

Prayer:

Father God,
You are a gracious and compassionate God, slow to anger, abounding in love, and relenting from sending calamity. Because of that You see our sin and love us anyway. God, I pray You would reveal to us the underlying cause of our outward emotions and actions that are defects in our character. Show us the areas of our lives that do not align with Your Word. Father, we desire to become more like You. Teach us how to seek You for knowledge that will change our hearts, and show us how to live like You daily. In Jesus' name I pray, Amen.

Questions:

1. List any negative emotions or actions that surface in your life on a regular basis. (For example, anger, irritation, overspending, gossiping, and so forth.)

2. Take a moment and do a word search on each of those areas to find a Scriptural reference that addresses the problem. Write them below.

3. What do you think is causing those "surface problems"? Ask God to reveal the underlying cause that may be raising those emotions or actions to the surface.

4. What does God's Word say about the hidden problem? What truth do you need to hold on to, in order to fix the problem, or what instruction do you need to practice? (For example, you may look up the need for control.) Write those Scripture verses associated with the hidden problem below, and repeat them to yourself over time so they become a tool with which God can renovate your heart.

*This article is an excerpt from *Like Me or Not*, (Nashville, Tenn.: Worthy Publishing, 2018). Used with permission.

Security Blanket

by Rosemarie Fitzsimmons

"Everything is permissible for me,"
but not everything is beneficial.
"Everything is permissible for me,"
but I will not be mastered by anything.
1 Corinthians 6:12 CSB

For the third time that week, she awoke in her daughter's bed. Kathryn sighed as she looked at the Cinderella clock on the bed stand, envious of the rest of the world for being able to sleep past five. Of course, if she'd only gone to bed a little earlier, she wouldn't be so tired, but she had been up late playing cards on her computer. Guiltily, she realized that if Melissa hadn't called out to her around 2 a.m., she probably wouldn't be upstairs even now.

She looked at little Melissa, sleeping peacefully after a fitful night. The child's damp, blonde curls were plastered against her sweet angel face, and her little mouth was drawn up in a precious pout. However, it was the empty hands that made Kathryn smile, and evoked a small surge of hope and victory within her. The hands were clenched in a tight ball as always, but they no longer clutched the familiar soft, raggedy yellow security blanket. It had been more than two weeks since the blanket had disappeared. The nights had been tough, but bit by bit, her precious little one was making the adjustment.

Kathryn and Mike had been trying to wean their daughter from that ratty yellow nuisance for months now, primarily because it was always in the way. At three and a half years old, the girl was just too busy for a blanket. Kathryn's heart soared at the prospect of a blanket-free life. No more one-handed activities, no more anxiety attacks while waiting for the washer/dryer cycles to end, no more cries in the middle of the night to retrieve it from under the bed. She knew Melissa was unable to see how much that blanket had been holding her back, and was thrilled to know how much life was about to improve for this child. She remembered with a chuckle, a recent finger-painting fiasco, and the mess it had made, and said a quick prayer of thanks for washable paint.

Kathryn tiptoed out of the room. Rather than risk waking Mike by going to bed, she turned left at the top of the stairs and went down to the den.

Even before she entered the room, Kathryn could see the computer lights blinking in the dark, calling to her with that familiar empty promise. Like hers, the computer's brain never slept. A few hands of solitaire might relax her.

She stepped carefully over some toys in the dark room and sat at the desk, and with a small nudge of the mouse, brought the machine to life. Then Kathryn began the monotonous task of not doing.

Black nine on red ten. King to the vacant space.

It was therapeutic, really, not doing. She idly wondered what she used to do with her worries, before the computer. An image flashed through her mind of sitting at the kitchen table pouring out the story of her day while Mike made dinner. How close they used to be . . . how they used to laugh and enjoy their time together. These days though, it seemed every spare minute was spent just getting through the day. At night it seemed he wanted to go up to bed just as she was settling down to relax.

"I'll be up in a few minutes," she'd say. Mike would shrug his shoulders and head up alone. By the time she got to bed he'd be sound asleep. Wondering how long it had been since they'd spent real, intimate time together, she toyed briefly with the idea of waking him sweetly, but decided he probably needed more sleep.

Four, five, six ... where's an ace when you need it? Okay, once more through the deck.

She thought again of little Melissa, and how wonderful it would be when the child could again sleep through the night. How fortuitous that fate had stepped in where she and Mike had failed. They had tried coaxing the girl to release her blanket voluntarily, to no avail. Then Kathryn cut small strips off the blanket every week or so until it was only a one-foot square. This had helped at first, but eventually Melissa must have become suspicious, because anxiety hit whenever it left her sight. Mike had tried being tough, ordering the poor child to leave it in the car when they went into stores and such. This usually resulted in a theatrical display of tearful shrieking and Mike's eventual relent.

When Melissa left her blanket behind at an amusement park, they had been unable to track it down. Neither she nor Mike would have had the heart to force its disappearance, but they cheered inwardly. Now they only had to help Melissa adjust and soon, hopefully, the child would no longer remember it.

Dead hand. Reshuffle, start afresh. Ah, lots of face cards ... this could be a good hand. She spent a few minutes concentrating, but eventually, all the moves played out and she was left with nothing. Again. Reshuffle. Here we go ...

The sky lightened outside. Kathryn could hear Mike upstairs showering for work. The children would be down soon. Just a few more hands and she'd go fix some coffee.

Shuffle, play, shuffle again.

A few hands later, she realized it was too late. Mike was already coming down the stairs, with six-year-old Kyle bouncing behind him. Where had the time gone? She wrenched herself away from the blinking box and dashed into the kitchen, greeting the boys with a smile.

Mike was sure looking good these days, now that he'd stopped smoking and started exercising. Why hadn't she noticed? She felt truly happy for him—it had been a tough addiction. He'd been smoking since he was a teenager . . . said it made him feel more confident. Now he seemed healthier, happier, and certainly no less confident. Plus, the house smelled fresh and the extra money they saved every month helped as well.

"Bye, Hon," said Mike, leaning over for a kiss as he picked up his briefcase. "Man, I must have slept hard. I didn't even hear you come to bed, let alone get up this morning."

As she closed the door behind Mike, Kathryn had little time to wonder why he was leaving so early before she felt a small tug at her sleeve.

"Mommy," said Kyle. "It's pancake day!"

Kathryn glanced at the clock and couldn't believe her eyes; it was already time for school. How could the morning have flown by so quickly?

"I'm sorry, Kyle, Sweetie," she said. "There's not enough time for pancakes this morning. We'll have to switch Pancake Day to Wednesday this week."

Kyle didn't hide his disappointment as she filled a bowl of cereal for him, but he quickly switched to a new topic.

"Did you make my Joseph costume last night? Don't forget I need it tomorrow."

Kathryn's hand flew to her mouth, her mind racing to calculate the remaining hours before the school play.

"Don't worry, Sweetie, it will be done in time."

Little Melissa toddled into the kitchen, arms piled high with stuffed animals.

"My, my," said Kathryn, "look what you can do, now that you have TWO hands to work with." She arranged the animals on the counter, set Melissa up to the table with a handful of cereal, and raced to pack Kyle's lunch. They met the school bus at the end of the driveway with seconds to spare.

Stepping back into the house, she leaned against the front door and closed her eyes. Was she imagining it, or were there images of playing cards flashing across her brain?

Kathryn cleaned up the kitchen, musing over the missed morning. Then she followed Melissa into the den, where the singing child quickly became engrossed in imaginary play. When had retiring to the den after breakfast become routine for Melissa?

The card game blinked at her from across the room. Entranced, she slowly moved to the computer, staring as if for the first time. Was this her thief? Surely she didn't spend all that much time here. Scoffing at the idea, she sat down, reshuffled, and began a new game.

But the thoughts continued. Black jack on a red—honestly! . . . How many hours a day did she spend at this? Certainly her family wasn't suffering. Or was it? She thought of the costume upstairs on the sewing table, the numerous lost mornings, sleepless nights, missed opportunities to be with Mike. What else had she missed?

Nonsense, she thought. It's not an addiction like Mike's cigarettes. I can stop if I want to! Didn't I stop that one time for Lent? I went without for forty days.

Ah, her thoughts countered, but on day forty-one you went right back to it. You aren't in control; the game is.

Kathryn stared at the screen. There was a red queen, begging to be moved onto the black king. It took every ounce of strength she had not to obey the command. Her eyes brimmed with tears as she thought of all the time wasted in the past—years? How could she not see what had been happening?

She pushed the mouse up to the top right corner and clicked the red box.

"Quit or Play Again?" The gray confirmation box offered her a chance to change her mind. Kathryn resolutely clicked the "Quit" button and sat there for a moment, staring mournfully at the blank screen. She felt lost. Empty. Even a little frightened. What would keep her from going back?

Melissa came to her side and reached her tiny hands upward. Kathryn lifted the child onto her lap and began stroking her velvety curls. The two rocked in silence for a few moments, each lost in thought.

"Mommy?" Melissa's sweet voice trembled. "I'm going to miss my blanket."

Kathryn kissed her daughter's forehead and murmured, "So am I, Sweetheart, so am I. But I think we'll be OK. We just have to pray, and ask Jesus to help us stop missing it. I'm sure He will. I'll bet He has something much better for us in mind, now that He's set us free."

Melissa's hopeful smile was all the confirmation she needed.

Discussion:

If it makes me happy and it's not hurting anyone, how can it be bad for me?

While it may be easy to see elements of bondage in the lives of those around us, sometimes it's a lot more difficult to see them in our own lives. One of Satan's best tools against us is his box of lies—the many lines he uses to make us think we need something more, or something better than what we have, or just something that will fill up our time so we have nothing left for the Lord.

Consider the following and fill in the blanks:

"I'd be a lot happier if I just had more _____."

"I can stop _____, but it's fun and it doesn't hurt anybody, so why should I?"

"I'd like to pursue God's will for me, but _____ takes up so much of my time."

Once we start down a path with this kind of logic, we can never become satisfied, because these paths are intended to take us further from God. Someone who starts down a path of pornography might begin by looking at seemingly harmless photographs, but after a while, the pictures do not satisfy. Then begins a quest for more—more graphic, more interesting, more exciting—and yet each time a new level is reached, the eyes quickly search for something better. Left unchecked, this could lead to some rather disastrous situations.

"But that's a lot more serious than what I'm doing," we justify, pulling another line from the box.

Is it? The controlling factor is not in what we do, but in why we do it. We can be held in bondage by money, video games, fashion, food, even something good, like education. Anything that we might define as strengthening or comforting, or that we pursue to excess in search of praise or self-promotion, can take control of our lives if we let it.

As He watches us grow, God can see these chains in our lives and He wants us to be free from them. He sees us finger-painting with one hand, and crying by the dryer for the blanket to be dry. He also knows what lies ahead for us if we let go, and He's rooting for us. He's there to help when we're ready.

Prayer:

Father,
Help us to discern the things in our lives that hinder our relationships and productivity. Help us to grow stronger in refusing what is wasteful or harmful and in choosing what is delightful and beneficial. May we be a blessing to You and to the people around us. In Jesus' name, Amen.

Questions:

1. Is there an activity or dependence in your life that might be controlling you, rather than the other way around?

2. What would you be free to do without this controlling factor in your life?

3. What's the worst thing that would happen if you give it up?

4. What is the best thing that could happen?

Scripture Reading:

> *"For I know the plans I have for you," declares the LORD, "plans to prosper you and not to harm you, plans to give you hope and a future."* (Jeremiah 29:11 NIV*)

> *I do not understand what I do. For what I want to do I do not do, but what I hate I do.* (Romans 7:15)

> *My flesh and my heart may fail, but God is the strength of my heart and my portion forever.* (Psalm 73:26)

*All Scripture verses are taken from the NIV unless otherwise indicated.

❖

The Hidden Work of Sanctification

by Jennifer DeFrates

I stood in the doorway with purpose. This strangely shaped little room in my ancient house just wasn't functional. The closet was too narrow to use for anything but piled junk. I had found a window behind the stored boxes, but I didn't have much use for a window hidden in a worthless closet. This room needed a renovation!

The safety goggles snapped against my face with a satisfying click. The new plastic smelled nostalgically of science class. Taking a practice swing with the heavy pry bar, I felt terribly professional, ready for demolition. I was excited.

I couldn't know I would end the day discouraged and overwhelmed or that this one room would reveal foundational issues throughout my house. Apparently, avidly watching HGTV hadn't prepared me for renovation reality.

Renovation is also an internal work.

Renovating our hearts is a beautiful growing process that God works in believers who humble themselves and seek Him. But the renovation of my heart constantly surprises me. Every time I think I've finally finished the demolition stage, I find I've only just begun. And if you're deadline-oriented like I am, a never-ending project is almost your worst nightmare. But I've learned to rest in the not yet and never finished because of this verse.

We all, with unveiled face, beholding the glory of the Lord,
are being transformed into the same image
from one degree of glory to another.
For this comes from the Lord who is the Spirit.
2 Corinthians 3:18 ESV

"We all, with unveiled face ..."

When we accept the truth that Christ is the only way to God, the Holy Spirit inhabits us. He removes the veil over our spiritual eyes so we can finally see God's righteousness and realize our lives have to change. Like my realization that the room was no longer useful. A coat of paint wasn't going to fix it. It needed a total overhaul.

For me, the moment when I realized that my life needed to change is crystal clear. I had moved away from my friends, family, and job; and my marriage was falling apart. I had been stripped of everything that was masking the real work I needed to do in my life. Sobbing, I finally stood before the Lord in prayer and surrendered everything to Him. As I stood in my dining room, my eyes were opened. I began to see the garbage that needed cleaning out of my heart.

Often in sanctification, we can see the work that lies ahead of removing such sins from our lives as sexual immorality, crude language, or substance abuse. We begin removing these big boxes of sin from our hearts only to realize that a deeper work is needed. We have to take down the walls and repair the foundation before our hearts can truly be renovated.

Before rebuilding my dysfunctional room, I had to tear down the lumpy, cracked, ancient plaster walls. In my head, this step was going to be fairly easy. Pry off plaster; put up new drywall. I couldn't know that the plaster was going to constantly break into tiny pieces, sometimes as small as my fist, the edges crumbling into fine dust that clung to everything. I couldn't see the layers upon layers of strange wall materials lurking beneath the surface plaster. Only time and hard work revealed the real issues.

Which takes us to the hard work of heart renovations, time spent ...

"... beholding the glory of the Lord ..."

How does God begin the work of renovating our hearts? We have to spend time in His presence, beholding His glory to understand His character. We spend time in God's presence through prayer, reading His word, and fellowship with mature believers.

Despite avidly watching home renovation shows, I was only prepared for unexpected issues to arise. I couldn't see the knob and tube wiring that was an imminent fire hazard and had to be replaced in the entire house. I had to spend time in the room, doing the hard work. I had to get past the plaster walls, past the layers of 1800s wallboard, past the wooden lathe to see the other issues.

Attending church or knowing all the Christian things to say never revealed some of the real heart issues lurking below the surface of my life. Only total surrender and dedicated time in God's word helped me see the real work I needed to do.

Once I grew spiritually past my obvious sins, I realized those sins were the product of selfishness. Then I realized that selfishness was born from pride in what I could do rather than submission to what God could do in me.

As I spent time with God in His word, His character was transforming my choices, then my thoughts.

"... [We] are being transformed into the same image from one degree of glory to another ..."

As an English teacher, I find the verb tense here important. We are BEING transformed, as in, continually. It is not work that is finished this side of heaven. As a deadline-oriented person, this gives me such tremendous freedom to rest in what God has called me to work on for today.

God intended this process of transformation to happen one degree at a time, revealing more to us as His Spirit works. I see the need for faith and humility in ways I didn't realize when I began this heart renovation. I'm reminded of the story from 2 Kings 6:8-17.

The king of Aram had sent chariots and horses and warriors to find and kill the prophet Elisha because God kept revealing their battle plans to him. When Elisha's servant saw the army against them, he was terrified. Until Elisha prayed for God to open his eyes. Then he saw the spiritual warriors protecting Elisha from the king's forces.

In many ways our heart renovations resemble Elisha's servant. We are operating based on only what we can see and know, until God opens our eyes and reveals the real warfare happening around us. The more I walk with Christ, the more I'm aware that the battles I'm fighting are not against flesh and blood, but neither is my help.

> The more I walk with Christ, the more I'm aware that the battles I'm fighting are not against flesh and blood, but neither is my help.

"… For this comes from the Lord who is the Spirit."

As new or renewed believers, we start pursuing God with a palpable fire and excitement. But we risk getting discouraged when the work turns out to be so much more intense and never ending than we anticipated. That is why Christ in John Chapter 14 promised us a helper, the Holy Spirit. We need His power to truly be transformed.

Just as using HGTV as a how-to guide didn't work for my home renovation project, trying to recognize and weed out sinful behaviors on our own doesn't work. We need the Spirit. As the walls of worldly thinking and desires come down, we see the plaster of sins like selfishness and pride that stubbornly coat everything else. We discover how our hard wiring as sinners fuels the fire of anger and bitterness.

Our heart renovation project continually reveals new areas that need work: old ideas rooted in our sinful nature that need to be tossed into the dumpster, and things like that old window that should have provided much needed light, but weren't being used well.

Remember that window, the one blocked by junk, hidden in the closet?

Once I took out the garbage, pulled the walls down, and restructured the space, that window offered a beautiful view of a gorgeous Eastern Redbud tree that blossomed each spring with vibrant fuchsia flowers.

My renovation project changed the room and reminds me often of the work the Spirit performs in us, taking us deeper and deeper still into a freeing and satisfying heart renovation. One which restores us and equips us to fulfill His amazing purposes for our lives.

Prayer:

Dear Lord,
Give me eyes to see and ears to hear so that I may correctly understand Your Word and recognize Your glory. Help me build time into each day to spend in Your presence. Transform me into Your glorious image degree by degree. Cleanse and renovate my heart for Your purpose through the work of the Holy Spirit. In Jesus' name, I pray.

Questions:

1. Have you ever started a project only to realize there were hidden obstacles? What were they?

2. Have you ever been aware of God removing a spiritual veil from your eyes? If so, how did it affect your heart, character, or life?

3. How can we move big boxes of sin out of our hearts? What part of the process is God's?

4. How does God bring our attention to some hidden boxes?

5. What are the benefits of spending time in God's presence? How does it transform you?

What's Eating You?

by Patty Schell

The floor in the kitchen of the small house had weakened over time. Just looking across the black and white linoleum-tiled room, there didn't seem to be a problem. Everything looked sound, but walking on it was a completely different matter. It creaked and bowed to the point of giving way. The unseen cause? Dry rot.

Beneath the surface, dry rot had done its worst and broken down the wood in the support joists of the floor. Dry rot is a fungus that weakens wood by digesting the parts of wood that give it its rigidity and strength. It eats away at what makes the wood sturdy and solid until it becomes weak and brittle. The spores themselves can be found on the building materials, and when they are exposed to an outside source of moisture, they start to grow, causing the damage.

A three-part process restores the structural integrity of a house ravaged by dry rot. First, find the trouble area. Next, remove all of the rotten boards and replace them with new ones. Finally, treat the new lumber to prevent another infection.

Quite often, Christians seem to be doing just fine as they are cruising along in life during the relatively peaceful times, but just below the surface trouble is brewing. They are like that kitchen floor that seems sound. The pictures on Zillow look great! But when pressure is applied, things start to crumble.

Our Invisible Danger

Hiding there along the foundation of our lives can be a bit of unrepentant sin. Inactive, yet potentially dangerous under the right circumstances, the sin has never quite been eradicated. No need to confess it. It was under control, and no one was the wiser. Instead of repenting, we tuck it away, concealed from view.

> *Whoever conceals their sins does not prosper, but the one who confesses and renounces them finds mercy.* (Proverbs 28:13 NIV,* emphasis mine)

The reasons may vary of why we would conceal our sin— embarrassment, fear of judgment, or shame. Perhaps we think the sin is just too big for God to forgive or we have to fix it on our own. Maybe it doesn't seem like a sin really, not according to society's standards anyway, yet in the back of our minds we know it doesn't quite line up with God's truth. Or maybe we've grown comfortable with our little secret and are not ready to let go of it.

Whatever the reasoning, the consequences of the sin will be the same if left untreated—a weakened spiritual life. How? It eats away at our connection with God.

In Psalm 32:3-4, David reveals how his sin affected his body and soul:

> *When I kept silent [about my sin], my bones wasted away through my groaning all day long. For day and night your hand was heavy on me; my strength was sapped as in the heat of summer.*

All that groaning sounds like the deteriorating floor joists in our little kitchen that are becoming weak and brittle. With any pressure, they threaten to give way. Interestingly enough, it is God who comes in as the Building Inspector to point out the trouble.

> *For day and night your hand was heavy on me . . .*

God has a way of getting right to the source of the problem and in this case, it's a big one. You see, God wants all of us, *every bit.* Even the parts of our hearts where we hide something that will only hurt ourselves. He wants us to have a sturdy foundation, a relationship that will not buckle under our weaknesses but is held firm in His strength.

Restoring Our Structural Integrity

What do we do with sin that we've hidden? Instead of tucking it away, we can bring it out into the open. Take another look at Proverbs 28:13 (emphasis mine): *Whoever conceals their sins does not prosper,* **but the one who confesses and renounces them finds mercy.**

As with the solution for the dry rot, we may find that there is also a step-by-step plan in this verse.

1. Confess

We have heard that sin grows in the dark. When it comes to fixing dry rot in our souls, we must expose the problem area. Often, we have shame and embarrassment about our sin, but we have never really voiced what the sin is. Guess what? God already knows all about it. He is never surprised. Putting it into words sometimes helps us by bringing clarity to what it really is.

2. Renounce

Here is where it gets a little tricky. This is where we get rid of the affected area in our lives. "Renounce" means "to refuse to follow, obey, or recognize any further."[1] When we harbor sin, it begins to *own* us. We become its slave. Romans 10:9 states, *If you declare with your mouth, 'Jesus is Lord,' and believe in your heart that God raised him from the dead, you will be saved.* The ultimate form of renouncing is changing what we love. Do we love Jesus more or our hidden sin? If "Jesus is Lord," there is no room for another master in our lives.

Often, this is easy in thought, but not always in deed. This part will take practice. Each time sin shows up to take over, we need to remind ourselves who's Lord of our lives. Jesus was raised from the dead to provide a way for us to no longer live with sin as our master. Daily we should remember the sacrifice, and live a life worthy of such a gift.

3. Commit

A wonderful surprise is found concealed within the wrappings of Proverbs 28:13. At first glance, we think we are the recipients of God's love and compassion, which in fact we are. But the most compassionate thing God graces us with through this process, is the ability to love deeply, have tender affection, and to be compassionate toward others who find themselves caught under the tyranny of sin. This is the redemption of our sins. The tender mercies of Jesus are transformed into actions in our lives as we have love and compassion for others. We know about the hope Jesus provides. We have experienced it first hand when we put our lives, warts and all, into His hands. This is what it takes to prevent future outbreaks of rot, weakness, and structural failure brought on by sin—giving our lives completely to God.

If we confess our sins, he is faithful and just and will forgive our sins and purify us from all unrighteousness. (1 John 1:9)

Prayer:

Dear God,
Search me, God, and know my heart: test me and know my anxious thoughts (Psalm 139:23).
I am sorry that I have held back any part of me from You. I was afraid and I didn't know how to let go.

See if there is any offensive way in me (Psalm 139:24a),
Show me the places I have hidden sin. I want to release them to You now so that they do not have any control over my life. Please forgive me.

and lead me in the way everlasting (Psalm 139:24b).
Thank You for Your faithfulness to lead me into living a life according to Your standard. Let my actions reflect Yours. I pray that Your love and compassion would be evident in me every

moment of every day. Allow me to tell others how much You loved me and how much You love them, too.

I love You. In Jesus' name, Amen.

Questions:

1.   Do you have unresolved sin tucked away?

2.   Have you accepted the gift of salvation?

3.   Read Ephesians 2:1-10.
     a.   According to this passage, what were you at one time?
     b.   What happened to change that?
     c.   What is the expected response to God's "renovation" in our lives?

4.   According to Mark 12:28-31, what action is greatest when it comes to doing good?

5.   First John 4:16 says, "And so we know and rely on the love God has for us. God is love. Whoever lives in love lives in God, and God in them." How can you start living that out today?

*All Scripture verses are taken from the NIV.

1. https://www.merriam-webster.com/dictionary/renounce.

The Revolving Door of Secret Perfectionism

by Jeannie Waters

Confessions of a Recovering Perfectionist

The mental alarm in the middle of the night made me leap out of bed, heart racing. Doubts pinged my brain.

What did I forget? Could I improve? Should I review the plan again?

Another evening, when the "alarm" buzzed, I planned to call a friend as worries badgered me.

Why did I say that? That's not what I meant. She probably thinks I'm irresponsible.

On yet a different night, sleep-robbing worries echoed.

What did I omit? Is my research thorough? What if the group doesn't approve?

Ongoing demand-bullets punctured me. Surely, I could do more or do better. My agenda was a "Must Do," not a "To Do" list. Each job required perfection. Task completion earned only momentary satisfaction because the list was perpetual.

There was no free time. No break. No reprieve.

A habitual watch-checker, I became more task focused than people focused. I savored family time, but spent late evening hours addressing greeting cards, planning church events, or preparing for work. I fretted over decisions, worrying about pleasing God and people.

After years of sleep deprivation and trudging toward the elusive goal of flawless performance, the malady of perfectionism gnawed at my health. Tension headaches, fatigue, and digestive issues annoyed me.

Nagging questions harassed my tired brain.

What can I omit? Where can I cut corners?

Short cuts were unthinkable because my performance scale had only two levels, perfect or failure. When I read "And whatever you do, do it heartily, as to the Lord and not to men" (Colossians 3:23 NKJV*), I knew excellence for God was appropriate, but I realized that the "perform better" echo was not from Him.

I was trapped secretly in my revolving door of mandates. I performed well, so no one knew I was rotating aimlessly in the spin cycle of endless expectations. I rued the miles I'd logged on the treadmill of perfectionism, yet attempts to escape seemed futile.

My heart throbbed with longing to cultivate more godly character, and sometimes I made progress with God's leading. However, the cruel master of perfectionism often thwarted progress as energy-draining self-evaluation persisted.

Contributing Causes of Perfectionism

How do we acquire this frenetic drive for perfect performance? What are the causes?

External influences like today's worldly standards magnified by social media images, clamor for excellence in financial security, physical fitness, appearance, test scores, parenting, and home design. They lure us into the performance trap like spiders catch flies.

Pride, people pleasing, fear, anxiety, and lack of faith also entice us to depend on impeccable behavior for satisfaction. When these sins wield their swords, we sometimes depend on our ways instead of God's for relief. Until we loosen our white-knuckled, fearful grip on gold-medal performance, we cannot totally trust God and allow Him to transform our character. "Without faith it is impossible to please Him" (Hebrews 11:6).

The good news is, that despite the sins that torment us, Christians have the promise, "If we confess our sins, He is faithful and just to forgive us our sins and to cleanse us from all unrighteousness" (1 John 1:9).

More Negative Effects

Just as one untreated health issue can aggravate another, perfectionism tends to foster legalism, self-reliance, unforgiveness, and a critical spirit. The further we wade into the cesspool of perfectionism, the more ungodly qualities may bubble to the surface. Repetitively grading our own performance can cause the cancer of perfectionism to metastasize until we become self-centered people pleasers, guilty of idolatry.

Furthermore, perfectionism encumbers our witness. When we trudge along fixated on error-free conduct, the voice of perfection blares through our earbuds playing the chorus of "never enough." That ruthless controller muffles the voice of God and hampers spiritual progress. Scripture teaches that we are to shine as lights so that others observe our lives and glorify God (Matthew 5:14-16). However, the fog of perfectionism often shrouds His glory in us.

Scriptural Blueprint to Freedom and Godly Character

Results of majoring on performance appear in the account of Jesus visiting a home. Mary sat near Him to listen, dismissing distractions and domestic duties for the sacred opportunity to learn from her Lord. Martha, in contrast, scurried around excessively tending to details. Perhaps Martha had perfectionistic tendencies. A current day "Martha" might insure uniform thickness of lemon slices for iced tea just before she re-irons the napkins while double-checking for dust under the table. Meal preparation is commendable, so why did Jesus confront her?

He spoke to Martha, not with condemnation, but with compassion as He longed for her to seek Him with abandon like her sister. "Martha, Martha, you are worried and troubled about many things. But one thing is needed, and Mary has chosen that good part" (Luke 10:41-42). Just as Jesus lovingly guided Martha toward freedom and His blueprint for godly character, He yearns for us to trust Him rather than our performance as we become more like Him.

> He yearns for us to trust Him rather than our performance.

Once God taught me that fixing my attention on Him in prayer and Bible study would release me from this trap, I followed the ideas below to victory. I sometimes slide back into old patterns but I recognize the Source of freedom.

6 Ways to Overcome Perfectionism

1. Evaluate your list of responsibilities daily. Who assigned them? Remember: "For My yoke is easy and My burden is light" (Matthew 11:30).

2. Pray verses like these:

    "Show me Your ways, O Lord; teach me Your paths." (Psalm 25:4)

    "Cause me to hear Your lovingkindness in the morning, for in You do I trust; cause me to know the way in which I should walk." (Psalm 143:8)

3. Write verses on cards to counteract old resurfacing thoughts.

    "For the weapons of our warfare are ... mighty in God for ... bringing every thought into captivity to the obedience of Christ." (2 Corinthians 10:4-5)

    "Be anxious for nothing, but in everything by prayer and supplication, with thanksgiving, let your requests be made known to God." (Philippians 4:6)

    "For there is not a just man on earth who does good and does not sin." (Ecclesiastes 7:20)

4. Celebrate the truths God teaches you as He renovates your heart.

5. Concentrate on God's love as you listen to praise music or take a walk. Breathe. The fresh air of God's love cleanses the soul of obsessive performance.

6. Give grace to others, and share your journey as God leads. Admit shortcomings, laugh about mistakes, and live a joyful life. Let His strength shine through your weak spots (2 Corinthians 12:9).

Are You Ready for Freedom?

Is Jesus speaking lovingly to you as He did to Martha about focusing on too many things? Do you long to shed the burden of excessive demands and grow in Christlikeness?

Ask God to liberate you from perfectionism's revolving door. Then relax in His love, the love that led Him to die for us and provide our freedom. "Therefore if the Son makes you free, you shall be free indeed" (John 8:36).

Exit that door! Sing praise to your Redeemer! Embrace the abundant life Jesus promises (John 10:10) as He renovates your heart and applies His blueprint to build godly character into you, His beloved child.

Prayer:

Heavenly Father,
I praise You, for You alone are perfect. Convict me of sin that misdirects my focus, and remind me to listen to You as Mary of Bethany did. I'm excited about Your promises to renovate my heart and build godly character traits into my life. Thank You for the freedom Jesus purchased on the cross. In His powerful name I pray, Amen.

Questions:

1. How does Philippians 1:6 give you assurance as you pursue godly character?

2. Which verses will you write on cards to fight sinful thoughts that lead to self-focus or perfectionism?

3. How will you focus more on Jesus as He encouraged Martha to do?

*All Scripture verses are taken from the NKJV.

Living above Reproach
by Patricia Luellen Nicholas

The steps of a good man are ordered by the LORD,
and He delights in his way.
Psalm 37:23 NKJV

On February 21, 2018, the world woke to the news that Billy Graham had passed away. I, like many that day and in the weeks that followed, marveled at the outpouring of love that was shown to the Graham family. The same love was bestowed on and felt by those who work for the Billy Graham Evangelistic Association.

We watched as the motorcade left the Cove in Asheville, North Carolina and made its way to Charlotte. Along the route, people waited for a chance to witness it, to pay their respects, and to mourn. Every overpass was covered with various fire departments in the "Crossed Ladder" formation, with the American flag hanging in the middle.

Just a few days later, we watched as Billy Graham became the fourth civilian to be given the honor of lying in the Capitol Rotunda. Then millions watched and mourned again as he was laid to rest in Charlotte.

What made Billy Graham so special? Was it the message that he preached? Was it the way he delivered the message? Was it that he was obedient to the call that God placed on him? My short answer to these questions is yes, but it is more than that. How, with so many other preachers falling by the wayside, or falling in sin and disgrace, did Billy Graham remain a man of integrity? Above reproach?

We all face hidden problems in life, and especially in ministry. Problems that seem to creep up out of nowhere. Often temptations can affect how we handle our money or business affairs. Temptation can strike in our work relationships, or how we deal with members of the opposite sex. Also creeping in unnoticed is the temptation to exaggerate, fib, or outright lie.

No one wakes up one morning saying, "I think I will wreck my marriage today," or "I think I will ruin my ministry with my actions." No, these things sneak up on us little by little if we are not careful.

In 1948 at the start of his ministry, Billy Graham asked several young men he had been working with to pray separately about hidden problems that come up in ministry. Temptations, if acted upon, cause devastation to the minister, as well as the ministry. He charged these men to seek God's guidance on every issue that they could think of that would derail a ministry. When they had prayed and were satisfied they had a comprehensive list, they agreed to come back together to discuss the problems as well as possible solutions.

They were surprised that each person had listed many of the same items. Everything centered around this one question: How can men traveling, preaching, and serving in ministry remain pure and full of integrity?

The answers to that question turned into what is now known as the Modesto Manifesto. They agreed to hold each other accountable in a series of resolutions.

1. To handle the ministry's money with integrity and above reproach. To down play offerings, and rely more on advanced donations that could be tracked and audited.

2. To be men of integrity in public with the opposite sex. To do this, they agreed to never travel or eat alone with women who weren't their wives.

3. To strive for good relations with local churches and clergy. To do this, they agreed to cooperate with any church that was willing to work with them.

4. To avoid negative publicity, they agreed on the need to be truthful about attendance numbers. They must never exaggerate or inflate this information.

We, as Christians, can and must continue the legacy of Dr. Graham. We are called by Jesus Himself to go to all the world and proclaim the good news of His gospel. We are commanded by Jesus to make disciples wherever we go.

Do we have the same hidden problems as traveling evangelists?

We may not face the same exact problems, but we are by no means free from temptations that can come our way. Managing money, the way we handle ourselves with members of the opposite sex, and the dilemmas of honesty will always tempt us in a myriad of ways.

Do we need to maintain the same strict policies that they did?

Certainly most of us will never have such a high profile ministry, but we can learn the lessons of living above reproach. Applying these principles to our lives builds godly character.

Just think of the impact we can have around us if we think and pray before we take a trip. Maybe it could be as simple as adjusting our plans by bringing someone else along so we are not put in compromising situations. Or we could ask a trusted friend to hold us accountable in certain areas of life in which we know we struggle.

Our lives may not have the impact for the kingdom of God that Billy Graham's life did, but we can follow his example of striving to live above reproach. Living as persons of integrity in our sphere of influence will please our Lord, guard our influence and testimony from encroaching sin, and keep us fit and ready to serve Him.

Prayer:

God,
I pray today that my life will be above reproach and reflect godly character. I pray for wisdom in the areas of my life that need to change so I will not give any appearance of compromise or cause suspicion. I pray that I will have integrity in handling the resources You have entrusted to me and that my conduct will in no way tarnish Your name. May the lives of Your people be a reflection of Your integrity. In Jesus' name, Amen.

Questions:

1. In what area do you struggle the most—money, living above reproach with members of the opposite sex, working well with others, truthfulness, or something else?

2. Is there one person you would feel comfortable in asking to hold you accountable?

3. In 1 Timothy 3:7, what is one of the requirements for an overseer or elder of the church?

4. What causes reproach according to Proverbs 14:34? In Proverbs 18:3?

5. In Isaiah 51:7, what advice does God give us if we are reproached by the world for His sake? Why, in v.8? In v.11-12, what can we look forward to?

6. In 1 Kings 9:4, what did God ask Solomon to do?

7. In Proverbs 20:7, what benefit does a life of integrity have?

Renovating Our Hearts
from Secret Sins

by Lyneta Smith

We smelled it before we saw it. The telltale scent of mildew assaulted us every time we opened the bathroom door.

"How can there be mildew already in our brand new house?" I asked my husband.

We'd chosen paint colors, carpet, and linoleum and then waited in anticipation as the builders completed our home. Everything was new and shiny when we moved in.

But over several weeks, mildew patches spread above the showerhead and on the other side of the wall, in our bedroom closet. Workers had to tear out huge chunks of drywall, repair the leak in the shower pipes, and then rebuild and paint the drywall.

How similar our home's mildew problem is to secret sins that can grow in our hearts. If we keep disobedience in the dark, it will eventually show itself after doing much damage.

King David, who tried to cover up hidden sin by having Uriah, Bathsheba's husband, killed in battle, eventually repented, then penned one of the most insightful passages of Scripture in the Bible:

Blessed is the one whose transgressions are forgiven, whose sins are covered. Blessed is the one whose sin the LORD does not count against them and in whose spirit is no deceit.

When I kept silent, my bones wasted away through my groaning all day long. For day and night your hand was heavy on me; my strength was sapped as in the heat of summer. Then I acknowledged my sin to you and did not cover up my iniquity. I said, "I will confess my transgressions to the LORD." And you forgave the guilt of my sin. (Psalm 32:1-5 NIV,* emphasis mine)

When we foster hidden sin in our lives, the very framework of our relationship with God wastes away. Like our mildew problem, we look good on the outside while the inside rots.

Many people struggle with lust, as King David did. Studies show half of the Christian men surveyed admitted to having a problem with pornography, and 28 percent of women view pornography regularly. Even some parts of mainstream media, such as *Game of Thrones* and *Fifty Shades of Grey*, feature lust-inducing scenes.

Perhaps your secret sin isn't lust. Maybe you battle greed, pride, or any number of ways the enemy wants to trip us up.

We don't have to let secret sins rot away our bones. Our bodies are God's temple. He is able to clean out whatever junk lurks in our hearts, just like we would care for our own houses. Just as a contractor uses a certain process to renovate a house, there are steps to renovate our hearts from secret sins.

Three Steps Help to Renovate Our Hearts from Secret Sins

1. Reduce Temptation

We live in a world where an enemy seeks to destroy us (1 Peter 5:8). Often, we fall into secret sins unintentionally, but our enemy is intentional about keeping us from God's best for our lives.

By the time we are ensnared, we have allowed many safekeeping boundaries to break down. The good news is, God shows us a way out of temptation.

> No temptation has overtaken you except what is common to mankind. And God is faithful; he will not let you be tempted beyond what you can bear. But when you are tempted, he will also provide a way out so that you can endure it. (1 Corinthians 10:13)

Here are a few examples of how we can reduce the tempting power of some common secret sins.

- Lust—Here is where we have to get radical, because our culture is permeated with gratuitous sexual images. Some families may need to cut off television reception entirely and unsubscribe from magazines with lingerie ads. Those traveling alone may find it necessary to store the hotel television cable and their laptop in the car's trunk overnight.

- Envy and greed—Those of us prone to coveting and comparing may reduce temptation by staying away from the mall and limiting social media time. Instead of focusing on what we don't have, we can appreciate what we do have by keeping a gratitude journal and beginning each prayer time with thanksgiving.

- Pride—Even if we don't often voice our thoughts out loud, sometimes we hold contempt for those who don't share our worldview. We can reduce the temptation to be prideful of our own opinions and tastes by avoiding discussions of those topics that tend to make us feel "right" or superior in our thinking. Such topics include politics, theology, or certain cultural hot-button issues.

2. Remember Your Purpose

Ephesians 1:12 tells us we're here to "be for the praise of [God's] glory." In other words, to worship.

Sometimes we think of worship as the twenty minutes in church when musicians lead us in song. But worship is more than singing; worship is adoration in all the things we do—work, service, or recreation. Whatever we are adoring is what we are worshiping. Our *general purpose* is to give God glory whatever we happen to be doing.

But each of us is created for a *specific purpose* that only we can fulfill. Jesus bought us with His blood so we can "do the good things he planned for us long ago" (Ephesians 2:10 NLT). We each have talents and gifts to equip us for our purpose (1 Corinthians 12:27-29). During different seasons of life, God fills our hearts with unique passions to meet the needs around us.

Remembering what we're here for, helps us to keep God's best for our lives in perspective when a secret sin threatens to upend everything we have to lose. A man I know who found victory over pornography formed an accountability/mentor group with several other men. He knew God wouldn't be able to use him in ministry if he remained in disobedience.

3. Refill Your Heart and Mind

Victory means more than purging sin. We've got to replace harmful habits with something else, because the sin is a symptom of an empty space not being filled by God. Getting rid of our secret sin isn't a magical, automatic solution. It involves God refining us as we cooperate with Him.

> Sin is a symptom of an empty space not being filled by God.

- Dig in deeper than ever to daily prayer and Bible meditation. Keeping a prayer journal allows us to see progress and be encouraged by answered prayer. God doesn't always speak in magnanimous ways when we study His word, but careful and diligent study always yields the message we need (Isaiah 55:11).

- Aside from reducing temptation, there are other habits we can change. What enjoyable activities have you been missing out on because your life has been full of secret sin? Reading, having coffee with friends, taking a hike or a bubble bath—replace the time you spent thinking about your secret sin with things that bring you joy and peace.

- <u>Above all, find a trusted accountability partner or group</u>. Someone who loves Jesus and cares about you, can help you scrub out the blight holding you back from God's best. Going through a book on the topic you're struggling with provides a framework to talk about all the issues. (An excellent resource for lust and pornography is *Surfing for God* by Michael John Cusick. Lysa TerKurst's *Made to Crave* is another great resource.)

Like mildew, secret sins thrive in darkness. The only way to break free is to shine truth on them. I don't advise sharing every deep, dark secret with the world at large, but without admitting the problem and activating the three Rs (reduce temptation, remember your purpose, and refill your heart and mind), secret sins will only grow worse. Sin is never static; either you're conquering disobedience or it's conquering you.

Prayer:

Heavenly Father,
I know there is no way I could ever be good enough to earn Your love, just as I know there's nothing I could ever do to make You love me any less. Thank You for sacrificing Your Son, so I could be righteous before You. I'm so grateful You redeemed me. Lord, help me to remember You're waiting, with arms wide open, for me to lean into You like never before to confess and repent of my secret sin. Let Your light chase away all darkness and make me clean. Amen.

Questions:

1. How would you choose an accountability partner? What traits would he or she have that could help guide you to freedom from secret sins?

2. How does the enemy use shame to keep us from dealing with secret sins?

3. Take some time to think about your passions and gifts. What's your purpose for this season?

*All Scripture verses are taken from the NIV unless otherwise indicated.

Constructing Character
that Overcomes
Life Issues

Weeks 3-4

When Change Happens to You, God Says, "I Will"

by Julie Lavender

"We're doing what?" I said to my husband when he announced, near the end of grad school, that he was considering a career in the Navy.

"But I don't want to leave home," I said through tears. "Our families are here. Friends. Our church—we've lived here our entire lives!" (Which wasn't exactly true, because my high school and college sweetheart had moved to MY hometown when he was five years old.)

"I don't want to go."

I've often wondered how Sarai felt when Abram first shared their relocation plans, as Moses recounted in Genesis 12:1 (NIV'):

> *The LORD had said to Abram, "Go from your country, your people and your father's household to the land I will show you."*

What a huge change that was in Abram's life! To leave the familiarity and comfortableness of home and family, and journey into the unknown. My, what a tough first step that must've been.

Yet, apparently from God's unerring Word, Abram didn't falter or stumble. He obeyed. He packed up and left his surroundings with complete trust in the Lord.

If Abram had questions initially, he didn't voice them within the verses of Genesis 12. Abram believed God when the Almighty Lord said, "I will."

God told Abram, "I will show you" (Gen 12:1), and Abram stepped out in faith, believing God would reveal the path He wanted Abram to take, as well as Abram's final destination.

God said, "I will make you into a great nation" (Gen 12:2), and Abram believed, even though he had no offspring at that time. A *great* nation—God had GREAT plans for Abram—not just mediocre ones.

"I will bless you" (Gen 12:2), God told Abram. God had plans for Abram, "plans to prosper [him] and not to harm [him], plans to give [him] hope and a future" (paraphrased from Jeremiah 29:11). God had good in mind through the changes Abram would encounter.

God promised Abram a great name, for "a good name is more desirable than great riches" (Proverbs 22:1). God had already blessed Abram with great riches, as referenced by the possessions and people he took with him on the journey.

"You will be a blessing" (Gen 12:2), God told Abram. Abram's address change meant he would encounter new faces, new families, unbelievers. God promised, planned, and expected Abram's blessing upon those he met.

"I will bless those who bless you and curse those who curse you" (Gen 12:3 TLB), God told Abram. Not only was the omniscient and Sovereign God of Abram familiar with all the ways of Abram, God, too, knew all the days ordained for each and every person in Abram's path. Those that might bless and those that would curse.

And lastly, when Abram took that first step of obedience, he did more than accept the changes God planned in his life. Abram opened the door for the greatest change for "all peoples on earth" (Gen 12:3), in the person of Jesus Christ, for it was through God's covenant with Abram that God secured His chosen people to prepare for the coming of His only Son, the Christ child.

When God said, "Go," Abram was obedient and knew change was inevitable. Abram trusted God to walk with him every step of the way on his journey.

Unlike me.

I loved the familiarity of home and the students I'd taught for two years while completing my master's degree. I enjoyed our small town and the fact that my address had only changed once.

What if I can't find another teaching job? Where will we live? We won't know anyone. I like *this* church.

I think what I feared most was change. I was afraid. Afraid of obeying God because I didn't know what lay ahead. I didn't trust God to journey with me. I'd only *known* God in Statesboro, Georgia—would He really go with me when everything about my life changed?

I don't know if Sarai stamped her feet in the dust when she followed Abram to the border of Haran, but by the time the moving van loaded our possessions—a very small moving van, because two broke college newlyweds hadn't accumulated much—the dust had settled on my rotten attitude, and I tried to look at my future as the adventure promised in the Navy recruitment posters.

Just like with most adventures in life, I loved a great deal of the changes that came during our twenty years in the Navy, and I struggled through a host of changes, too. But you know what? With every address change, God was there! Why had I ever doubted?

God surrounded us in Florida at Naval Air Station Jacksonville, much like the St. John's River that sloshed ashore nearby. God protected us at Camp Lejeune, North Carolina, during Operation Desert Storm, when my husband deployed for war.

God encouraged us in Stafford, Virginia, when David spent more hours studying than he did being a dad, but fortunately, that tour of duty only lasted twelve months.

God blessed us in Oceanside, California with a church that became like family, when we journeyed farther from our loved ones than we'd ever been, and He changed the course of eternity for our eldest son and daughter when they accepted Jesus as their Saviour.

God directed us in Poulsbo, Washington, and showed us another corner of His beautiful world, just before our ship sailed back to our hometown when David's twenty-year career came to an end.

And guess what? The change from military life back to civilian life was equally difficult for me, but this time I trusted God with the journey. By now, I'd figured out that God would accompany me through every change, small or huge, no matter what corner of the world I called home.

Though I don't always get it right, I try to remember the story of Abram when I'm faced with some sort of change in my life. I want to be a blessing to others. I want my name to be greater than whatever riches I might have acquired. I want to walk in faith and obedience, trusting God with each step. Wherever that change takes me, I want to meet God there and worship Him with my thoughts and actions and words and deeds.

> Wherever change takes me, I want to meet God there and worship Him with my thoughts and actions and words and deeds.

I've learned that the blessings that come from obeying God far outweigh whatever negatives I perceive from an unwanted change. Sometimes, that change might be the first step of the best adventure of my life! And because God said, "I will," well, that settles it for me!

Prayer:

Dear God,
Sometimes change is exhilarating and adventurous; sometimes it's terrifying and unwanted. Help me to realize that nothing catches You off-guard—You know what "changes" are coming my way. Lord, help me trust You completely and obey You faithfully with each step of my journey.

Questions:

1. What is the biggest change you've experienced? Did you view it as a positive change or negative change?

2. When you're faced with change, what's your first course of action?

3. How can the story of Abram encourage you to be obedient to God's calling, even if it means unwanted or frightening changes in your life?

*All Scripture verses are taken from the NIV unless otherwise indicated.

JUST. MUST. TRUST.

by Lisa Kibler

I sat in the waiting room, my book lying untouched on my lap. After an hour, I was called back to see my husband, Sam, following his diagnostic colonoscopy. The doctor looked at me, closed his eyes, and shook his head.

"I'm afraid it's cancer."

I grabbed his arm and squeezed.

Make that news go right back in your mouth, I screamed inside.

"Wha…?" I couldn't form a complete word.

Sam, even in the cloud of the anesthetic, looked at me and said, "I heard him."

Sam's haze transferred to me; I don't even remember driving us home. We called no one; we just stretched out together, and I hugged him with all that was in me.

And we prayed, "Lord, whatever You bring, we are in."

Throughout the remaining four years God gave us together, our faith wavered a bit, but it didn't disappear. God never failed us as He led us through that "valley of the shadow of death." Our hearts were full of love for the Lord and for each other.

When Sam's body had enough, the Lord took him home, and He held me in His grip—in an impenetrable grace-fog against the flames of death that surrounded me.

Lord, what will I do without him?

The Lord spoke to my heart, "Child, I have turned your grievous earthly loss into Sam's greatest gain, heaven. He is in glory, rejoice in that." During this process, God has revealed life-changing markers to grow in faith.

1. Acknowledge your loss.

As grief ascends from smolders to whiffs of bittersweet memories, the patterns of my life change. That incredible fog that God placed around me lasted for months. I learned to allow the tears an exit and to let the people who love me, take care of me. In your time of grief, it's important to pour out your heart to the Lord, just as King David did. He trusted God especially in his most dire moments. It's no wonder Psalm 23 is the passage so many turn to in times of trouble. Verse 4 (NKJV) says,

> Yea, though I walk through the valley of the shadow of death,
> I will fear no evil;
> For You are with me;
> Your rod and Your staff, they comfort me.

God cares for us in every way. He knows what we will face at every moment in our lives, and He stands ready to comfort us. Notice the verse says, "the *shadow* of death" (emphasis mine). As sinners saved by the grace of the Lord Jesus, we are kept from death. We will all stand in its shadow and feel the pangs of it, yet through Jesus we are alive forever. That's good news! That's what God our Father wants us to remember. He is our Shepherd, and as a shepherd tenderly cares for his flock, so too the Lord keeps us safe in the confines of His tender mercies. The acknowledgment is a key, because our Father shows us how He fills our grief-weary souls.

2. Thank God.

Every morning, I thank God for the day He has given me to serve Him, and I thank Him that even though I miss him every day, I know where Sam is. Knowing Jesus and trusting His promises make all the difference.

> Through the LORD's mercies we are not consumed,
> Because His compassions fail not.
> They are new every morning;
> Great is Your faithfulness.
> "The LORD is my portion," says my soul,
> "Therefore I hope in Him!" (Lamentations 3:22-24)

When we thank God, we express our deepest hope in Him. He is merciful, compassionate, and faithful, and He is enough!

> In everything give thanks; for this is the will of God in Christ Jesus for you. (1 Thessalonians 5:18)

Wow! Everything means everything. That means even when we face our deepest losses, we are to thank God. We don't thank Him for the losses (and there will be more than one), but we thank Him as He leads us through them. It's His will, and it draws us closer to Him.

3. Be courageous.

It takes great courage to deal with loss, and we must be patient with ourselves as we go through the process. It's all part of the journey of sanctification. We, as humans, need time to accept and cope with what we cannot control. Jesus is the only One who can bear everything. Part of being courageous is trusting God and giving up the emotional chains that threaten to overwhelm us. He bids us in Matthew 11:28-30:

> Come to Me, all you who labor
> and are heavy laden, and I will give you rest.
> Take My yoke upon you and learn from Me,
> for I am gentle and lowly in heart, and you will find rest for

your souls.
For My yoke is easy and My burden is light.

Yes, I have wailed in the agony of my loneliness. That was the hardest thing for me to bear, so much so that I couldn't look at the grief etched on my face. But for those who belong to Jesus, the blazing heartache is assuaged by the power and the presence of Him who loves us. I did go to Him; I go to Him every day, and I feel His presence. He is patient with me as I lean in and learn from Him what it means to face this life without the man He gave me. It was huge for me to give Sam back to God; it took guts to give him up as my husband. And in doing that, I gained peace from Jesus. Grieving is not holding on; it is letting go.

> Have I not commanded you? Be strong and of good courage; do not be afraid, nor be dismayed, for the LORD your God is with you wherever you go. (Joshua 1:9)

The courage I have is not mine; it is solely from the Lord, and it is mine (and ours) to receive.

4. Be patient; *wait on the Lord.*

Many times I feel like people are thinking, *Come on, girl! Suck it up and get back to living.* Not a one has said that to me, and I highly doubt my incredible family and friends have thought it. I'm the one who gets the most impatient with me, and we must be patient with ourselves as we go through the process.

Lord, it's been almost three years. Shouldn't I be healed of this by now?

And my spirit testifies with His that it's all in His time, not mine. The important thing, as this passage from Isaiah says, is to "wait on the Lord."

> But those who wait on the LORD
> Shall renew their strength;
> They shall mount up with wings like eagles,

They shall run and not be weary,
They shall walk and not faint. (Isaiah 40:31)

It's a beautiful passage that promises our strength will be renewed! It doesn't say we *might;* it says we *shall.* That's a promise from God. Can you imagine soaring about like a mighty eagle?

The memories linger, and some of them bring stinging pain, no matter how long a loved one has been with the Lord. We can hold on to the memories, although we have no choice but to let go of a person's closeness. We can hug a pillow, or smell a closet full of clothes, but that essence is not them. Truly, given the choice, a loved one who has gone home to heaven would not come back.

Waiting on the Lord means praying, reading His Word, and learning more about God. In the midst of life's trials and heartaches, who else would we ever want to beseech for peace?

Waiting on the Lord means listening as His "still small voice" (1 Kings 19:12) whispers thundering truths to our souls. He speaks—He says, "My child, you can mourn your loss, and I will help you grow as a result of what you are experiencing. I love you. I am here."

God exacts a heavy sentence on grief when we wait on Him. He renews us—He makes us fly like an eagle, buttressed by His Holy Spirit, Jesus' presence in us, His Word, and His church. His strength in us is more than enough to carry us through any loss this life can deliver. Yes, "I can do all things through Christ who strengthens me" (Philippians 4:13).

5. Rest in the Lord.

Come to Me, all you who labor
and are heavy laden, and I will give you rest.
Take My yoke upon you and learn from Me,
for I am gentle and lowly in heart, and you will find rest for your souls.
For My yoke is easy and My burden is light. (Matthew 11:28-30)

As we rest in Him, He lets us know He hears us by what He does. Loss makes for a weary soul because we are heartsick. Tears release some of the stress, but only Jesus can erase the paralyzing anguish.

In Psalm 40:1-3, as David focused on God, he saw his anguish turn into worship as a new song of praise emerged. He knew that his actions and reactions spoke of how he viewed the Lord. When we rest in the Lord, not only are we encouraged and strengthened, but our witness for the Lord is enhanced. Because of Jesus, we can walk the path of loss knowing He is always in front, lighting the way.

> Because of Jesus, we can walk the path of loss knowing He is always in front, lighting the way.

6. Find your peace in Jesus.

Jesus said, "Peace I leave with you, My peace I give to you; not as the world gives do I give to you. Let not your heart be troubled, neither let it be afraid" (John 14:27).

His peace is overwhelming my loneliness, and since He wastes nothing, He has given me a charge for the Kingdom, and I am to use what He has allowed for His glory and my good. With His peace, our hearts can remain calm, and we need not be afraid. As I wait, He is changing my "mourning into dancing" (Psalm 30:11). That's a call for worship!

Losing a loved one can make anyone's faith waver, even a mature believer's. But God has provided avenues for our anguish that point us right back to the One who is sovereign over all. Knowing Jesus and trusting in His promises sets our hearts in sync with the Father's. One of the phrases we can cling to is one I repeat often: Just. Must. Trust.

Prayer:

Lord God Almighty, blessed Father of all,
We thank You for this season in our lives, much as it hurts, for You bring the healing as the world can never do. You restore our hope

as You strengthen our faith in You. We praise You for Jesus and the peace He has left with us. We don't want to "do life" without Him or Your Holy Spirit; we thank You that we don't have to. Help us as we mourn losses in our lives and change us as we grow in the grace and knowledge of our Redeemer. In Jesus' name, Amen.

Questions:

1. Make a list of the ways God has manifested His presence in your life. How has that helped you as you grieve?

2. Read Psalm 30. David's adversaries were flesh and blood, but as we deal with loss, spiritual enemies also seek to destroy our faith and joy in the Lord. Re-write that prayer with personal pronouns.

3. How can you dance in the presence of Jesus today?

*All Scripture verses are taken from the NKJV.

Finding Gems in the Midst of the Junk of Life

by Denise Roberts

Rejoice always, pray continually, give thanks in all circumstances; for this is God's will for you in Christ Jesus. (1 Thessalonians 5:16-18 NIV)

After two wearisome days of travel, a flat tire was the last thing I needed at 10:30 p.m. My nice clothes were wilting in the oppressive heat and humidity of Atlanta in July. And, I had never changed my own tire before. This kind of junk invites me to melt down.

I might have, if it had not been for a text I received early the day before.

I was on seven different standby lists to seven different cities trying to get home from a conference. The flights were all oversold, standby lists were growing, and frustration was escalating each time I was on the airport side of a closed boarding door.

I was whining via text to my husband when "enjoy your circumstances" popped up on the screen of my phone. Inhaling deeply and deliberately exhaling the mounting tension between my shoulder blades, I recalled Paul's instructions tucked in his first letter to the Thessalonians. *Rejoice. Pray. Give thanks.*

Paul does not say that we need to be thankful for the junk, but to practice joyfulness in the junk. How? Find the gems and pray thankfulness.

Minor irritations like oversold flights are a training ground preparing us for when life's hard crises strike. Our natural response to life's junk is to whine, blame, and get angry. We must seize the opportunities to practice mining the beautiful gems of thankfulness when the stakes are not high so that we will instinctively seek them when relationships struggle, illness invades, or job loss threatens.

> Mining the gems of thankfulness creates fertile ground for the seeds of peace and joy to take deep root.

Mining the gems of thankfulness creates fertile ground for the seeds of peace and joy to take deep root. The very things we need to sustain us through the junk.

"Enjoy your circumstances" was the prompt I needed to find gems and give thanks. In this, joy promised to bubble up and override the frustration.

The following gems of thankfulness are excerpts from my journal.

Day 1 - The day started mighty early, Lord. Even though the birds weren't up yet, thank You for my husband's job that provides this benefit. This is a minor inconvenience compared to missing the bigger blessing of the conference. Thank You that security lines were short at that hour and that Einstein's was open for coffee.

All direct flights are oversold. This will not be simple. Lord, thank You for free Wi-Fi that works, plugs near chairs, and mobile technology that lets me manage the possibilities.

Moving from gate to gate together, a young couple, new to standby travel, asked for tips on navigating the system. Lord, thank You that I was approachable because Your joy in me was evident.

Twelve hours at the airport and the temptation to whine was strong. Lord, thank You for family that rearranged their day to come fetch me at the airport. Thank You that I can take a shower, have a bed to sleep in, and for my great neighbor helping with my dog.

Day 2 - Hope grew elusive again. Lord, thank You for Bill Panky, in his Hawaiian shirt, inviting laughter when he introduced himself as "Bill Panky, you know, like hanky-panky."

That flat tire challenged me to keep finding thankful gems. Lord, thank You that I am in a well-lit parking lot and not on the side of the interstate. Thank You that it is not raining, that I could get those lug nuts off, and please don't let my tire fall off on the way home.

Arriving home I was greeted with dog hugs and kisses. I realized I was not tired despite the long day. I am surprised by how content and peaceful I feel. Have felt all along.

Peace. Joy. Contentment.

This is what God wants for us. Mining the gems of thankfulness and praying them back to the Lord is how we cultivate a heart ready to receive His peace and joy in the midst of our trying circumstances. This will be harder to do in some times than others. We must practice in the less trying times to be established in this when the harder times come.

Prayer:

Holy God,
You are a faithful God. We claim Your promise to never leave us nor forsake us. Lord, please forgive us that we do not show You the same faithfulness. When life gets hard, it gets easy to forget that You are working in the midst of our junk. Lord, enlighten the eyes of our hearts so that we may see the gems in the midst of our junk and teach our hearts to praise You in thankfulness.

Questions:

1. What circumstances in your life are robbing you of joy, peace, and contentment?

2. What has your response been to these circumstances so far?

3. Mining the gems takes practice. Sometimes they can be hard to see. Take time to list five gems (or more) you can identify in the midst of the junk of your circumstance.

4. For each gem, write or speak out loud a statement of thankfulness. There is power in writing them down so we can go back and recall God's faithfulness. There is power in the spoken word. As we hear words of thankfulness, they will influence our thoughts.

My Wallet, God's Money
by Laura W. Watts

When I belonged to the I-want-it-now society, I needed the latest and greatest of everything. Buying something better, faster, or prettier than what I owned fed an insatiable appetite deep in my soul.

My heart's desire to find fulfillment by owning more stuff created a mountain of debt from credits cards, finance companies, and personal loans. I didn't know about God's principles for financial freedom, and I made a lot of mistakes. My lack of money management skills created a slippery slope into the pitfall of debt and contributed to a bitter divorce. My life needed a major rescue.

Fast forward seven years. I married a godly man. We volunteered in our church, gave the first ten percent tithe of income, and hoped the rest would fall into place. Although we believed God would provide for our needs, we didn't put feet to our faith in that promise. Our debt load from student loans, cars, and credit cards mirrored the average American household. We thought we could handle our personal finances on our own. As a CPA, I should know how to manage money. Wrong. Throughout six years of college, I never learned anything about personal money management.

Admitting our failure, we committed to seek God's help. We searched and found what was missing—our view of God was wrong. We allowed God into every area of our life except the money part.

How we view God is paramount to how well we manage what He gives us. After taking a money management class at church, we made these changes immediately:

- Stopped using credit cards
- Saved $1000
- Quit buying on impulse, prayed, and waited 24 hours before deciding to buy
- Called each other before any purchase over $50
- Applied excess cash to pay down bills

Doing it God's way completely transformed our finances and strengthened our marriage. God's promises worked for us, and they can do the same for you.

The Cornerstone Truth

Do you know God cares about every dollar we earn and spend? The Almighty King of the universe knows every aspect of our lives and promises to provide what we need. The Lord wants to be involved in our finances.

A typical church member knows about the 10 percent tithe, but most are not aware the Bible gives us a complete set of principles to help us manage the remaining 90 percent of income.

The most important principle for money management is found in 2 Chronicles 29:11-12 (TLB):

Everything in the heavens and earth is yours, O Lord, and this is your kingdom. We adore you as being in control of everything. Riches and honor come from you alone, and you are the ruler of all mankind; your hand controls power and might and it is at your discretion that men are made great and given strength.

God owns everything. He's in control and opens the doors for us to get jobs, promotions, and raises.

If we believe God owns everything, this means our money doesn't belong to us. God owns it, and *He* gave it to us. We need to relinquish ownership back to Him. This sounds easy, but it requires a radical change in attitude. God owns more than our money. He owns our houses, cars, clothes, jobs. Everything. Understanding this cornerstone truth prepares our hearts to embrace an attitude called contentment.

A Root Cause

Contentment doesn't mean we have to live an austere lifestyle. Enjoying the good things of life is part of God's plan for us, because He richly provides us with everything for our enjoyment (1 Timothy 6:17). In God's plan, we may wait longer to buy so we can save and pay cash, but following God's way acknowledges His lordship over our money. He knows what is best for us, because He sees our tomorrows.

To determine your level of contentment, take some time to review the *when, what,* and *why* of your most recent spending. The results may reveal some areas of discontentment.

When do I buy? Buying on impulse when we find something appealing instead of planning ahead for a specific item, often leads to overspending. Shopping to boost self-esteem or ease emotions such as loneliness, may provide temporary relief, but these habits will send the budget into the red zone. Using credit cards to get something now instead of waiting until we can pay cash indicates we trust our own wisdom more than God's.

What do I buy? Gadgets, electronics, designer clothes, luxury cars, and so forth exceed the basic needs of life. Buying these things to impress others or to prove financial status shows we need to find our identity in our possessions. Our true identity is found in God and our relationship with Him. Contentment comes from knowing God and understanding who we are based on His truth.

Why do I buy? Needs, wants, and desires are the three reasons we buy things. We *need* to buy the essentials such as food, clothes, and a place to live. But when we *want* and *desire* material possessions in excess of genuine need *and* we use debt to get them, we need to examine our motives. Are we allowing God to be Lord over our money?

The Heart of a Faithful Steward

The next principle of financial wisdom is our role.

In Matthew 25:14-30, Jesus told a parable about money and stewardship. In summary, a master gave money to three of his servants before he went on a long trip and instructed them to manage it while he was away. He gave different amounts to each servant based on their ability to manage. Right away, the first two servants invested the money, but the third servant buried his. When the master returned, he called the servants to see how they managed. The two who invested had doubled their master's money, and he praised each one saying, "Well done, my good and faithful servant." (Matthew 25:21 NLT). He rewarded their obedience with more responsibilities and celebrated their successes.

The master found great pleasure in these wise servants, but not with the one who buried his money. He called him wicked and lazy. He took back the money and gave it to the first servant. Then he threw the lazy servant out into the darkness.

God is looking for a faithful steward—someone He can trust to obey Him. The Lord wants us to manage what He gives us and use it for His purposes. Sometimes, He gives a surplus to those He can trust so they can help others in need. Like the good and faithful servants, we can honor God through wise choices and reflect faith, integrity, and values to others.

A faithful steward loves God first. Jesus said we can't serve both God and money, because we will hate one and love the other (Luke 16:13). The love of money competes with God for our affection. When we accept God as the owner of everything, His truth transforms our hearts. We make decisions as good stewards and not as selfish owners.

Great Financial Advice

The Bible has much more to say about how to spend, save, invest, and enjoy a debt-free life.

- Honor God with the tithe (Malachi 3:10, Proverbs 3:9-10).
- Know the condition of your finances (Proverbs 27:23-27).
- Determine goals for spending, saving, and giving (Proverbs 4:25-27).
- Plan a budget to reach goals (Proverbs 16:3 NLT)
- Take care of your family (1 Timothy 5:8).
- Stay away from debt (Proverbs 22:7, 1 Corinthians 7:23).
- Work hard (Colossians 3:23-24 TLB).
- Save consistently (Proverbs 21:5 ESV)
- Give a portion of surplus money to others (2 Corinthians 8:14-15).
- Diversify—don't put all the eggs in one basket (Ecclesiastes 11:2, 6 NLT).

We experience contentment by resting in God's love and knowing He ordains tomorrow. The immense storehouse of heaven reveals God's Father's heart toward us and draws us to depend on His resources and wisdom, not our own.

Prayer:

Father, I acknowledge You as Creator of everything. I want to be a good and faithful servant and honor You as Lord of my wallet. Teach me to follow Your ways and not my own. Help me to find peace and contentment in You. In Jesus' name, Amen.

Questions:

1. Read 1 Chronicles 29:11-12. What actions or attributes of God impact our financial well-being? Our jobs?

2. Read Psalm 24:1, Psalm 50:10-12, and Haggai 2:8, and write down the things God owns.

3. Considering all that Gods owns, make a list of the things you own.

4. In Luke 16:10 (ISV), Jesus said "Whoever is faithful with very little is also faithful with a lot, and whoever is dishonest with very little is also dishonest with a lot." Do you believe this verse applies to money alone or to all areas of life? Explain.

5. Read Matthew 25:14-30. What does God expect us to do with everything He gives us?

6. Read 1 Timothy 6:17. What does this verse say about why God provides for us?

7. Read 2 Corinthians 8:14-15 and 1 Timothy 6:8-9. Why does God bless us with a surplus of money and possessions?

Regret! Release It—Don't Relive It
by Billie Corley

"Forget regret, or life is yours to miss."[1]

As we travel the path toward Christian maturity, making a wrong choice is inevitable, but it isn't the finish line. It doesn't disqualify us from continuing. It may take us longer to reach our destination, but it's definitely not the end. We can't let failure stop us in our tracks. We can't let regret paralyze us. With God's grace, we can confess the wrong, make amends where we can, and move forward, as we see in the lives of Peter, Paul, and others.

Thousands came to know Jesus as their personal Savior under Peter's preaching. His life, however, was not void of poor choices. Peter learned a painful lesson about self-confidence. He was confident that even though all men would stumble in faith, he wouldn't (Matthew 26:33). Yet, when the pressure was on, he faltered. As soon as the words of denial were out of his mouth, the agony of his actions hurled him into the horrifying trenches of remorse. Thankfully, this was short-lived. With Jesus' help, he was able to move forward to become a powerful preacher of the gospel.

What lessons can we learn from Peter's experience?

- Jesus wasn't surprised when Peter denied Him. He knew Satan would "sift" Peter, and He knew how Peter would respond (Luke 22:31-32).

- Jesus cushioned Peter's fall with prayer. Jesus didn't pray that Peter wouldn't stumble, rather, He prayed his faith wouldn't fail (Luke 22:32).

- Jesus didn't regard Peter's denials as the end of his ministry. He knew that Peter would return to Him. He didn't say to Peter *if* you return to Me, but *when* (Luke 22:32).

In his epistle, Peter cautions Christians to be sober-minded and watchful (1 Peter 5:8) against a powerful enemy. Satan's strategy is to hold Christians captive within the confines of their own minds. When we continually drag up wrong choices (whether ours or someone else's), we're traveling a road to nowhere. But remaining alert will expose and eradicate the works of the devil.

Satan seeks to rob us of the joys of today by trapping us in the regrets of the past. But Paul didn't buy into that tactic. Even though he had persecuted Christians before he believed in Jesus, he didn't let it stop him from spreading the gospel and building up the church. We can use Paul's words from Philippians 3:13-14 (NKJV) to devise strategies that will help us to guard against the enemy and debilitating regret.

- *Brethren, I do not count myself to have apprehended* (v.13). Remember that Christian growth is a process that has ups and downs. Perfection will only be realized once we enter Heaven's gates.

- *But one thing I do* (v.13). Live in the moment. Accomplishments are achieved by taking one step at a time.

- *Forgetting those things which are behind* (v.13). Put the past where it belongs—behind you.

- *Reaching forward to those things which are ahead* (v.13). Keep your eyes on the goal.

- *I press toward the goal* (v.14). Keep moving toward it.

- *I press ... for the prize of the upward call of God in Christ Jesus* (v.14). Continue pursuing God's calling upon your life.

Another person who released regret is Jason Kent, son of the author Carol Kent. He was sentenced to life in prison without parole. One day he told his mom, "I hate prison, but I'm not going to waste it."[2] Because of his choice, God opened doors for a thriving ministry within the confines of the prison walls. His parents have also transformed their misery into an effective ministry in which many are encouraged for God's glory.

We can either allow our mistakes to define us or refine us. Perhaps you are in the trenches of regret. It's time to R-E-L-E-A-S-E it and allow God's forgiveness and grace to lift you up and fortify your course. Tap into the power of these seven steps to gain release from the bondage of regret.

R-E-L-E-A-S-E Your Regret

1. REFUSE to allow destructive thoughts to dwell in your mind by bringing every thought captive to the obedience of Christ (2 Corinthians 10:5).

2. EMBRACE responsibility for your choices. The process toward freedom mandates owning the decision that was made (Psalm 51:4).

3. LET GO of past mistakes (Psalm 51:3). For example, write a letter or record the experience, seek forgiveness, grant yourself the freedom to make mistakes, or make amends.

4. EXAMINE the reason for the mistake or wrong choice. Also, what did you learn and how can you apply this knowledge as you move forward (Psalm 51:6)?

5. ACCEPT "it-is-what-it-is." It is impossible to undo an action no matter how much you agonize or fret. A word spoken cannot be taken back; an act cannot be reversed.

Acknowledge the slip-up and look forward to brighter days (Philippians 3:13a).

6. Recognize the SOURCE of spirit-depleting thoughts. Discern whether the enemy is speaking, by measuring your thoughts against God's Word.

7. EXPECT to make more mistakes. It's a certain part of growing into the image of Christ. But determine to choose God's way next time. Choose from this point forward to walk with God as best you can, depending on Him to help you.

> "Success is not final, failure is not fatal: it is the courage to continue that counts."
> - Winston Churchill

Remember: "Success is not final, failure is not fatal: it is the courage to continue that counts."[3]

It is not how many days we have ... it is how we live our days. Regret is unavoidable. Don't relive it. Release it into God's hands and patiently wait as He works all things together for good.

The next time you find yourself in the pit of regret, say, "I didn't come this far, only to come this far." Reach out and grab hold of God's rope of hope. Pull yourself up out of the pit of regret and continue on ... until Jesus comes.

Prayer:

Heavenly Father,
I thank You for creating me by Your wisdom. Life is a set of choices and sometimes I mess up. Your word teaches I will fall, but not be utterly cast down. You are the Anchor of my hope and the God of my tomorrows. Thank You for providing a way of escape against the torments of my mind. When I'm tempted to relive my mistake, I choose to release it into Your mighty hands and wait as You work all things together for good. Yes, even my mistakes. Thank You, Heavenly Father, for Your gift of grace, unfailing love, and infinite power. In Jesus' almighty name I pray, Amen.

Questions:

1.   Review and right down the seven methods of release.

2.   Which steps seem the most effective to you in enabling us to release regret?

3.   What do these Scriptures teach us about avoiding regret?
    - Psalm 32:8
    - Proverbs 3:5-6
    - 1 Thessalonians 5:17
    - 1 Corinthians 10:13

4.   When we make a wrong choice, what action should we take?
    - Psalm 51:1-2
    - 1 John 1:9

5.   What do these Scriptures teach about hope?
    - Psalm 146:5
    - Romans 15:13

6.   Regret threatens to stop us in our tracks. Acts 20:24 tells us what to do when we are tempted to quit. How can you apply this to your situation?

*All Scripture verses are taken from the NKJV.

1. Jonathan Larson, www.wiseoldsayings.com/regret-quotes.

2. From a speech by Carol Kent at Epworth by the Sea, Saint Simons Island, Georgia, in April 2015. Used by permission.

3. Winston Churchill, https://www.brainyquote.com/quotes/winston_churchill_124653.

Surviving Grief

by Patricia Luellen Nicholas

"I don't know how you've survived." I was having a conversation with a friend, and when the subject turns to my losses, I often get similar comments. "You sure are strong to have gotten through," or "A lesser person would not have made it." There have been days that I wondered myself how I have made it through.

Five years ago, I came home from work to discover my husband Dave, unresponsive. We lost him that day unexpectedly to a heart attack. While that alone would be enough to send any person into a deep grief, just two days later, I lost my father to an illness he had been battling for over a year. I went from a normal person with everyday cares, to one who had fallen into the deepest darkest pit of sadness and despair. I was hit by wave after wave of grief until I thought I would never be able to stand upright again.

I pleaded with God to take away my sadness which felt like more than I could bear, much like Paul pleaded with God to take away his thorn in the flesh.

And lest I should be exalted above measure by the abundance of the revelations, a thorn in the flesh was given to me, a messenger of Satan to buffet me, lest I be exalted above measure. Concerning this thing I pleaded with the Lord three times that it might depart from me. And He said to me, "My grace is sufficient for you, for My strength is made perfect in weakness." Therefore most gladly I will rather boast in my infirmities, that the power of Christ may rest upon me. Therefore I take pleasure in infirmities, in reproaches, in needs, in persecutions, in distresses, for Christ's sake. For when I am weak, then I am strong. (2 Corinthians 12:7-10 NKJV)

This passage is amazing, because it is so counter to how we think God should work in our lives. Paul asked God *three* times to take away the "thorn in the flesh," but God told him no, that "My grace is sufficient for you." That is not really what we want to hear at first, but if we truly listen to what God is saying, He is telling us that He will be with us through the trial, that it is His strength that will carry us. He also never promised that our lives would be free of trial, in fact, quite the opposite.

Of course God lead me to see that in my weakness, He wanted to shine His strength through me.

These things I have spoken to you, that in Me you may have peace. In the world you will have tribulation; but be of good cheer, I have overcome the world. (John 16:33)

I asked God, "If You have overcome the world, promised us peace, and promised that Your grace would be sufficient, why do I not feel it?" The still small voice that I heard in my soul lead me to one more passage in His word.

But the fruit of the Spirit is love, joy, peace, longsuffering, kindness, goodness, faithfulness, gentleness, self-control. Against such there is no law. (Galatians 5:22-23)

God was telling me that when I became a Christian and was adopted as His child, He gave me gifts, two of which were joy and peace. While I wondered if I would ever experience joy again, He was saying I already had it. When I wondered where my peace went to, He said, "It never left you." So I began to pray every day through each of the fruits, listing them one by one in a prayer much like this.

Heavenly Father,

Help me to love Your people the way You love them. Help me to love the unlovable when they say insensitive things.

Restore my joy. Help me to see that joy has never left me, it is just hidden by my grief. Help me to have joy in little things throughout the day. Help me to see that joy is not dependent on my emotions, but it is a gift from You, and for Your glory.

Help me to have patience and longsuffering to let the grief process work through me. Let me not miss a step, or miss a lesson You are teaching me. Help me to use this time to grow closer to You as You hold me.

Help me to be kind to others even though I may not feel like it. Put a smile on my face to brighten someone's day, thereby brightening mine.

I thank You for Your goodness all around me. I thank You for friends whom You have given me, I thank You that *You* are good, and that even though this does not *feel* like it, I know You will use this for *my* good. I pray that You will help me to be good to others today.

I pray that I will remain faithful. I pray that in my hardest day my faith will remain true, that it will grow as I see You give me strength moment by moment, hour by hour, and day by day.

Help me to be gentle as I interact with Your people today. Spirit, will You work through me and let Your gentleness shine a light on others today that may not know You, that they be won by Your gentle spirit in me?

Finally, help me to have self-control; help me to exhibit this quality to everyone around me, whether at work, at church, or at home.

After praying through this list of "fruits" every day for about six months, I began to see a significant difference in my life. My joy was returning, and where I once felt deep, dark grief, I had peace when nothing could explain it. I began to love others who, not long ago, would have aggravated me, and I had patience and self-control when before I would have "given them a piece of my mind." On and on it went, until I totally felt like a new person.

God truly had given me sufficient grace to get through one of the hardest times in my life. Do I still have times of grief? Yes, it is something that will always be part of me, but I am significantly better than I was even a year ago. His grace is sufficient to heal, but it is also sufficient to get through each wave of grief as it hits, and like ocean tides that come and go, my "grief waves" are receding and do not knock me off my feet as they used to.

Prayer:

O Heavenly Father,
I know every trial, every tear, and everything that You have allowed in my life will be used for Your glory. Be my strength today, let Your light shine through the cracks in my life, and be glorified. Comforter, Holy Spirit, help me to use the gifts that You have bestowed on me in the form of various fruits, to grow. Give me sufficient grace to get through the trial You have given me, and not just get through, but to be a shining example to others. Amen.

Questions:

1. In what ways have you experienced a "thorn in the flesh"?

2. How have you seen God's sufficient grace displayed in your life?

3. What fruit of the Spirit do you wish to experience more?

4. What trial is God wanting to use in your life to shine through and to display His glory to the world? Will you let Him?

*All Scripture verses are taken from the NKJV.

Silencing the Noise of Loneliness
by Adria Wilkins

I never realized how much noise my kids made until they went off to college.

Babbling, chatter, and questions are the noises we hear as our children grow from the stages of baby, toddler, and tween. Kids seem to get louder as they grow. Walking through the house, closing doors and kitchen cabinets, and talking all become part of the sounds we hear. Between running through the house, Nerf gun competitions, and video games, the noise can get out of control. We long for silence and a hot bath at the end of the day.

We don't realize how precious the noises are to our ears until we are in the car and it is filled to the brim with dorm room supplies. We pull into the college parking lot and unload our child's things into their new home away from home. After we shut the trunk and start the drive home, the stillness in the air can turn to loneliness.

Loneliness hits us no matter our age, lifestyle, or job. It can be triggered by the loss of a loved one, a job relocation, or a relationship breakup.

Jesus, who came as a man and experienced all the things we do here on earth, knows and understands loneliness. He lost a friend, Lazarus, and wept as He approached the grave. He even had a disciple that betrayed and denied Him. He was also left alone to die for us. Matthew 27:46 (NIV) says, "About three in the afternoon

Jesus cried out in a loud voice, *'Eli, Eli, lema sabachthani?'* (which means 'My God, my God, why have you forsaken me?')."

The good news is we have ammunition to fight this loneliness.

- Meeting with other believers for encouragement and support. Hebrews 10:24-25 says, "And let us consider how we may spur one another on toward love and good deeds, not giving up meeting together, as some are in the habit of doing, but encouraging one another—and all the more as you see the Day approaching."

- Communicating with God through praise music. Psalm 13:6 says, "I will sing the LORD's praise, for he has been good to me." Or, if you know how to play an instrument, Psalm 33:2 says, "Praise the LORD with the harp; make music to him on the ten-stringed lyre."

- Praying and writing your thoughts in a journal. Psalm 17:6 says, "I call on you, my God, for you will answer me; turn your ear to me and hear my prayer."

- Reading or listening to an audio stream of the Bible. Romans 10:17 (KJV) says, "So then faith cometh by hearing, and hearing by the word of God."

- Doing an act of kindness to encourage others. Proverbs 11:25 says, "A generous person will prosper; whoever refreshes others will be refreshed." The act of kindness tool is one of my favorites for silencing loneliness. Taking a meal to someone who is sick or helping with chores allows me to take the focus off myself and encourage someone who may be just as lonely.

You may have heard the quote, "If you fail to plan, you are planning to fail." It would be wise to plan or determine our response when loneliness tries to creep up on us. There are times when I feel lonely but I have learned that my response to this invasion is the key to overcoming it. I begin by talking with God and allowing His Word to speak to me. My prayer might begin like this, "God, I know You are here with me. I am not alone."

> Spending time with God will fill vacant places in our lives.

We may be *alone* with no one around, but that doesn't mean we have to be *lonely*. A simple pleasure in life is being alone in the presence of God. Spending time with Him will fill vacant places in our lives. Psalm 16:11 says, "You make known to me the path of life; you will fill me with joy in your presence, with eternal pleasures at your right hand."

Jesus dwells with us at all times. He is our companion that sticks closer than a brother. Psalm 91:1 says, "Whoever dwells in the shelter of the Most High will rest in the shadow of the Almighty." To *dwell* means "to live or continue in a given condition or state, ... to linger over, emphasize, or ponder in thought, speech, or writing."[1] Staying or dwelling in His presence and lingering a while with Jesus, will allow us to feel the abiding love of God.

In order to get to know someone, you have to spend time with them.

I learned years ago that in order to have friends you have to be willing to invest time in a friend. You have to set time aside to listen, talk, laugh, and cry. Jesus has all the time in His hands. He sees beyond our loneliness and loves us because we are His. He is a loving Father who wants to be close to us. He will listen as we share our deepest concerns with Him. And yes, even our babbling about the same thing that upsets us, over and over.

When we don't take the time to talk with God, I believe He misses us just like I miss my kids when they are away at school. Psalm 139:1-3 says, "You have searched me, LORD, and you know me. You know when I sit and when I rise; you perceive my thoughts from afar. You discern my going out and my lying down; you are familiar with all my ways."

Even though I don't know what all my children are doing while they are away at school, I can take the time to think about the laughter that filled our house when they were home. We enjoyed playing board games like Sorry and Monopoly. We laughed as we sprayed each other with the water hose in the backyard on a warm summer day. The memories will turn into a smile and maybe a chuckle, silencing the noise of loneliness.

Prayer:

God, I want to dwell in the shadow of Your wings today and every day. Help me on the days when I feel lonely, to remember that You will never leave me or forsake me.

Questions:

1. When do you feel loneliness?

2. What action will you take the next time loneliness tries to creep in on you?

3. Memorize Psalm 139:1-3 and journal what the verse means to you personally.

4. Take time this week and talk with God and share with Him some of your deepest concerns.

5. What does Psalm 91:1 tell us to do?

*All Scripture verses are taken from the NIV unless otherwise indicated.

1. www.dictionary.com/browse/dwell?s=t.

Work with Joy

by Katherine M. Pasour

Many years ago, before the advent of computers and cell phones, people held a writing implement in hand, wrote real words on paper, and sent the letter through the US mail. In my teenage and adult years, this method (now known as snail mail) was a major mode of communication. I suppose young folks cannot imagine a world without email, cell phones, text messaging, or social media.

One summer I wrote my best friend, Sharon, a letter bemoaning my daily work. I lived on a farm with a large garden. My rant went something like this: "Besides everything else I have to do on the farm, I'm stuck with the garden. I had to plant it, hoe it, weed it, pick the vegetables, snap the beans, shell the peas, and shuck the corn. Then I have to freeze it all!"

Whine, whine, whine …

Sharon got a kick out of my letter. Years later we still laugh about it.

Now I have a garden—a BIG garden. I do the same work and more. But, now I enjoy it—it's no longer drudgery, but more like therapy.

What's the difference?

Perspective.

How we view our work makes all the difference. By work, I'm referring to labor in the home and careers in the public sphere, both paid and unpaid work.

Whatever you do, work at it with all your heart, as working for the Lord, not for human masters, since you know that you will receive an inheritance from the Lord as a reward. It is the Lord Christ you are serving. (Colossians 3:23-24 NIV)

Working with Joy

1. **Be sure to select a career, job, or vocation that honors God.** We should prayerfully consider work decisions (both paid and unpaid) before making career, marriage, or volunteer labor decisions. If our career doesn't honor God, we should find another profession. Taking our concerns about our work to the Lord can assist us in making difficult decisions.

2. **Give your work the honor it deserves.** Be punctual and dependable. Always do your best. Even if we are going through a rough patch (being passed over for promotion, treated with disrespect, assigned a repugnant task, feeling unappreciated, and so on), we still should give our very best. If we can't give our best, it's time to make some changes or look for a different workplace. Advice from Steve Jobs: "The only way to do great work is to love what you do. If you haven't found it yet, keep looking. Don't settle! As with all matters of the heart, you'll know when you find it."[1] Of course, if we are working from home, our options may not include changing our workplace, but we can prayerfully seek to change our attitude toward our domestic chores.

3. **Demonstrate the Fruit of the Spirit in the workplace and at home.** Demonstrate "love, joy, peace, forbearance, kindness, goodness, faithfulness, gentleness, and self-control" (Galatians 5:22-23) to your coworkers, superiors,

clients, and everyone within the workplace, as well as in the home. Be respectful, loving, kind, and fair to all.

4. **Focus on the positive rather than dwelling on the negative**. No matter where we work, there will be good days and bad days, aspects of our work that thrill us or make us angry, and occurrences that lead us to shout—"I love my job"—or growl—"I can't wait until I leave this place." We need to recognize the good and the bad in every situation and not allow the negative aspects to overpower the positives. Look for the best and you're likely to find it. The same holds true for the negative—if we always focus on the bad, we *will* find it.

5. **Keep the lines of communication open—in both directions**. When we have good relationships in the work setting and at home, we are able to speak freely and openly with our colleagues and family. Whenever possible, we should praise in public and criticize (only if needed) in private. When a coworker or family member completes a task well, let them know. However, if correction is needed, do so appropriately (not with anger or accusation) in a private setting. Avoid gossip—don't start it or spread gossip if someone shares with you. Better yet—ask the gossiper not to share hurtful news with you or others. "Make every effort to live in peace with everyone and to be holy; without holiness no one will see the Lord. See to it that no one falls short of the grace of God and that no bitter root grows up to cause trouble and defile many" (Hebrews 12:14-15).

6. **Honor those who work in unpaid settings** (stay-at-home mothers and fathers, caregivers, volunteer workers). Sometimes it's hardest to find joy in domestic chores. When we wash the dishes, scrub the floors, and clean the bathroom, what happens? Often, no one notices, everything is soon dirty again, and we have to start all over. Unpaid work can become drudgery quickly! Remember to thank workers who do menial tasks for you (custodians,

maintenance workers, servers in restaurants) or provide unpaid services for you (your family or volunteer workers).

7. **Keep our work in perspective**. Jesus addressed the issue of work in His conversation with Mary and Martha when He visited their home. Mary sat at the feet of Jesus—listening—but Martha was distracted by all the domestic tasks she had to do in caring for her guests. When Martha complained to Jesus about Mary's lack of help, Jesus responded, "Martha, Martha, ... you are worried and upset about many things, but few things are needed—or indeed only one. Mary has chosen what is better, and it will not be taken away from her" (Luke 10:41-42). Our work shouldn't interfere with our relationship with our Lord.

8. **Rest.** Our work should honor God, but so should our rest. "There remains, then, a Sabbath-rest for the people of God; for anyone who enters God's rest also rests from their works, just as God did from his. Let us, therefore, make every effort to enter that rest, so that no one will perish by following their example of disobedience" (Hebrews 4:9-11). We need adequate rest and sleep, we need time with God, and we need time away from work. God recognized this and reminds His people to rest from their work (Exodus 20:8-11, Exodus 23:12, Exodus 34:21, Deuteronomy 5:12-14).

Most of the time, going to work should be something we look forward to. Our work should be a blessing to us and to others. We should find joy in service. If we cannot—if our job is a drudgery—we should prayerfully examine if our career, workplace, or setting is right. Perhaps God is calling us in a different direction or asking us to change our attitude.

Prayer:

Father,
I want to work for You with all my heart in all aspects of my life.

Help me discover those areas in which I may not be honoring You with my work, and guide me to make the changes that will honor You. I pray that You will guide me to live by the Fruit or the Spirit as I work at home and out in the world. Help me be an encourager to others and a light for Jesus in all that I do.

Questions:

1. Consider the response Jesus made to Martha, "You are worried and upset about many things, but few things are needed—or indeed only one." Are you worried about many things? How would you describe the "one thing" to which Jesus is referring? How would your life change if you incorporated this "one thing" into your daily life?

2. Sometimes, no matter how hard we try to avoid gossip, a coworker, friend, or family member will share information that is negative about a person. Even if a statement about an individual is true, it can still be harmful if spread unnecessarily. What are some strategies we can use to help each other not say harmful things about others?

3. How would you describe your feelings (perspective) about your work? Please review Colossians 3:23-24 above. Are you working with "all your heart"? Are you "working for the Lord"? If not, what needs to change?

4. It is important to find balance and harmony in all aspects of our lives. Sometimes our work can demand long, stressful hours. This can include public work and domestic duties. What are some strategies that have worked for you in maintaining balance between work demands, family needs, and personal time?

*All Scripture verses are taken from the NIV.

1. Steve Jobs' 13 Most Inspiring Quotes, https://www.inc.com/dylan-love/steve-jobs-most-inspiring-quotes.html.

❈

From Hostile to Holy, Part 1
by Katy Kauffman

Angie couldn't take it anymore. Two cubicles over, Veronica's laughter invaded her thoughts, making her lose her train of thought. Angie's presentation, less than two hours away, had been assigned just that morning, and she didn't have time for distractions. Or dealing with a difficult person.

Veronica had a serious competition problem and didn't mind showing it. Last week Angie finally managed a "Hello, how are you?" to Derek who always smiled at her but never said anything. When Derek paused at Angie's cubicle, Veronica called his name and asked him to figure out what was wrong with her printer. (The printer was brand new.)

"Of course, I like to run," Veronica said. "Every day before work."

That's a lie, Angie thought as she turned in the direction of Veronica's voice. *She must be talking to some guy on the phone. At work.* Everyone knew Veronica loathed running or any form of exercise. She had boasted recently that she didn't need to work out because she "just came slim."

Veronica's voice sounded again above the chatter and ringing phones in the office. "Sure, I'd like to go out. ... Saturday? Fantastic. Just give me a call later about the time. ... OK, bye!"

A chair squeaked on its hinges, and Veronica's raven-colored hair popped into view. Angie whipped her attention back to her notebook on her desk. The sound of footsteps made her cringe.

"That's three dates in three days," Veronica said behind her. Angie swiveled her chair to face her. Veronica's eyes gleamed with challenge. "I'm sure you've never had that kind of luck, huh, Angie?"

I don't advertise myself everywhere I go, Angie thought but managed not to say. Just then, she realized how hostile her thoughts were becoming against her co-worker. *God, help me to say the right thing*, she prayed silently.

"I like to get know a guy a little before accepting a date," Angie stated calmly. "You never know what he's going to turn out to be like. My friend showed me a picture of her Facebook friend and asked if I wanted her to set up a date with him. He was a Christian and not bad looking, so I said OK. Turns out the picture was fifteen years old. I was shocked when I saw him in person. But besides that, he wasn't the kind of man I would go out with again. He just wasn't honest or sincere."

"Man, that's horrible," Veronica replied. Her eyes started to bulge, and she put her hand over her mouth. "I need to see whether guy #2 has put his birth date on Facebook. Thanks, Angie!"

Veronica ran back to her cubicle and landed. A squeak escaped from her chair, and a sigh escaped from Angie.

Common ground. Thank You, God. Maybe we're making progress.

When You Can't Avoid Difficult People

An easy solution to handling difficult people is to avoid them, but that's not always possible. Sometimes they frequent our work places. Even our churches or homes. So how can we practice godly character and respond to them in holiness instead of hostility? What initiatives can we take to make the environment in which we encounter them less ... difficult?

1.   See them from God's perspective.

A teacher once shared a way to overcome the fear of speaking in front of people, and it works for handling difficult people, too. Look at them with God's love. If we stop long enough to consider how much God loves a person who causes trouble, patience and grace can ease irritation and angst.

Jesus didn't die for just the people who get along with everyone, or for the ones who say the right thing at the right time. He died for those who speak without thinking, for the ones who get focused on a problem so much that they can't see a solution, and for the ones who blow up at the slightest mistake. He loves each of us, all of us. And He strives for the soul of each person He has created so we all may know Him. No one is shut out of God's love. No one. Aren't we grateful that includes us?

> Jesus didn't die for just the people who get along with everyone, or for the ones who say the right thing at the right time.

Seeing someone through God's eyes helps us to remember their worth—a creation of God and someone Jesus died for. Keeping this mindset releases some steam. Instead of replaying our conversations with a difficult person in our minds again and again, we can ask God how to affirm their value and respond to them in a Christlike way.

2.   Follow Jesus' advice.

Love and prayer. Jesus taught that loving our enemies identifies us as God's children. No way would a child of the world love his enemy. People will know we're different when we choose love instead of retaliation. "Love your enemies, bless those who curse you, do good to those who hate you, and pray for those who spitefully use you … that you may be sons of your Father in heaven" (Matthew 5:44-45 NKJV). Because we belong to God, we have a higher agenda that getting even or being angry—we have God's agenda, a powerful one. Loving those who aren't easy to love.

What do we get when we love those who are unlovable? We become more and more like our Father in heaven (Matt 5:48), and we please His heart. We stay useful to Him because we're keeping a cool head about us. We can listen to what they're going through and point them to God. Even if we can't say something pleasant to them, we can pray for them. We can appeal to God to help them with things we don't even know about, which leads to a third way that we can relate to difficult people.

3.   Be aware of the invisible.

A battle may be raging in someone's heart, and some of the overflow of that may get sprayed in our direction. If we become the victim of someone's tirade or ill will, we can evaluate whether we've done something to warrant it. If we haven't, we can pray for the person in case they are wrestling with some private issues.

Sometimes spiritual warfare is the cause of tension and stress. Satan may be coming after the people around us to isolate them from everyone else or to put friction between them and us. He thrives in chaos and seeks to wreak havoc everywhere he goes. Wisdom asks God for help and direction. We don't want to help Satan's agenda of harming someone, but we also want to guard our own hearts and proceed carefully. Being mindful that there may be unseen causes of tension, helps us to have compassion instead of anger.

More to Come

Tomorrow we will continue to look at how to relate to difficult people God's way. Godly character is mindful of people's value and seeks to relate to them as Jesus would. Unlike us, He can see what we can't—all that is going on in their lives to cause stress. He can help us to choose godly responses and to take godly initiatives, as we'll discuss tomorrow. Instead of perpetuating hostility, we can choose holiness—God's way of handling difficulties, surprises, and ambushes. What we reap is the good *He* can do in someone's life, and ours. What a privilege to see that and to be a part of it.

Prayer:

Dear God,
Please help me to choose Your way of handling difficult situations and people. I want to see what You can do in those relationships. Give me Your grace and wisdom to know what to say and how to act. Help me to see them as You do and to show the love of Christ as You direct me. Help me to be a part of Your team helping others when the enemy or troubles are harassing them. In Jesus' name, Amen.

Questions:

1. Our culture programs us to respond to hurtful words with more hurtful words. How can seeing someone as God does, reprogram our responses to difficult people?

2. According to Proverbs 15:1 (NKJV), what kind of answer "turns away wrath"?

3. If someone speaks to us in anger, what are some things we can immediately say to dispel anger and help bring peace to the situation?

4. Has there been a time when you said something unkind but didn't mean to? Was there a private struggle that was fueling your feelings and words, and it bubbled up to the surface?

5. If someone intentionally or unintentionally hurts us, how can we pray for them, obeying what Jesus said in Matthew 5:44-45?

6. If we were going through a difficult time and letting outbursts of anger or stress get the best of us, what we would want someone to pray for us?

From Hostile to Holy, Part 2
by Katy Kauffman

Jenny had felt like an outsider. Back in middle school, the girls she wanted to know wouldn't let her in their tight circle. Wasn't she "cool" enough? It wasn't until she was in her twenties that she understood why she never meshed with those girls.

Now, as a middle school teacher, she observed how the pre-teen girls at her school treated each other. One day, short little Marissa stood at the edge of the schoolyard and watched the rest of the class play kickball. Jenny walked over to her, and watched the game for a minute.

Then she asked Marissa, "Don't you want to play?"

Marissa shrugged and looked up at her. "I don't think they like me. They look at me and then say stuff."

"Who doesn't like you?"

Marissa turned her gaze to the group of chatty girls on the bench. "I know they gossip about me," she said.

My life all over again, Jenny thought.

"Have you ever talked to Christina or Elizabeth?" she asked Marissa.

The girl's eyebrows furrowed as she scanned the kids for the two girls. They stood in line to kick the ball.

"Well, not really," she replied.

Jenny smiled. "They like art as much as you do. You remember last month's bulletin board in our room that was decorated with watercolor pictures of different countries' flags? Christina stayed late one day and helped me to paint those for our social studies emphasis."

"Oh, I loved those!"

"You should tell her. Last summer their moms put them in an art camp, and when school started, they brought some of their paintings to school to show me. Maybe they'd tell you about it. You could also ask your mom if they could see her art studio in your basement. I bet they would love that."

A light sparkled in Marissa's eyes, and Jenny knew there was hope for her to feel like she belonged somewhere. It wasn't a matter of being cool, but finding the right group to be cool with. And showing a little kindness.

Three More Ways to Relate to Difficult People

4. Initiate kindness, and appeal to God.

For years my mindset was to expect others to be kind first, and then I understood that God wanted me to take that initiative. When we initiate kindness toward a difficult person, it can build a bridge that ushers us into friendship or at least a ceasefire in our dealings with them.

A mini-handbook for relationships especially within the Church, Romans Chapter 12 guides us to choose kindness over revenge. The following passage shows us how to respond to challenging people and situations.

Repay no one evil for evil.
Have regard for good things in the sight of all men.
If it is possible, as much as depends on you,
live peaceably with all men.
Beloved, do not avenge yourselves, but rather give place to wrath;
for it is written, "Vengeance is Mine, I will repay," says the Lord.
Therefore "If your enemy is hungry, feed him;
If he is thirsty, give him a drink;
For in so doing you will heap coals of fire on his head."
Do not be overcome by evil, but overcome evil with good.
Romans 12:17-21 NKJV

Since God is faithful to fight for us when we need it, we are free to show kindness to others. Instead of avenging ourselves, we can "give place to wrath," as verse 19 says, meaning that we give the matter over to an authority to handle so they can execute justice.[1] If our authority is not willing to set things right or can't, then we can appeal to God. He fights for His own.

As we wait for the situation to change or improve, we can help our enemy at the point of their need. According to godly wisdom, of course. Heaping coals of fire on someone's head always sounded like a punishment to me instead of a help, but it means that our kindness may melt the opposition "into penitence and love."[2] It may be that God uses our kindness to soften a person's heart. Second Timothy 2:24-26 (NKJV) talks about being "gentle to all" and using humility to correct those who oppose us in case they turn from their sin and God forgives them. Better that someone be rescued from wreaking destruction on others and themselves, than we demand justice our way.

5.   Compartmentalize the trouble.

Sometimes the person we're seeking to be kind to, won't respond in like manner. Sometimes the other party is just not willing to make amends. The godly response is not to let the difficulty take over life. Oh, it may seem like life revolves around some difficult situation or another, but we can make our lives revolve around God and practice His way of thinking, feeling, and acting. We can depend on His strength and His Spirit to respond to a difficult person in a way that is contrary to human nature. We can remember how much we have to live for and what God's good purposes are in the world. We can remember all the good that surrounds us and seek to be good and do good to those we come into contact with. We can remember that this difficult relationship is one part of life, and not life itself. Until the day comes that our difficult person moves on or we are no longer affected by what they do, we can focus on the good in our lives and depend on God as our unfailing source of strength, wisdom, and love.

6. Set up boundaries.

"Nice" has boundaries. Difficulties occur when those boundaries are violated. When a difficult person goes past "nice" to annoying, abrasive, or worse, we can observe God's boundaries of integrity, honor, and goodness. We can seek the grace from Him to contribute the good that we are not receiving, and to operate on earth as a citizen of heaven and a child of our loving Father. We can choose to operate within the boundaries of godliness and to affirm the worth of the other person. We can behave ourselves as if God were with us and watching or listening to the whole encounter, because He is. We can choose God's ways of relating to people. Even difficult ones.

Appreciating God's Love and Giving It Out

When I think about withholding kindness or forgiveness from someone, I am reminded that God didn't withhold those from me. I would be in a very different place in my life without God's gentleness and patience. Because we are grateful for the love He has shown us, we can choose to respond in godliness towards those who set us on edge, and we can seek and follow His direction for knowing how to deal with them. Wouldn't it be something if God used our love and prayers to save people from the unseen battles and heartaches they could have been facing? Wouldn't it be like God to use blessings to resolve difficult situations, and to help people experience the good of valuing others and living and working together agreeably?

The more we cooperate with God's renovation of our hearts, the purer and stronger our godly character will be. The more we say yes to God and His ways, the more we will contribute to changing the world around us from hostile to holy.

Prayer:

Dear God,
Please help us deal with difficult people out of godly love and kindness. Help us to see them from Your perspective and to obey Jesus' command to love others. Make us aware that unseen forces may be at work to stir up trouble, or unseen struggles may be taking a toll on a person's goodwill. Remind us to initiate kindness and to persevere in it. Teach us to compartmentalize difficulties so that they don't overshadow all of life, and help us to abide within the boundaries that recover relationships. In Jesus' name, Amen.

Questions:

1. Have you ever witnessed the triumph of godly ways over worldly ways? Do you know any of the benefits that came from that? If not, what might they be?

2. If you've been trying to deal with a difficult person recently, which of these six ways would help ease the situation or help you to move forward even if the person isn't willing to fix things?

3. Think of someone in the Bible who handled a difficult person with godliness, and answer the following questions.

    a. What did that person do to bring peace to the situation or relationship?
    b. What character qualities did the godly person have to possess in order to initiate peace?
    c. Did the other person respond well?
    d. If he or she didn't, what did the godly person do, and what can we learn from that?

1. Adam Clarke, *Adam Clarke's Commentary*, quoted in Phil Lindner, *Power Bible CD*, CD-ROM (Bronson, Mich.: Online Publishing, Inc., 2007), Romans 12:19.
2. *Family Bible Notes*, quoted in Phil Lindner, *Power Bible CD*, CD-ROM (Bronson, Mich.: Online Publishing, Inc., 2007), Romans 12:20.

Blueprints of Character: People in the Bible

Week 5

When God Interrupts Your Status Quo
by Jenifer Kitchens

Our little family is great. Dad, Mom, and two girls: nine and four. We are finally at a place where the girls are gaining independence. We've been out of diapers for a few years, and the girls play well together and can do so for hours. I can go for a run up and down our street and they play in the yard where I can see them. We have created a culture in our home in which we can talk with our girls and they can come to us. The girls are learning about God, and discipleship is happening every day. Things are tight, like space and money, but God provides. I love our life and wouldn't change it. And then this happened …

Things were a little off two months ago. Last month, I went to my OB/GYN for a yearly visit, and left with news that shook my husband and me to the core. I called my mom after the appointment. She heard the tremor in my voice and asked if I was OK. I heard myself say it for the first time in five years. "I'm pregnant."

Things are changing … and this is only the beginning. We're trying to figure out where to put another person in this house. This will probably include bunk beds. I'm searching online for used baby gear because any of ours that we didn't sell was donated to the local crisis pregnancy center, including my maternity clothes. My energy level has dropped, and the exercise routine I've fought years for was the first thing to go. I feel like everything I've worked so hard for is disappearing.

Can you tell I'm a bit of a control addict? I like controlling what is coming and having a plan to face it. Here lately, though, it feels like our whole world has been turned upside down. Every so often, I remind myself, "Only God can create life. He is doing something, and we get to be front and center. He has intentionally trusted us with another child! He has a plan for this life and has trusted us to raise it!"

Gideon, from the book of Judges, was just living life when out of nowhere, his life changed. (I can identify with Gideon a little!) God interrupted Gideon's status quo with a plan, and Gideon had to let go of what he had to accept something different, something not even on his radar. (Now this is getting personal here! Can you identify, too?)

Gideon's status quo was mere existence. The Midianites were oppressing the Israelites to the point that Gideon was threshing wheat in the pit of a winepress to keep the Midianites from stealing it. This is where Gideon's life was interrupted. The angel of the Lord greeted him, saying, "The LORD is with you, O valiant warrior" (Judges 6:12 NASB). Gideon explained to God's messenger why it felt like they had been abandoned by God. The messenger responded by telling Gideon to go and deliver Israel from the oppression of the Midianites. Gideon wasn't very receptive to this plan, yet. He listed reasons why he was not the man for the job.

How many times has God interrupted our status quo with an opportunity to be His representative, to show His love, and we respond by listing all the valid reasons (and some invalid ones) why we aren't the one God wants to use. But aren't they all really invalid reasons? God has a plan and in His sovereignty He wants to use us. God says to invite someone over for dinner to reach out, and we answer with how dirty our house is. God tells us to pay for someone's meal, and we remind Him how much we have in our bank account. God makes it obvious that we need to share Christ with someone, and we tell God that we aren't the person for the job because we aren't eloquent and we would probably trip over the words. Even Moses tried to use this excuse (Exodus 4:10).

God knows all these things before He calls us. He doesn't call us in spite of them, but because of them. In our weakness we depend more on Him, and His power shines through us all the more (2 Corinthians 12:9-10).

In Judges Chapter Seven, the time came to fight the Midianites. Gideon and his army of 32,000 had camped south of the army of Midianites, who were as numerous as the locusts (Judges 7:12). God wasn't finished preparing him for the battle, though. He said there were too many Israelites in the army. If God were to give the Midianites to this many Israelites, they would boast as if they had accomplished it themselves (Judges 7:2). God reduced the number of the Israelite army from 32,000 to 10,000 to 300 (Judges 7:3-8). Gideon would fight a massive army with only 300 men.

This was another opportunity in which Gideon had to conform to God's agenda. The circumstances were in place for God to receive the glory, not Gideon or his army. Has there ever been a time when the circumstances seemed stacked against you? Allow yourself to bend to God's plan, and don't try to be the hero. God will work in ways that bring Him glory, that allow Him to be our hero.

That night Gideon and his men surrounded the Midianite camp holding trumpets and torches covered by pitchers (Judges 7:16-18). At Gideon's cue, they blew the trumpets and broke the pitchers, revealing light. The Midianites were confused and started killing each other, crying out as they ran away (Judges 7:21-22).

Three hundred men won a battle against an innumerable army because they did it God's way. No strategist would have ever encouraged the cutting of an army to just over 0.9 percent of the original number and initiating the battle by surrounding the opposition with torches and trumpets. God doesn't consult strategists, though.

God has a plan not only for my life, but for the lives of every person around me. God is, by His very nature, good, and He cannot go against His nature. So ultimately, all His plans are good even though they may not feel that way. We have such a narrow view of our place in eternity, who are we to evaluate His plan?

I was not expecting to have a baby at this stage of life, but I praise God for this tiny person growing. And by the way, telling our four-year-old that a baby is joining our family has reminded us of the joy that babies bring. She has accepted God's plan readily and loves to hug and kiss my ever-expanding abdomen to show love to her sibling. Oh, that we all were as trusting as four-year-olds!

Prayer:

Sovereign God,
Your ways are higher than my ways, and Your thoughts are far beyond what I can comprehend. Please forgive me, Lord, when I don't trust Your plan and when I don't take action to obey You. Please help me to let go of my attempt to control and instead to embrace whatever You have for me. Your Son modeled this for me when He gave up Heaven to die on the cross, and I thank You for His sacrifice. Help me to seek Your kingdom, Lord, rather than my comfort.

Questions:

1. Do I believe that God is good and wants good things for me?

2. Which Bible verses confirm that?

3. Is there any part of my life that God wants me to handle His way, but I am resistant?

4. Will I trust in the nature of God and in His sovereignty?

5. Will I bend to and embrace His plan?

Strength for the Furnace
by Julie Lavender

Pastor Kenny Grant, Senior Pastor at Calvary Baptist Temple in Savannah, Georgia, was shocked when his daughter, Kameron, shared an early college experience.

"Dad," she said to her pastor-father. "My professor started class with these words: 'I'm here to challenge everything you know about God. To change what you believe. To change what you think about God.'

"I was so stunned by his boldness," she continued, "that I couldn't think straight at first. No one said anything. He just kept making bold statements. We all sat in silence.

"Dad, after a couple of minutes, I raised my hand and, respectfully, stood up to his words. I told him that I stood firm in what I know about God. And guess what? When I spoke up, some of the other students joined me. We pushed against him, Dad. We didn't give up."

Kameron told her father that once the professor realized that the students were confident in what they believed, he backed down and changed the subject.

I'm reminded of the story of three strong young men in the Bible who stood firm—literally—and refused to bow down to a golden image. The young men pushed against a command to renounce God and worship the image of King Nebuchadnezzar instead. Their resolve to worship only God landed them in a fiery furnace.

I can't imagine how Shadrach, Meshach, and Abednego felt while trapped inside the burning furnace. When I read their story in Daniel Chapter 3, I am amazed at their strength while facing imminent death.

Shadrach, Meshach and Abednego replied to him, "King Nebuchadnezzar, we do not need to defend ourselves before you in this matter. If we are thrown into the blazing furnace, the God we serve is able to deliver us from it, and he will deliver us from Your Majesty's hand. But even if he does not, we want you to know, Your Majesty, that we will not serve your gods or worship the image of gold you have set up." (Daniel 3:16-18 NIV')

To the unbeliever, Shadrach, Meshach, and Abednego's comments must have sounded like reckless abandonment and would surely signal their death in the furnace. The three young men, however, had experienced God's faithfulness before in their lives, which gave them the strength to have total commitment and complete devotion to the Almighty God now. God's unwavering faithfulness to the young men during their days of captivity gave them the confidence and strength to say without hesitation, "Our God will save us."

"Our God will save us."

Though they had the faith to believe He could and would, their next words—"But even if he does not"— blatantly proclaimed their trust and loyalty. With great strength and resolve, the three men believed that even if God chose not to rescue them at that moment, they would be with the Lord eternally, whatever His method of "saving."

3 Promises that Build Blazing Strength

1. "For I know the plans I have for you," declares the LORD, "plans to prosper you and not to harm you, plans to give you hope and a future" (Jeremiah 29:11).

God promises us plans for our good. You and I can count on His plans—they're gonna be good! Remembering this promise helps us to say with boldness like those three young men, "God is our refuge and strength, an ever-present help in trouble" (Psalm 46:1). God indeed walks before us into the fiery furnace, with us in the furnace, and leads us out of the furnace. God is bigger than any of life's fires that we face.

> God is bigger than any of life's fires that we face.

He [King Nebuchadnezzar] said, "Look! I see four men walking around in the fire, unbound and unharmed, and the fourth looks like a son of the gods." Nebuchadnezzar then approached the opening of the blazing furnace and shouted, "Shadrach, Meshach, and Abednego, servants of the Most High God, come out! Come here!"

So Shadrach, Meshach, and Abednego came out of the fire and the satraps, prefects, governors, and royal advisers crowded around them. They saw that the fire had not harmed their bodies, nor was a hair of their heads singed; their robes were not scorched, and there was no smell of fire on them.

Then Nebuchadnezzar said, "Praise be to the God of Shadrach, Meshach, and Abednego, who has sent his angel and rescued his servants! They trusted in him and defied the king's command and were willing to give up their lives rather than serve or worship any god except their own God." (Daniel 3:25-28)

2. "The LORD himself goes before you and will be with you; he will never leave you nor forsake you. Do not be afraid; do not be discouraged" (Deuteronomy 31:8).

God promises to never leave or forsake us. He didn't abandon Shadrach, Meshach, and Abednego, and He has no intentions of abandoning us, either. We can count on God to be by our side at all times and in all places. God's overwhelming, magnificent presence enables us to stand tall in the fires of life, to battle the blazes with Him by our side.

3. "Have I not commanded you? Be strong and courageous. Do not be afraid; do not be discouraged, for the LORD your God will be with you wherever you go" (Joshua 1:9).

Wherever. And God means just that—He proved that promise when He walked with Shadrach, Meshach, and Abednego in the fiery furnace.

God's word—His assurance and promise to never leave us—gives us the confidence and strength to boldly step into the furnace, whether that's to battle cancer with rounds of chemotherapy, face the onslaught of an approaching hurricane, or stand tall when ridiculed or persecuted for worshiping the one true God.

Depending on God's strength to get me through each day instead of my strength, helps me not to grow weary in doing good and opens my eyes to His wisdom for handling relationships and daily challenges. Knowing that it's God's strength that helps me prepare one more meal when I'm tired after a long day, or answer one more question from my children, or listen to one more diagnosis about my mom's health—that knowledge is a breath of fresh air in a sometimes smoky world.

God gave Shadrach, Meshach, and Abednego the strength to stand up to King Nebuchadnezzar and to survive a heated furnace. A steady and unyielding relationship with God gave Kameron the strength to stand up to her professor, thus encouraging the strength of her classmates to do the same. And the One who gives me strength stands ready—daily—to walk with me through any fire.

Prayer:

Dear God,
Sometimes it feels like the "furnace" here on earth gets mighty hot! Please give me the strength to face my challenges and difficulties by completely trusting Your promise to never leave me nor forsake me. Thank You for that promise, God. In Jesus' name, Amen.

Questions:

1. What challenging or difficult circumstances have you faced recently?

2. How does God's promise to "never leave you nor forsake you" (Deut 31:8), encourage you in your day-to-day activities?

3. What situations give you the most difficulty in trusting the Lord?

4. What can you do to change that lack of trust?

5. Look up some of the following verses on trusting God, and record what they tell us.
   a. 2 Samuel 22:31
   b. Psalm 5:11, 18:2, 31:19, 56:3, 91:2, 143:8
   c. Isaiah 26:4

*All Scripture verses are taken from the NIV.

An Indispensable Guide
for Building Godly Character

by Jeannie Waters

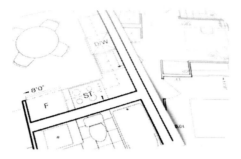

A small problem left unattended, can have big costs. Just like our kitchen renovation project.

Did you know American homes lose one trillion gallons of water annually due to minor leaks? That's the amount of water used in 11 million homes each year![1] A one-eighth inch crack in a plumbing pipe can leak 250 gallons of water per day.[2]

Water loss and subsequent damage is costly and can lead to health issues and weakened support structures. When hidden, deterioration may become extensive. For example ...

Our Kitchen Renovation Project

Step One: Demolition. My husband pried off the counter top and removed the first section of cabinets to make room for the new ones. Our excitement grew as we envisioned a brand new kitchen.

Step Two: Discovery. We stared in disbelief at the now-exposed wall behind the sink. Ugly black mold had created a dappled design on the sheetrock! Our enthusiasm waned as we anticipated additional cost.

Step Three: Distress. My handyman examined the wet sheetrock which crumbled into his hands and revealed partially rotted wall studs. Our elation morphed into disappointment.

Step Four: Deductible. We searched our homeowner's policy for the deductible amount and called the insurance company. Our eagerness to proceed with renovation had come to a screeching halt.

The Process

When the demolition crew removed the flooring under the sink, they discovered wet subflooring. Several floor joists had to be ripped out. Their removal triggered cracks in the ceramic tile we had intended to keep. One problem led to another.

The restoration company removed damaged materials, and insured the area was dry and mold free before reconstruction began. A small amount of moisture or bits of mold spores left behind could have caused future problems.

The culprit for this devastation? An old iron pipe behind the sheetrock of our sixty-two-year-old home had rusted and allowed water to escape. No evidence of the insidious ruin appeared until the cabinets were removed. A hidden problem had damaged a vital part of our home one layer at a time!

Heart Damage

Disdain for God's laws was hidden in the hearts of some Judean leaders. This adversely influenced their people, resulted in rampant idol worship, and provoked God's wrath against the entire nation. King Josiah lamented the deterioration of the moral fabric of his people which led to judgment (2 Kings 22:11-17).

Although some of his predecessors ignored God's laws, Josiah "began to seek the God of his father David" (2 Chronicles 34:3 NASB*) when he was sixteen. At age twenty, Josiah ordered the destruction of all forms of idolatry in Judah. Can you imagine the shock waves that must have traveled through Jerusalem that day?

Perhaps Josiah watched from a palace window as workers followed his instructions. They destroyed incense altars, ground pieces of wooden and metal images into powder, and then sprinkled the remains over the graves of idol worshippers (2 Chron 34:3-7). The wise king left no trace of idolatrous worship. Like mold spores hidden behind a wall, particles of sin lodged in a heart can grow rapidly and result in ungodly practices.

Once all evidence of idol worship had been eradicated, the then twenty-six-year-old king ordered carpenters and masons to repair the temple his forefathers had neglected (2 Chron 34:8-11). As temple restoration began, Hilkiah, the high priest, discovered "the book of the law of the LORD" (2 Chron 34:14).

As a scribe read the law, Josiah's response probably stunned members of the court. Upon hearing the words of God, he tore his clothes as a dramatic symbol of sorrow. He then commanded his advisors, "Go, inquire of the LORD for me and for those who are left in Israel and in Judah, concerning the words of the book which has been found; for great is the wrath of the LORD which is poured out on us because our fathers have not observed the word of the LORD" (2 Chron 34:21). The king's emissaries sought God's response from a prophetess (2 Chron 34:22). Imagine Josiah's anguish when he received God's message.

> Behold, I bring evil on this place and on its inhabitants, even all the words of the book which the king of Judah has read. Because they have forsaken Me and have burned incense to other gods that they might provoke Me to anger with all the work of their hands. (2 Kings 22:16-17)

Josiah gathered the people and read "all the words of the book of the covenant" (2 Kings 23:2). Then, he "made a covenant before the LORD, to walk after the LORD, and to keep His commandments ... with all his heart and all his soul" (2 Kings 23:3). Furthermore, the king reinstated proper celebration of Passover (2 Kings 23:21). Josiah placed a high priority on God's Word. What an example for anyone seeking godly character!

Consider Josiah's legacy recorded in Scripture. "He did right in the sight of the LORD . . . and did not turn aside to the right or to the left" (2 Chron 34:2). "Before him there was no king like him who turned to the LORD with all his heart and with all his soul and with all his might, . . . nor did any like him arise after him" (2 Kings 23:25). God commended Josiah for his tender heart, his humility, and his weeping over sin (2 Kings 22:18-19). May his legacy inspire us.

Four Ways to Develop Godly Character Like Josiah's

1.   **Place a high priority on God's Word.**
     Obeying Scripture that we already know and studying to learn more, changes our hearts. Churches and reliable online sources afford access to sermons and Bible studies. Waking up a few minutes earlier for prayer can align our thoughts and actions to the Word of God.

2.   **Destroy all evidence of idolatry.**
     An idol can be a person or thing we spend significant time or focus on each week. Has something or someone crept in as an idol? Purging our hearts of idolatry is a step toward godly character.

3.   **Repair "the temple," restore relationships, and reinstate godly practices.**
     Our bodies are temples of the Holy Spirit (1 Corinthians 6:19). We can enhance our physical health with proper diet, rest, and exercise. With God's guidance and humility in our hearts, we can do our part to restore broken relationships. Perhaps the practice of a quiet time, writing in a prayer journal, or worship times can be reinstated into our daily schedule.

4.   **Humble your heart before God.**
     Reading Psalms and acknowledging the majesty of God orders our perspective. God honored Josiah's humble heart.

Refurbishing our kitchen required removal of mold and damaged materials. Restoring a high priority on God's laws among the people of Judah required ruthless removal of every sign of idolatry. Renovation of our hearts requires confession and dependence on God to cleanse us of idolatry and other sin. Let's place a high priority on God's Word as Josiah did, regarding it as our indispensable guide for building godly character.

Prayer:

Dear Father,
Purge our hearts of every particle of hidden idolatry and other sin. Teach us to place a higher priority on Your Word, and then use it to renovate and restore our hearts. May Scripture become our daily navigational tool. In the name of Jesus, Amen.

Questions:

1. How can you place a higher priority on God's Word? What is the meaning of Psalms 119:105?

2. Josiah removed every trace of idol worship. Can you think of signs of idolatry in your own heart?

3. Prayerfully create a plan for heart renovation based on Josiah's actions. Are there practices to reinstate or relationships to restore?

*All Scripture verses are taken from the NASB.

1. "Fix a Leak Week," United States Environmental Protection Agency, last modified June 28, 2017, https://www.epa.gov/watersense/fix-leak-week.
2. "Water Damage by the Numbers," Water Damage Defense, last modified 2017, https://www.waterdamagedefense.com/pages/water-damage-by-the-numbers.

❃

Freedom through Forgiveness
by Jean Wilund

One morning in Benton Harbor, Michigan, Police Officer Andrew Collins set a goal. By the end of the day he'd land another drug arrest no matter what it took. Even if he had to destroy a life to do it. And he did.[1]

That day Andrew arrested Jameel McGee on false charges of drug dealing. Jameel lost everything. Despair led him to thoughts of suicide. Hatred of Andrew consumed him with plans for revenge. But before he got out of prison, the truth caught up with the crooked cop.

The courts sent Andrew away and released Jameel. Andrew served a mere eighteen months for his many crimes. Jameel served four long years and lost everything for nothing. Except, it wasn't for nothing because while he was in prison, Jameel met Jesus and placed his faith in Him for the forgiveness of his sins. Andrew also turned to Jesus in prison and became a new man.

Some time after his release, Jameel took a job at a small coffee shop—the same coffee shop where the crooked ex-cop worked.[2] It was as if God had delivered Andrew right into Jameel's hands. He walked into the perfect opportunity for revenge.

A few thousand years earlier, David, a former shepherd boy and future king of Israel, faced a similar opportunity. God had delivered his archenemy, the current and crooked King Saul of

Israel, into his hands. The savory taste of revenge tempted him when an unaccompanied Saul walked into the very cave in which David and his men were hiding. This was the same Saul who years earlier had set a goal to hunt David down and destroy him for no more than achieving success and popularity as the king's faithful servant—more success and popularity than Saul.

In Saul's quest to kill David, he attempted to pin David to a wall with a spear (I Samuel 18:11, 19:10) and kill him in his home (1 Samuel 19:11) where he lived with his wife, Saul's daughter. He even tried to drive a spear through his own son, Jonathan, because of Jonathan's friendship with David (I Samuel 20:33). He later ordered the slaughter of 85 innocent priests and every man, woman, and infant in their city because one innocent priest had helped David (I Samuel Ch. 21). And now, Saul sent out an army of 3,000 men to kill one man—David (I Samuel 24:2).

These appalling memories no doubt gnawed at David as he faced his decision. Would he kill this unstable king and stop his murderous rampage or forgive him and trust God to deal with Saul in His own time and way?

With his eyes fixed on the Lord, David chose to trust God and forgive Saul. Fast forward a couple millennia, Jameel McGee fixed his eyes on Christ, chose to trust God, and forgave ex-officer Andrew Collins. In David and Jameel, we witness two innocent, yet condemned, men forgive their guilty, yet free, conspirators because they trusted in the better way, the way of the cross, the way of Jesus—grace and forgiveness.

Jesus, more innocent than either David or Jameel, stood silent before Pilate and His accusers. He neither defended Himself nor demanded justice. He remained quiet and accepted the thirty-nine flesh-ripping lashes and the nails driven into His hands and feet. And as He hung and bled on the cross, He paid the penalty for the sin of the world and broke the chains of sin and death.

While Andrew and Jameel were both in prison, their hearts experienced a radical renovation once they met Jesus. And the moment Andrew told Jameel, "I'm sorry," Jameel forgave Andrew and set them both free to enjoy a surprising friendship. Jameel laid down his anger and thirst for revenge and picked up a close friendship that continues today—a David and Jonathan caliber friendship. They not only continued to work together, they've now traveled the country sharing their story of an uncommon friendship because of their wholly uncommon Savior, Jesus Christ.

Sadly, David and Saul's relationship didn't come to a happy end. In fact, nothing in Saul's life ended well. While David enjoyed God's pleasure, Saul refused to truly repent, and died on a battlefield by his own sword at the hand of his stubborn pride (I Samuel 31:4).

We don't have the power to free anyone from sin—only Christ can do that—but we can offer them the forgiveness Christ gave us. And we can pray as Jesus did, "Father, forgive them; for they do not know what they are doing" (Luke 23:34 NASB). They think they know, and we think they know, but they don't. If they truly saw the undistorted reality of God's penetrating holiness and the abject misery of their sin, their shame before such a holy God would likely knock them to the ground. Our sin of rebellion against God's command to forgive would bring us to our knees as well. We think we're holding our offenders in a prison of unforgiveness only to discover we're the ones imprisoned.

Forgiveness isn't always easy, but it's always right. And it sets us free.

Prayer:

You, O Lord, are the righteous and holy One, and You're fair when You judge our sins. Thank You for Your extravagant grace that has cast all my sins from me as far as the east is from the west. Change my heart, Lord. Change me. Make me more like You, eager to love and forgive. In Your name I pray. Amen.

Questions:

1. Forgiveness often helps the giver more than the receiver. Many compare withholding forgiveness to drinking poison and waiting for the other person to die. Matthew describes it as being tormented by the torturers. Not much fun either way.

   Read Matthew 18:21-35 and answer these questions:
   a. Who wound up tortured in prison in the end (v. 34)?
   b. The servant owed 10,000 talents (Matthew 18:24). One talent was "more than fifteen years' wages of a laborer."[3]
      i. Could the man ever pay his debt to the king in his lifetime?
      ii. What does Romans 13:8-10 tell us we should owe man?
   c. Why do you think the man who owed the massive debt didn't extend mercy to the man who owed only a small debt? (Consider Proverbs 11:2, Proverbs 21:24.)

2. Many are resistant to forgive, at least until their offender has suffered as much as they have. Read 2 Corinthians 5:10 and Hebrews 13:20-21. What do you think David knew about God that enabled him to forgive King Saul and not seek revenge?

3. Read about an encounter between David and Saul in I Samuel 24:1-22. Notice verse 22.

   a. After Saul admitted his sin to David, even calling David his son through tears, where did David go? Why do you think David chose to forgive Saul but still keep his distance from him?
   b. Considering David's example in 1 Samuel 24:22, read John 2:23-25 and Romans 5:8. We often confuse forgiveness and trust. Forgiveness doesn't have to be earned, but trust does. God calls us to forgive our offender, but He doesn't call us to place ourselves back in harm's way. Is there anyone you need to fully forgive, even if you still can't trust the person?

4. Record what these verses teach us about God and/or His forgiveness:
    a. Psalm 86:5
    b. Psalm 103:8, 10-12
    c. Isaiah 1:18

5. Based on what you've read today, how much renovation do you think your heart still needs in the area of forgiveness?

6. How would your life be different today if you forgave like David and Jameel? If you forgave like Christ?

1. CBS Evening News. "Crooked Cop Paired Up with the Man He Framed," YouTube, April 15, 2016, https://www.youtube.com/watch?v=7wffHBQKq74. Web, July 5, 2017.
2. Steve Rempe, "A Tale of Forgiveness," *Prison Fellowship*, April 19, 2016. Web, July 5, 2017.
3. B. M. Newman and P. C. Stine, *A Handbook on the Gospel of Matthew* (New York: United Bible Societies, 1992), 578.

Becoming a Leader of Godly Character
by Katy Kauffman

"Bayonets!"

Although the cry could have meant certain death, Union soldiers followed Colonel Joshua Chamberlain once more into battle. Their orders were to defend Little Round Top, a small hill near Gettysburg, Virginia. With half of their men dead and little ammunition left after an onslaught of five Confederate attacks, they were outnumbered four to one. And yet, they charged.

What kind of leader ignites such courage in his men?

Shortly before this battle, the men who followed Chamberlain had wanted to go home. After fighting for two years of a three-year agreement, they witnessed other soldiers released from duty. Two hundred and twenty Union soldiers refused to fight. A serious offense for a soldier in time of war. So the Union authorities executed forty of them to motivate the others to return to fighting. It didn't work.

Then they put the group under Chamberlain's command. He listened to the mutineers who were sent to him from another regiment, and he appealed to the governor of Maine on their behalf.[1] He rallied them at Little Round Top, and his so-called "insane courage"[2] led them to victory.

What kind of character is needed for one man to take 180 mutineers and turn ninety-nine percent of them into obedient soldiers, men who would help the Union ultimately win the Civil War?

A man of vision and determination. One who could see what was at stake and communicate that to those who had an opportunity to make a historical difference to a fledgling nation. A man of courage with keen fighting skills and effective strategies, who could lead his followers to victory. A leader who was fair-minded and willing to listen. One who would speak up for the welfare of his men.

If Little Round Top had been overrun by Confederate soldiers, it's likely that the Battle of Gettysburg would have ended in a Southern victory, and the South would have won the war. Yet Chamberlain was the right leader for the 20th Maine Infantry Regiment.

"I had the inability to do nothing," Chamberlain said about that historic day on July 2, 1863. "I would not die with a bullet in my back."

Do we have the courage and character to lead the people in our circle of influence to progress God's plans and win the victory over opposition? Would the people that we work or live with, follow us into battle?

A Servant Became a Leader

Another leader who had compassion, wisdom, and grit is Nehemiah. He stepped onto the scene in Jerusalem at a time that God's people were desperate for leadership and protection. The walls of Jerusalem lay in ruins even though the temple had been rebuilt. In Persia as the cupbearer to the king, Nehemiah heard about the condition of God's people and prayed. At the right time, he appealed to the king to send him to Jerusalem to rebuild the wall. Because of God's work behind the scenes, the king permitted Nehemiah to go back, and we gained an example of godly leadership in this cupbearer turned governor, wall builder, and hero.

His Mindset toward the People

Nehemiah had a "we" mentality. When enemies of the Jews threatened them, he refused to be afraid. In Nehemiah 2:20 (NKJV'), he identified with God's people and appealed to God for protection and success:

> *So I answered them, and said to them,*
> *"The God of heaven Himself will prosper us;*
> *therefore we His servants will arise and build ..."*

Nehemiah saw himself and the people as God's servants. When we work with other Christians to further the gospel and build up the Church, we are serving God's interests on earth. He is our Leader, and we are His servants. When we keep a "with" mentality as we work with those entrusted to our care, there will be no room for jealousy and competition. Our spiritual enemy won't be able to tear us apart because we are linked by the love of Christ which is *the bond of perfection* (Colossians 3:14).

As leaders, we build a "we" mentality when we value each worker. Concerned for the safety of God's people, Nehemiah armed each man who worked on the wall. He set them according to their families, so each family would work together and protect its members (Nehemiah 4:13-14). Like Colonel Joshua Chamberlain, when we listen to our group members' concerns and act to help them, they will know that we are on their side, that we care, and that we will go to the trouble to help them.

What kind of leaders do God's people need? Ones who are guided by the truth. They have the word of God as their high standard for right and wrong, a standard that shows us how to love one another and how to live and fight for God in this world. Godly leaders are faithful to maintain boundaries based on God's word. Those who stay within the boundaries will be the most blessed and productive. Those who violate the boundaries will probably lead their people into defeat, and perhaps disgrace. A wise leader will always guard the purpose and fellowship of the group. A foolish leader will allow divisions, distractions, and damage to persist and tear down the strength and effectiveness of the team.

His Mindset toward the Enemy

Nehemiah didn't let the enemy gain any ground among God's people. The rest of Nehemiah 2:20 shows how he dealt with the enemy.

> *So I answered them, and said to them,*
> *"The God of heaven Himself will prosper us;*
> *therefore we His servants will arise and build,*
> *but you have no heritage or right or memorial in Jerusalem."*

As spiritual enemies seek to hurt God's people today and hinder the work of God's kingdom, the job of a godly leader is to guard His people as much as possible. Just as Nehemiah gave the enemy no claim to Jerusalem and no base of operation within the city, leaders today can limit the enemy's influence by being faithful to teach the truth, uphold honor and boundaries, and following God's guidance. Leaders and their people can work together to give Satan no room to work in their minds, hearts, and lives.

His Mindset toward God

From the first day that Nehemiah heard about God's people living in reproach and the wall lying in ruins, he prayed. Prayer was never a last resort for him, but the first action to take. Nehemiah understood the greatness of God, His power, and His love for His people. He called God the *LORD God of heaven* (Neh 1:5), the *great and awesome God* (1:5), *my God* (6:14), and *our God* (6:16). He understood that the Maker of all things cared about the welfare of one small nation, and would protect them as they made their home again in the promised land.

A godly leader will be effective only as much he stays connected to the great and awesome God and follows His lead. What God wants above all else for His people—whether we are leaders or followers—is that we love Him with all that we are

> Knowledge may make us smart, and power may make us mighty. But love makes us great.

(Mark 12:30) and love one another as Jesus has loved us (John 13:34). Knowledge may make us smart, and power may make us mighty. But love makes us great—great and useful to God and His eternal purposes. The greatness of a leader can be measured by the greatness of his or her love and dependence on God.

Becoming that Kind of Leader

How did Nehemiah come to the place that he was the right man for the job of overseeing the rebuilding of Jerusalem's walls? How did Joshua Chamberlain grow in courage so that he called for the bayonets at just the right moment and charged into battle?

We become the leaders that God wants us to be, by doing life with Him. We choose God when all is quiet and the battle is far off. We faithfully study His word and spend time with Him in prayer. We choose God's way in the small things, because life's challenges won't stay small. The battle won't stay far off.

And we keep choosing Him. When the enemy's attacks keep coming and we're running low on ammunition. When the enemy taunts us and tries to hinder God's work. We set our sights on staying close to God, following His lead, and doing what's right for the good of those around us. We don't allow the enemy to have any place in our own minds, hearts, and lives. We decide the battle is worth the cost, and God can work good out of anything. We plunge ahead, holding His hand, making a difference in His name. Then perhaps we will leave this world a little better than we found it, a little brighter, and a little safer for future generations. We will pass on a legacy of godliness and courage, of determination and conviction. We can arrive at the end of our lives and know that we used our power for good and for God.

Prayer:

O great and awesome God,
Be the leader that we follow into battle. Arm us with Your truth and Your love. Help us to limit the enemy's influence in our own lives and in our circles of influence. Build within us a heart of courage so that we can be the leaders You want us to be. In Jesus' name, Amen.

Questions:

1. What traits do you think qualify someone as a godly leader?

2. What godly leaders have you had in your life, and how did they help you to be a better person?

3. In what ways are you a leader in your sphere of influence?

4. How can the right mindset about people help you to be a good leader?

5. What might the enemy be doing to thwart God's purposes in your sphere of influence?

6. How can depending on God defeat the enemy's plans?

*All Scripture verses are taken from NKJV.

1. Jared Peatman, *Joshua Lawrence Chamberlain*, Essential Civil War Curriculum, http://www.essentialcivilwarcurriculum.com/joshua-lawrence-chamberlain.html.
2. Charles Billingsley's sermon delivered on February 11, 2018 at Shadow Mountain Community Church, El Cajon, California.

Christ: The Model of
Godly Character

Week 6

Launched and In Flight

by Katy Kauffman

Launched is the goal. But the weight of a space shuttle—about 165,000 pounds, or the weight of forty-one cars—is the problem.

To propel that much weight off the surface of the earth, takes some power. How do you achieve flight and adventure when that much weight is keeping you grounded? NASA's answer was two rocket boosters and an external fuel tank. But the solution compounds the problem. The fuel to produce that power is also heavy. Now the weight totals around 4.3 million pounds, or the weight of 846 elephants. That's a lot of fuel. And elephants.

Space shuttles won't go anywhere unless the fuel is ignited. First comes the countdown for launch, then the igniters in the rocket boosters shoot flames down the center of the cylinders. The solid fuel burns from the inside out, sending gas through the throat of each rocket booster and out the exhaust. Fuel is also burned from the shuttle's massive external tank and ... liftoff!

Sometimes God calls us to do something that we know will either take a lot of work or involve a lot of obstacles. Our "space shuttle" sits on the ground, as we contemplate the possible adventure ahead. What launches us from our state of comfort and propels us into the great unknown? A commitment to God that is willing to overcome any outside force pulling us down. A zeal for Him and His great purposes. A loyalty that chooses "flight" over "grounded," what's hard over what's easy, and what's helpful over what's convenient. How do we fill our tanks with enough fuel that will see us through the assignment? How can we sustain flight and complete our mission? A look at Jesus' commitment and loyalty holds the answer.

Jesus' Propelling Commitment to God

He had an incredible mission—save the world. In order to do that, Jesus first had to humble Himself and be born as one of us, fragile and human. Then He had to live a sinless life, never once saying a harsh word, never complaining or grumbling or fretting, never giving in to temptation. He always chose God's way, the right way, over what would have been easy, lazy, or selfish.

His commitment to God propelled Him forward, through crowds of hungry souls, through mobs of vehement religious leaders. He didn't let the pull of fame distract Him from being God's servant. He didn't let the temptations of Satan short-circuit God's plan. He chose to be all in for God though it would cost Him His life. Jesus lived every day of His life on earth knowing that the cross was His destination. We don't know how often He thought about it, but we do know that the cross was planned before the foundation of the world (1 Peter 1:18-20). For all of mankind's existence, Jesus knew that He would die. Yet He was committed.

The Igniter of His Commitment and Ours

What ignited Jesus' commitment to God? What made Him continue forward, heading to the cross without choosing an alternate destiny? Love, joy, and our need.

His love. Jesus' love for God and people moved Him to accept the mission of the cross. In the Garden of Gethsemane, He dreaded being separated from God. But He said yes to God's plan for our sakes and because of His great love for us (John 15:9, 1 John 4:19, Romans 5:8). The pain, anguish, humiliation, and suffering of the cross were bearable because He knew what He was winning for us—forgiveness, life, and closeness. Freedom, healing, and renewal. And great joy.

His joy. Jesus stayed committed for the "joy that was set before Him" (Hebrews 12:2 NKJV). What a Lord and Savior we have that He has joy over seeing people repent of their sins and turn to Him. People who commit their lives to Him. When He sees that our hearts are sincere, He in turn commits Himself to us (John 1:12-13, 2:23-25). Then we are blessed with reconciliation, renewal, and relationship. When we believe in Christ, we become new creations in Him (2 Corinthians 5:17) and we are set on a new course—God's course for our lives. We achieve "flight"—a life that we can't live apart from Him. And the same flame that ignited Jesus' commitment to the Father, ignites ours—love and joy.

Our need. We needed God, so Jesus committed Himself to go to the cross. We needed Someone to take our sin and bear its penalty. God's own Son stepped forward as the substitutionary sacrifice for our sins (Hebrews 7:26-27, 9:14, 9:28, 10:12; Isaiah 53:10). We live in a world that needs Him, that needs to hear the gospel and accept it. How strong is your love today? Do you see the need of those around you, and can you picture the joy that's to be had when they discover their need is met in God?

Sustaining Flight

Just as Jesus encountered obstacles in God's mission for Him, we encounter obstacles today. Fatigue and weariness pull at our hearts. Persecution and rejection tempt us to slow down and "land." Sin and struggles corrode our engines. But the love of God, the joy of life with Him, and people's need can keep our commitment burning. We know that we desperately need God, both for salvation and everyday life. We who have firsthand knowledge of the goodness and greatness of God can continue to fly forward because we want others to know Him, too. We can sustain "flight" because we believe in the daily missions God gives us and we want to be useful to His plan.

Jesus didn't let anything deter Him from fulfilling God's will for His life, and He enables us to keep flying forward to fulfill God's will for ours. A closeness to Jesus reinforced with dependence on

Him keeps our passion for God and people burning strongly and sustains our commitment. Even when the ride gets bumpy. Even when we lose some power and feel like we're going to crash. When we ask Jesus for help and choose "flight" over "grounded," He builds within us a loyalty to God that overcomes all opposing forces.

> When we ask Jesus for help and choose "flight" over "grounded," He builds within us a loyalty to God that overcomes all opposing forces.

Are you ready to fly today? When we say yes to God, the great unknown is not really unknown. God sees what's ahead, both the challenges and the victories. He will help us to sustain flight as our hearts grow in being fully committed to Him.

Prayer:

Dear Lord,
Thank You for staying committed to God's mission. Thank You for facing the cross and enduring it so we could know You. Reinforce our commitment to You with Your love and joy, and help us to remember the great needs of the people around us. We want them to find in You the strength, help, and hope we have discovered. Use us for Your purposes, and keep us flying steadily along. In Your name I pray, Amen.

Questions:

1. According to Hebrews 12:1-2, what do we need to set aside to sustain "flight" (or run our race), and where do we need to keep our focus?

2. According to Philippians 3:13-14, what is a key for pressing forward?

3. What kinds of things in our past may try to keep us from being committed to God?

4. How does God's wisdom in Scripture tear down those obstacles?

5. Besides love, joy, and people's need, what else can ignite a commitment to God and keep it burning?

6. How far do you want God to propel you this year? What would you like to see Him do, or where would you like Him to lead you? List some things that you want to be "on mission" for, and ask God to show you which assignments He has for you. And then liftoff!

Assaulted in the Wilderness
by Ron Gallagher

I might have been a kid, but I had seen enough westerns to know what an attack was. An attack was something that happened to wagon trains in the old west. Attacks began with hordes of mounted Native Americans (we didn't call them that back then, of course) suddenly beginning to emerge over a hilltop in full headdress and war paint. They'd pause just long enough for the chief to take a dramatic look in each direction to survey his forces, at which point the wagon train people would notice them and begin to panic. Then the chief would poke his spear up in the air and let out a war cry to signal that it was time for all the ordinary, non-office-holding Native Americans to kick their horses in the ribs and go barreling down the hill, whooping to the top of their lungs, and firing their rifles or shooting arrows in the general direction of the hapless wagon train in the valley below.

Thankfully, the brave pioneers knew exactly what to do. At the first sign of guys on horseback dressed in loincloths, wearing face paint, and sporting feathers on their heads, the lead wagon driver would make a hard left and get all the wagons into a big circle. Then the intrepid settlers would return gunfire as the Native Americans rode 'round and 'round, shooting and yelling until the cavalry finally showed up to chase them off. That's what it meant to have an "attack"—simple.

A New Kind of Attack

You can imagine my confusion when I heard one of my uncles mention that someone he knew died from a "heart attack." "What," I inquired of myself, "could that possibly mean? How does a 'heart' get 'attacked'?"

I was not about to leave this conundrum unattended, so I asked my grandpa what this new kind of attack was all about. He told me that it just meant that something happened to the man's heart that kept it from working like it was supposed to. "People sometimes call that a 'heart attack,'" he said. Grandpa's response was simplistic, but it was basically accurate, and it was a lot easier than attempting to explain coronary disorders and malfunctions to a six-year-old.

In any case, that early introduction to what it meant to have a "heart attack" was a lesson in broadening perspectives. I came away understanding that what constitutes an "attack" was much more expansive than I had suspected. Enemies apparently existed that I never knew about, and human hearts were vulnerable.

Another Expanded Perspective

What constitutes a "heart" to God is another lesson in expanded perspectives. He has much to say about them, and most of it has nothing to do with that organ pulsating in our chest. For instance, there is this significant and familiar admonition: *Keep your heart with all diligence, for out of it spring the issues of life* (Proverbs 4:23 NKJV).

There is a tone of gravity in Solomon's charge evident in his use of the word "keep." In that context, it means to defend, to protect, to watch over, or to safeguard something—in this case, our "heart." Such a challenge would be pointless in the absence of a real and prevalent threat, and that raises other questions:

- Who or what constitutes "the enemy"?
- When, where, and how is this adversary likely to launch his offensive?
- What is his objective?
- What weapons will be used?
- From which direction is he most likely to come?
- And most importantly, what counteractive resources do we have, and what strategies do we need to apply in order to mount a viable and effective defense?

There is one episode in Jesus' life that, while not exposing every detail of every possible attack, does provide an effective defense against all of them.

The "Heart" of "Character"

With apologies to Solomon and to God, let me respectfully offer this expanded paraphrase of the admonition quoted above. "Watch over that core internal concept of who you are with extreme diligence and protect it at all costs, for the most important decisions you make will emerge from it, will define your 'character,' and will reveal to the world a composite picture of who you really are and what your life is about." Character is not just a cumulative compilation constructed from past behavioral trends, it becomes a basis for predicting future trustworthiness and provides evidence that either validates or denies claims about our life. From God's perspective, the "heart" that Solomon mentioned is more than just one of the elements associated with what we call "character"—it is the wellspring of it, and as such, it becomes the enemy's primary objective.

After His baptism, the Spirit led (literally "drove") Jesus into the wilderness (Mark 1:12-13) where He was left without companionship or physical nourishment for forty days. It was there that He was confronted by Satan and subjected to what we might call the ultimate cosmic "heart attack."

The Enemy's Primary Target

Satan wanted to incite a response from Jesus that would do irreparable damage to any future claim that He was the perfectly obedient Son of God. Every component of his attack targeted that objective. Satan's attack involved physical responses, but it wasn't the physical heart he was after. The heart attacks that pose the most extensive threat to us human beings have nothing to do with our coronary arteries. They are attacks that seek to damage, dismantle, or destroy those beliefs that define who we are. Our great hope for surviving a "heart attack" like Jesus endured in the wilderness lies in understanding how they work and applying the strategy He applied. These familiar elements from that event are worth highlighting again:

- The attack began to unfold following a major public statement about who Jesus was. Be prepared and be aware that open expressions about our relationship to God are open provocations for satanic attack.

- The focused assault began when Jesus was isolated relationally, weakened physically, and deprived of material support. All those situations make our hearts more vulnerable and as such, invite attacks. In those situations, remembering who we are is vital.

- John categorized Satan's enticements as *the lust of the flesh, the lust of the eyes, and the pride of life* (1 John 2:16 NKJV). They still comprise his favorite areas to probe and the place where his attacks have been most devastating.

- The attack may have seemed behavioral and/or circumstantial on the surface, but the primary objective was relational. So rather than statements like, "If you're hungry …," Satan began with, *If You're the Son of God.* So it is with us. He will use our weaknesses as an opening, but it is ultimately the power of our relationship with God that he wants to dismantle because it comprises the greatest threat to the supremacy he covets.

God does warn us to guard against behavioral transgressions, but when we fail in those areas, it isn't just our mouths or some individual body part that gets tainted—it's our character, it's our heart, it's our claim of association with God. Once "who we are" becomes subject to doubt, what we say and do will be questioned as well, and when our own concept of who we are is damaged, our primary defense is weakened, and our behavior will follow suit.

Surviving a "Heart Attack"

It is often pointed out that Jesus applied the Word of God as His defense, and that is obviously true, but there's a principle in it that we don't want to miss. It wasn't that simply enunciating the words released some kind of anti-satanic magic. After all, the devil used God's words, too. The difference was that the Words of God weren't just manipulative mechanisms to Jesus. They were a living part of Him, and they defined who He was. When faith in Jesus Christ becomes personal, it does something religious dogma can never do. It makes us family and changes our identity. That becomes a defense against "heart attacks" that cannot be had otherwise, even if we happen to be in a wilderness when they come.

> The Words of God weren't just manipulative mechanisms to Jesus. They were a living part of Him, and they defined who He was.

Prayer:

Thank you, Father, for the incredible privilege of calling You Father, and for the awful price Jesus paid to allow this relationship. Forgive me for the times I have failed to recognize the power that my relationship with You has to defend me against Satan's temptations, and please help me to see that Your Words are more than terms to memorize and recite. Help me to internalize them as living definitions of who I am.

Questions:

1. Which condition do you think makes us the most vulnerable to the enemy—isolated relationally, weakened physically, or deprived of material support?

2. Which of Satan's tactics—*the lust of the flesh, the lust of the eyes, and the pride of life* (1 John 2:16 NKJV)—do you think is the most enticing to Christians today?

3. In what other ways does Satan seek to undermine our relationship with God?

4. What steps can we take to guard ourselves against these heart attacks?

5. What practical steps can we take to make Scripture a living part of who we are?

Self-Sacrifice: No Greater Love
by Lauren Craft

I like to picture myself there, gathered around Jesus. No crowds are around, and He's only speaking to His closest followers. His face is lit only by firelight, and all eyes are fixed on Him. Everyone's ears are tuned to His words, words that would be passed down through the ages.

As Jesus neared the end of His life, He spoke alone with His disciples for a time of teaching (John Chapters 13-17). It was then Jesus explained the meaning of real love, a kind that places others before self. He said, "Greater love has no one than this: to lay down one's life for one's friends" (John 15:13 NIV').

When I first read "lay down one's life," I pictured myself jumping in front of a bullet to save a friend's life. Or maybe lunging at a lion to save my younger brother. That way little Matthew would have time to run away.

But self-sacrifice can also mean a lifestyle of giving up many small things. First John 3:16 says, "This is how we know what love is: Jesus Christ laid down his life for us. And we ought to lay down our lives for our brothers and sisters." So how can we lay down our lives if a bullet or lion isn't headed in our direction?

Many of the things Jesus sacrificed—time, comfort, and honor—offer practical examples for us to follow. During His ministry, Jesus didn't have a bed of His own to lay His head on at night (Luke 9:58). He gave up food, water, and other comforts when He was tempted in the wilderness (Matthew 4:1-11). Later, He handed over His position of honor when He washed the disciples' feet (John 13:5).

We can lay down many of the same things. When we offer our seat on the bus or let someone ahead of us in line, we sacrifice our own comfort. We can give up time by devoting hours to serving the less fortunate or sharing the gospel. And we can give up honor when we're quicker to credit others than ourselves.

Self-sacrifice isn't easy. All of us hold onto certain things too tightly, placing us in a tug-of-war between what we want and what God wants. One of my weak spots is time on the weekends. I work full time, and I'm tired when Saturday rolls around. I feel like I "deserve" to relax and sleep in. When the alarm goes off those mornings, I sit and stew for a few minutes. But I know God wants me to wake up early—and *cheerfully*—to bless the seniors, many who don't have family nearby.

Jesus taught us to think of ways to serve, not what we think we deserve. One day, Zebedee's wife asked Jesus to promise that her two sons would sit at His right and left hands in heaven. Jesus replied, "Whoever wants to become great among you must be your servant, and whoever wants to be first must be your slave; just as the Son of Man did not come to be served, but to serve, and to give his life as a ransom for many" (Matthew 20:26-28).

Another common trap is the idea that others haven't earned what we give up for them. Yet Jesus' way of self-sacrifice doesn't have conditions. Romans 5:8 says, "But God demonstrates his own love for us in this: While we were still sinners, Christ died for us."

Jesus didn't wait until people stopped sinning before He died on the cross for us; He did it while many were insulting Him, abusing Him, and still rejecting the gospel. In a similar way, we can show kindness to everyone, even those who have been unkind to us. We can show love to prisoners no matter what they did in the past, or volunteer at a homeless shelter even if some residents could have prevented their situation.

> When we sacrifice the things we love, God doesn't leave us with an empty spot in our hearts. He replaces what we've sacrificed with a new joy, a new purpose.

Here's the best part: when we sacrifice the things we love, God doesn't leave us with an empty spot in our hearts. He replaces what we've sacrificed with a new joy, a new purpose.

Think back to a time you've seen someone who's just been shown mercy. Their face brightens and every muscle in their body seems to relax at once. Doesn't that make us want to be generous with grace, no matter the cost? Maybe you've seen the light in the eyes of a person whose life has just been committed to Christ. Doesn't that encourage us to give more hours to sharing Jesus? And think how it feels to give a friend a ride home at night. Wasn't it worth driving out of the way to see them step inside that doorway safely?

First John 5:3 says, "In fact, this is love for God: to keep his commands. And his commands are not burdensome." Self-sacrifice isn't a burden because God has something greater planned instead. Instead of only pleasing ourselves, self-sacrifice gives us a role in His Kingdom. We witness His work unfold right before our eyes.

When we see the ways God uses our sacrifices, the things we've given up don't seem important at all. In fact, we'll probably forget what they were.

Prayer:

Lord, I may never know all the sacrifices You've made for my sake yesterday, today, and tomorrow. Because of You, I can know abundant life and trust in Your promise for eternal life. I want to follow Your example, giving up my desires for the sake of others You love. Help me see any sacrifice—big or small—as an opportunity to make You known. In Jesus' name, Amen.

Questions:

1. When you were growing up, what did your parents or caregivers give up? How did their sacrifices benefit you?

2. How do you sacrifice for your own family? If you don't have kids, think of things you can do for aging parents or your nieces and nephews.

3. How can you show self-sacrifice to those outside your family, such as friends, neighbors, and co-workers?

4. Is it difficult to make sacrifices when you aren't sure if you'll be thanked? If so, what strategies would help you serve others no matter what?

5. What's something you're gripping tightly that God wants you to give up? What better things might He be planning instead?

*All Scripture verses are taken from the NIV.

Praying Like Jesus
by Evelyn Wells

As Jesus walked up into the craggy hills to pray, He must have been tired in body, mind, and spirit. He just had to get away from all the crowds and lay His burdens down and talk to Abba.

When I was a teenager, our pastor told us that if we wanted to have an effective prayer life, we needed to learn to pray like Jesus. Really? *How* like Jesus? He went on to say that Jesus found it necessary to pray, spending much-needed time with His heavenly Father. Pastor told us that Jesus was an awesome prayer warrior. He went on to say that if Jesus spent a lot of time praying, then how much more should *we* be spending time in prayer.

We looked at each other. It seemed such an impossible task! After all, He was God. He had a perfect relationship with His Father before He left heaven to come to earth. Our Pastor told us that God wants each of us to have a close relationship with the Father, in which we go to Him with confidence and love.

> Go to God with confidence and love.

Heart renovation happens as we seek to draw close to God and listen for His leading and instruction in our quiet times. Prayer shapes our character to be more like Christ. And a big part of godly character is staying in an attitude of prayer all day long.

Jesus' Instructions for Prayer

As a Jew, Jesus grew up in the tradition of public prayer and would have been taught the piety of prayer. Although He did not condemn praying in public, Jesus stressed the importance of private prayer (Matthew 6:5-6). He used an example of those who liked to stand in the synagogues and on street corners and pray so they would be seen by others. He instructed them to go into their room, shut the door, and pray to the Father in private.

Jesus said we're not to heap up empty phrases (Matthew 6:7-8). He was referring to pagans who repeated the names of their gods over and over, using empty phrases when they prayed. He wants us to pray meaningful and sincere prayers, straight from our heart to the heart of God.

Jesus' Model Prayer

In the Sermon on the Mount, Jesus gave us a pattern for prayer in "The Lord's Prayer" (Matthew 6:9-13). He begins by acknowledging who God is, honoring the holiness of His name, and petitioning God's kingdom to dwell in our hearts. Then, Jesus added petitions which focus on personal and community needs. He prayed ...

Our Father in heaven (v.9 ESV*) – When we address God as *Father*, we are acknowledging Him as loving, approachable, and caring. Heaven reminds us of God's eternal reign and our eternal life there, if we belong to Him.

Hallowed be Your name (v.9) – We honor God and set Him apart in our minds as holy.

Your kingdom come (v.10) – We pray for God's kingdom to reign in our hearts and to rule our lives. We should also ask Jesus to reign in our churches and homes, so we live as a reflection of Him, in which we increasingly honor Him, show His love, do good to others, and share the message of salvation. His character governs our own.

Your will be done (v.10) – Just as God's will is carried out in Heaven, He desires that we carry it out here on earth. We can pray that we will be faithful in carrying out God's will and be obedient to His instructions as we live out His salvation. As we learn to seek God's will above our own, we will find it easier to practice the things He has taught us. As a result, our character will shine.

Give us ... our daily bread (v.11) – God knows our hopes and dreams and our basic needs. He wants us to ask for what we need and to depend on Him to provide it. By doing this we show we have confidence in Him.

Forgive us our debts (v.12) – By asking this, we are acknowledging God's great forgiveness of all of our sins. We are to do likewise to those who have wronged us.

Lead us not into temptation (v.13) – Scripture tells us that God doesn't tempt anyone to do evil (James 1:13). This phrase in the prayer is asking God to keep us from being overcome by temptation, whether it comes from our own appetites, the enemy, or others—to lead us so that we do not succumb to temptation.

Deliver us from evil (v.13) – We are to pray for God to lead us in the paths we should take and help us not to be influenced by the evil one, Satan.

Jesus' Prayer in the Garden

Jesus was overwhelmed on the night of His betrayal by His impending death on the cross (Luke 22:39-46). As He prayed in the Garden of Gethsemane, His distress and sorrow were so overwhelming that He asked Peter, James, and John to pray. These three formed His inner circle of disciples, and they were His best friends here on earth. He wanted them to intercede for Him.

Jesus fell on His face, showing the ultimate humility as He talked to His Father about what He faced. Jesus was assigned to take humanity's sins upon Himself and to die a criminal's death on a cross. He was so distraught, He even sweated drops of blood.

He asked God if it was possible to take this task away from Him, but immediately afterwards Jesus said, "Not my will, but yours, be done" (Luke 22:42).

He prayed three times for the "cup" to pass from Him, and each time relented by saying He would be obedient to God's will. When Jesus found Peter, James, and John sleeping, He asked, "Why are you sleeping? Rise and pray that you may not enter into temptation" (Luke 22:46).

Although we will never have to accomplish the same mission as Jesus, we all face trials from time to time that send us to our knees. There are times when we are desperate for God, for His comfort or His forgiveness. When we or a family member face sickness or upheaval, we know we have a Heavenly Father who cares. He is the One we can depend on.

Giving Thanks in Prayer

We know Jesus valued giving thanks before eating, since it is recorded in Matthew 14:19 where He gave thanks to God before distributing the loaves and fish to the 5000. In Matthew 26:26, He gave thanks before breaking the bread at the Passover meal, which we call the Lord's Supper or the Last Supper.

Jesus gave us good examples for giving thanks for our food. He delights in meeting our needs and in giving us good gifts. We are to express our thanks to God every day for meeting our needs and for all He provides. Most importantly, we should express our thanks every day for the sacrifice Jesus made on the cross for us.

The most important aspect of prayer is bowing before the throne of God's wonderful grace and visiting with Him. We can come to Him with anything. In fact, He wants us to come into His presence. He loves being with us. Psalm 95:2 tells us to go into God's presence with thanksgiving and to make a joyful noise with songs of praise. After we have given thanks to Him, we are to offer praise to the Most High God.

The Privilege of Prayer

Prayer is not meant to be an unpleasant task or something to hurry through. If we have accepted God's free gift of salvation, we have the privilege of developing a close relationship with Him. Yes, we can have a close relationship with Him like Jesus did when He walked the earth.

Jesus met with His Father in prayer, and we can only imagine the conversations They had! He would have been excited to talk with His Father. And God was surely thrilled to hear from His Son. As we grow closer to Him, we want to be with Him more and more.

Prayer:

Loving Father,
Thank You for Your saving grace which enables me to live eternally with You. Thank You for this new day, a day full of promise and hope. Thank You for meeting my needs today and for Your divine protection. I praise You today and lift Your name on high. Lead me in the way You would have me go. Help me to be kind today and to represent You well. Please forgive my sins and help me to be obedient to You today. In the sweet name of Jesus, Amen.

Questions:

1. Have you ever thought what it would be like to pray like Jesus? In what ways, that are not mentioned above, can we pray like Him—for ourselves, for others, and for His purposes on earth?

2. What do you particularly appreciate about what Jesus included in the Lord's Prayer?

3. In your prayer time, do you spend time in thanksgiving? In praise? Do you ever sing to God?

4. Is your prayer time like having a conversation with a dear friend?

*All Scripture verses are taken from the ESV.

Compassion from the Ground Up
by Lyneta L. Smith

A Crazy-Desperate Mom

Rumors of a Miracle Man from Judah circled for months. He could heal the sick and make the blind see. Some said He even cast out evil spirits.

And now He was in Tyre? The Canaanite woman barely heard the news before throwing on her veil and taking to the streets in search of Him. If others had seen Him, there was a chance she'd find Him. Could He take away her daughter's demon?

For years, the little girl had fallen into screaming fits for no apparent reason. They came out of nowhere. Lately, she had holed herself up near the fire. No amount of coaxing could entice her to her bed at night, or anywhere near the dark.

No one in the house had slept for days. Fatigued as she was, there was no stopping until the despondent mother found the Miracle Man from Judah.

Up ahead, a crowd gathered around a house. It had to be Him! She darted toward the door, pushing through the people, squirming her way through until she saw Him.

"Son of David," she cried. "Have mercy on me!" (Matthew 15:22 NIV'). She couldn't move any closer because of the crowd, but she kept shouting.

Jesus didn't answer. Didn't even look at her. Another Jew whispered something in His ear.

Couldn't He hear her?

Finally, He spoke. "I was sent only to the lost people of Israel."

Those standing in her way moved aside to let her closer. She fell at His feet and pressed her forehead onto the cold floor. "Lord, help me!"

Her veil slipped a little and tears ran down her cheeks, but she didn't care.

Jesus finally said, "First let the children eat all they want … for it is not right to take the children's bread and toss it to the dogs."

She jerked her head up, eyes wide. "Even the dogs eat the crumbs that fall from their master's table."

Her heart pounded. She expected Him to ask some of the men to grab her by the arms and toss her out. Instead, He looked at her as though He could see right into her core. "Woman, you have great faith! Your request is granted."

She let out a cry of relief. "What?"

He laid a hand on her shoulder. "You may go. The demon has left your daughter."

In a flash, she shot to her feet. "Thank you!" The crowd let her pass through easily this time, and she sprinted home to find her daughter lying on her bed. The demon was gone.

A Bedraggled and Weary Healer

Jesus didn't go to Tyre for ministry; He went for rest. He didn't want anyone to know He was at the house (Mark 7:24). It was not time yet for the Gentiles to receive the gift of the Messiah. He first needed to reach the Jews, God's chosen people.

Knowing He'd walked for days just to get a respite, the disciples urged Him to send the Canaanite woman away. Whether that meant grant her request so that she would leave them alone, or shoo her off without healing her daughter, we can't know. But their thoughts were not of compassion for the woman, only secrecy and respite for their teacher.

Despite His fatigue, despite her Gentile-ness, despite the disciples' urging, Jesus said words that changed her life. His actions are the blueprint for us to follow when building the character trait of compassion.

Though most of us can't heal with a word, we can follow Jesus' example and use our gifts and talents to show compassion. Like the disciples, we may lack it, especially during stressful circumstances. But there's good news: even an amateur can build compassion.

Tearing Out Misconceptions

First, as happens in any renovation, we have to remove the rotten parts before we can install new elements. In this case, what's rotting is the lies we've told ourselves about compassion.

1. The need is too great. What can one person do? It's easy to be overwhelmed by the needs of others. But all or nothing thinking makes us powerless, when in truth, we have supernatural power to make a big difference. Thinking we're expected to help everyone keeps us from helping the one we're supposed to help in the moment. Every time the Bible says Jesus had compassion, it was a time when He was surrounded by overwhelming hordes of people.

2. I have enough troubles of my own. How can I add more? Showing compassion to someone else doesn't mean taking on their troubles. It simply means sympathizing with them and relieving their pain if we can. Helping someone, or even listening with a sympathetic ear, forges a connection that relieves our own pain as well. Jesus healed the sick and fed 5,000 even while withdrawing to grieve the beheading of His cousin, John the Baptist (Matthew 14:13-15).

3. Won't I be enabling them to make bad choices if I show compassion? In some cases, the most compassionate choice is not to give what's requested. For example, giving a drug addict cash could do them more harm than good. But being ready to offer the most helpful thing (for example, a ride to a rehabilitation center, a sandwich, or prayer) shows compassion without doing further harm.

Installing Compassionate Habits

After we've cleaned out the rotting untruths about compassion, we can begin to build it up in our lives. But which materials do we use?

We don't want to mistake philanthropy for compassion; that's like using particleboard instead of two by fours. It's easy to check something off our list and claim we've done our good deed for the day.

But true compassion comes from deep within. The Greek word for compassion (*splagxnízomai*) comes from splanxna, meaning "the inward parts, especially the nobler entrails—heart, lungs, liver, and kidneys."[1] Another definition of compassion is "to be moved as to one's bowels ... (the seat of love and pity)."[2]

> When we are moved to our innermost core, compassion overflows.

When we are moved to our innermost core, compassion overflows. Each act of compassion is as individual as each giver and recipient. It could be a cool cup of water one day, and a hot meal the next. Another time, it could be sponsoring an impoverished child overseas.

Building compassion means looking to Jesus' example as our blueprint, and then relying on the Holy Spirit to show us the areas in our lives where we need it the most.

Prayer:

Compassionate Heavenly Father,
So many around me are desperate like the Canaanite woman. I pray You would move me from my core to offer them compassion. Give me eyes to see where others lack, and fill the needs. Show me who needs a kind word or a hug. Grant me ears to hear their cries. Like the builders who create spacious and lovely homes, I pray You'll use my hands and feet to build a kingdom of kindness with compassionate acts. In Jesus' name, Amen.

Questions:

1. In Mark 1:40, Jesus had compassion on the leper. Most Christians we know haven't encountered literal leprosy. What other conditions have made people outcasts and in need of compassion?

2. Several times Jesus had compassion on those "sheep without a shepherd" (Mark 6:34, 9:36). What ways can we offer compassion to un-churched people today?

3. Jesus had compassion on those who didn't have anything to eat (Mark 8:2, Matthew 15:32). How can we practice offering compassion to impoverished people?

*Quotations or paraphrases in the story are from Matthew 15:21-28 and Mark 7:24-30.

1. Bible Hub, *Helps Word Studies*, http://biblehub.com/greek/4697.htm.
2. Bible Hub, *Thayer's Greek Lexicon*, http://biblehub.com/greek/4697.htm.

Construction Zone:

Helping Our Children
to Grow in Godly Character

Weeks 7-8

Pray without Ceasing
by Julie Lavender

My firstborn, Jeremy, was a kindhearted, gentle preschooler with a vivid imagination. His sensitive nature led me, as an inexperienced mom, to avoid certain topics and issues that I thought might upset him.

We didn't discuss homeless people, I never defined the word "orphan," and I skirted the subject of divorce. I thought I was sheltering him from the adult hurts and sufferings that he would probably learn about all too soon. But then a vacation to San Diego changed my viewpoint.

My husband David, four-year-old Jeremy, one-year-old Jenifer, and I visited the usual tourist spots: the San Diego Zoo, the La Jolla coastline, and the world-famous Coronado Hotel.

We spent our last sightseeing day at Balboa Park. After visiting a couple of museums, we passed an outdoor fountain, spewing water into a concrete pool dotted with pennies and other coins. I gazed at throngs of children, remembering field trips from former teaching days when I was the one responsible for that many students.

I thought Jeremy was watching them too. When I followed his gaze to see which child had interested him, I realized he was staring at a man lying on his stomach next to the fountain, wearing an old, tattered flannel shirt, torn grey-green pants, dingy white socks with no shoes, and using a yellowed newspaper for a pillow.

Because this was Jeremy's first experience with an apparently homeless man, I felt I could no longer avoid the topic. I tried to be delicate, for I knew Jeremy would add this to his list of worries that sometimes accompanied his "fearsome fours," as the parenting books called it.

I explained that he probably had no home, no money or job, and perhaps not enough to eat.

Jeremy listened intently to every word and said without hesitation, "But doesn't he have a mommy?"

His voice was a little shaky, as was mine when I answered, "I guess not."

Our next stop was a fast-food place for lunch. Once again, we encountered someone in need, as her "Homeless and Hungry" cardboard sign announced to anyone willing to glance her way. This time, I broached the subject first, as we stood in line for burgers, and we discussed her possible desires and how we might could help.

We bought coupons for free meals in addition to our sandwiches, and I gave them to Jeremy to hand out when we left.

Both kids snoozed on the drive back to the hotel, and I thought about the experience. I was wrong to use Jeremy's sensitivity to shelter him. I decided that day to capitalize on it, instead, to build a compassionate spirit, to construct a caring heart, not just a kind one.

I planned to be more specific when I told him how his tithe and offerings were used. I decided to share with him the reason we gave money to a children's home and clothes to children whose mother abandoned them and whose father was in prison. I chose to explain what a soup kitchen does and vowed to take him with me the next time I volunteered.

But most importantly, I wanted to teach my kids to pray with sensitivity and compassion—and to do it without ceasing. First Thessalonians 5:17 (NKJV) commands just that: "Pray without ceasing."

Obviously, Paul didn't mean a 24/7, eyes-closed conversation with God—even Paul had to take time out of his day to preach and make tents.

Through Paul's words, God teaches us to keep our minds on Him, from sunup until sundown. To keep our focus on Him. To be aware that God is with us always. To recognize that God hears our utterances and sees our actions. To give God continuous glory and honor and praise, with everything we say or do. To pray lengthy praises and petitions and intercessions during a set-aside devotional time, yes, but also to pray short one-liner requests and praises without ceasing, throughout the day and night.

One way I found to incorporate that attitude with my children was to take advantage of visual cues, to use those as reminders to pray compassionately for others. Almost as if every person or creation or situation bore a post-it note reminder for prayer.

Individuals with cardboard signs accepting our coins at a traffic light reminded us to pray for those who are hungry and have no place to sleep at night.

A school zone sign taught us to pray for teachers and students.

A siren or flashing red light encouraged us to pray for ambulance drivers and the sick or injured person inside the vehicle. Sometimes, I silently prayed before one of my children prayed aloud, if I spotted the light first.

Once, I saw the light-bearing vehicle long before my kids did and prayed silently. But as we neared the slow-moving vehicle, I laughed aloud.

"What's funny, Mommy?" Jeb Daniel asked.

"Well, Mommy's eyes aren't as good as they used to be, and I just prayed for that mail carrier."

"I guess he needed prayers, too," my oldest responded.

A playground called for prayers for families; a uniform with a badge solicited prayers for first responders' safety.

Large green tractors puttering across a field, turning rich brown soil into patchwork designs, warranted petitions for farmers and those that supply food and sustenance to our world.

A water jug taught us to pray for those who do not have safe drinking water and encouraged us to donate to those who are building wells in various places overseas.

Pray without ceasing. It's really not that hard to do when you're surrounded by so many with petitions and needs.

And, we made it a practice to share just as many praise-prayers, too. A majestic, snow-topped mountain prompted us to praise Him for His creations.

A beautiful sunset reminded us to thank God for the gift of sight, just as a barking dog brought to mind the gift of hearing.

Checking out books at the library taught my children to praise God for teachers and education and the ability to read.

Over the years, I've treasured the sound of my children's prayers. That sensitive four-year-old is now an elementary school counselor, listening compassionately to little ones with needs and concerns. The second child, married now, serves on the care team at her church, because her pastor recognized the compassion she had for others.

My third child, the future accountant, volunteers with the music and media ministry at church. And the fourth child teaches dance to little ones and encourages fellow college students through her council positions at church and on campus with the Baptist Collegiate Ministries.

Though they're no longer "kids," I pray without ceasing that my children will continue to build and grow their compassionate spirit through prayer and actions, and I look forward to the future births of their own construction projects!

Prayer:

Dear God,
Your word says to "pray without ceasing." Remind me during the day of Your presence with a gentle nudge or a loud awareness, and help that prompt me to turn to You in prayer—in praise and honor and petition and supplication.

Questions:

1. What does "pray without ceasing" mean to you?

2. How can you build compassion for others in your children?

3. What kinds of things do you do as a family to serve others locally or internationally?

4. Be on the lookout for prayer reminders throughout the day. What new visual cues did you encounter that will encourage you to pray?

When Your Child Suffers

by Julie Coleman

The year we switched schools was agonizing for my son. In place of the small, sheltered environment he had left behind, Adam entered a school of larger classes and total strangers. Seventh grade boys can be thoughtless or downright cruel, and the boys in my son's class were no exception. As the new kid, he found it hard to fit in. One night, several months into the school year, Adam approached me. He was not a complainer. But that night he had tears in his eyes and a heavy heart. "Mom, why do you think people are so mean?"

We talked into the night. For the first time I learned about the difficulties Adam was having with the harsh words and actions of his classmates. We prayed together, and though I was sick at heart, I encouraged him as best I could. When the conversation ended, I went out on the front porch, sat alone on the swing, and sobbed.

The next morning I went into action. I marched straight to the middle school principal's office and told her what I knew. My emotions were in turmoil. I was grieved I had moved my children to this school. Guilt overwhelmed me as I wondered if my husband and I had possibly made the wrong choice. Anger at the unjust treatment my son was experiencing consumed me. I wanted heads to roll. I didn't know what I could do, but I was going to do something.

Any parent knows that seeing your child in that kind of pain is excruciating. We would gladly take the pain and suffering on ourselves rather than see our precious children hurt in any way. A parent's first instinctive response is to protect at all costs.

After hearing my emotional plea for help, the principal promised to look into the matter. Then she gave me advice that would flavor my parenting for the rest of my life. She gently said, "Pain in a child's life is not bad, just hard. You don't want a child who has never experienced pain in his life. He would be insensitive, self-centered, and useless. God uses pain to develop us into mature, godly people."

Even though it went against every protective instinct in me as a mother, I knew she was right. James writes about this process in James 1:2-4 (NIV):

> Consider it pure joy, my brothers and sisters, whenever you face trials of many kinds, because you know that the testing of your faith produces perseverance. Let perseverance finish its work so that you may be mature and complete, not lacking anything.

There are several ways that pain and suffering are used by God in our children's lives.

1. Pain develops perseverance.

We must never lose sight of the fact that God is at work in our children. He purposefully and lovingly brings difficulty along at times in their lives. As they struggle though that circumstance, God develops perseverance in our child. Without that perseverance, our child would never be mature or complete. He would lack an essential character trait which is a mark of a mature Christian.

2. God uses pain to draw your child closer to Him.

As your child wrestles with a difficult circumstance, he will be driven to cry out to God in prayer. When we need, we look to the Lord. A deeper relationship with God as well as a stronger dependence on Him develops as he learns to trust God with his heartfelt pleas. Paul wrote about this in II Corinthians 1:9, "This happened that we might not rely on ourselves but on God."

3. Pain gives insight.

First Peter 4:1 tells us, "Whoever suffers in the body is done with sin." When we are in pain, suddenly the frivolous parts of our existence fade away, and the important things become crystal clear. Suffering gives our child insight and understanding he did not have before the pain. God also uses pain to open a child's eyes to those who suffer around him "so that we can comfort those in any trouble with the comfort we ourselves receive from God" (II Corinthians 1:4).

As Adam strove to survive that very difficult year, my husband and I did all we could to support him. He needed hope. We let him know he was not alone, that we were behind him 100 percent, and that the Lord had not abandoned him. And we prayed, every day, with him and for him.

Two long years passed before things started to look up. The start of high school gave Adam a place to shine and a chance to make new friends. He began to regain his confidence and optimistic spirit. He emerged from those difficult years a young man who loved the Lord deeply. Sensitive to the needs of others, his Christian character was widely recognized by his classmates and teachers. He became a leader among his peers. God faithfully used the adversity in Adam's experience to mold him into the likeness of Jesus Christ.

> God faithfully used the adversity in Adam's experience to mold him into the likeness of Jesus Christ.

Of course, there are extreme situations that require adult intervention and help. However, much of the pain our children experience does not fall into that category. Our children will face hardships like an unfair teacher, an adversarial peer, or even academic struggles.

Our first instinct as parents is to rush in and solve the problem. Rather than immediately doing this, pray instead that God would give your child endurance. Then find ways to support him so he will not be alone in the struggle. Give your support through a listening ear, prayer, and godly advice.

God is faithful. Have confidence that the Lord is carrying out a work in your child that is important to his development of mature, godly character; "being confident of this, that he who began a good work in [him] will carry it on to completion until the day of Christ Jesus" (Philippians 1: 6).

Prayer:

Dear Lord,
No one knows better than You how heartbreaking it is to watch your child suffer. We remember that You endured this very agony in order to save us from the consequences of our sin. Please give us wisdom and help as we work with our children to understand Your kind intentions as well as the promises in Your Word. Give us faith to trust You with their lives and to remember that Your love for them is perfect. Thank You for Your faithful presence with them and for how You will use hardships to develop them into mature and complete people. In Jesus' Name, Amen.

Questions:

1.   When your child suffers, what do we know about God's power over their peers' harsh words or actions? See Genesis 50:20 and Romans 8:28.

2.   What can you tell your child about God's ultimate intention toward them? See Romans 8:29.

3.   Scripture has a lot to say about suffering. Use Peter's counsel to give your child hope.

     1 Peter 3:14, 1 Peter 5:10

4. Pain is a tool used by God to transform us. Find what He accomplishes in us through pain.

    James 1:2-4, 2 Corinthians 4:17-18, 1 Peter 4:1

5. Let your child know that while they may *feel* lonely when experiencing painful rejection, they are never alone.

    Psalm 9:10, Hebrews 13:5

6. Talk over these verses with your child. Print them on index cards or sticky notes, and post them where they can be a continual reminder to call on God for help.

    Psalm 46:1, Isaiah 40:28-31, Hebrews 2:18; 4:15-16
    2 Corinthians 1:5, 2 Corinthians 4:8-11, 2 Corinthians 12:7-10

Help for the Helicopter Parent
by Cherrilynn Bisbano

Even a child makes himself known by his acts,
by whether his conduct is pure and upright.
Proverbs 20:11 ESV

"You are a hover mom, please stop!" my son said as he pulled his hand out of mine. The Walmart parking lot is a dangerous place. I had to protect him.

"When have I been a hover mom?" I asked my 13-year-old autistic son.

"Right now, and a million other times!"

"Can you give me another example?"

"At the gym the other day you kept trying to help me even when I knew how to use the chest press machine. Also, yesterday you put your arm around me as we were walking. Did you think I was going to get hit by a car? You even order for me at the restaurant."

I got the point. I guess I am a hover mom or what others call a helicopter parent. I don't want to be. I so desperately want my son to succeed and not use his autism as an excuse to limit himself. I have been the one sabotaging his independence by being over-protective.

I was crushed when I read that hovering can cause psychological harm to a child. A University of Washington study reported that children with micromanaging/helicopter parents had an increased risk of depression and anxiety.

I desire my son to be independent and to make good choices. How can he when I continue to make choices for him? Do I trust my parenting skills? Did I teach him well? How does a hover mom stay grounded so her child can take flight?

I love acrostics so I came up with this one to help those, like me, who hover.

H—Holy Spirit's guidance: "But when he, the Spirit of truth, comes, he will guide you into all the truth" (John 16:13 NIV).

"Mom, can I have this game?" We were at a yard sale and the game was $1.

"I'm sorry, Michael, but we have games at home you never play. Please find something else."

"But I'll play this one," he said.

"Put it back, please."

A few minutes passed.

"Mom, how about this game? I'll play this one!"

"Michael, you said that about all the other games and you never play them. Please put it back."

As I was speaking with the homeowner about her move, my son showed me a deck of cards in a small leather case. It was old and had a score pad with it.

"That was my mother's," the homeowner said. "You can have it for being such a good boy."

She was watching as my son obediently put the games back when I said no.

"Thank you for the cards," Michael said. "Can I still look around, Mom?"

"Of course, we'll leave in a few minutes."

I looked and found a few treasures.

"Mom, look what I found!" My son handed me sixteen dollars.

"I found it tucked away in the card case."

"Wow, Michael, thank you for your honesty. Let's go give it to the lady."

"I found this in the card case," Michael said, as he handed the woman the money.

"My mother tucked money away everywhere. Thank you for being so honest." The woman had a tear in her eye.

"Can I give your son those two games he wanted?"

Those big blue eyes looked into mine. How could I resist?

"Go get the games. I'm so proud of you for being honest and not pocketing the money."

When we drove away I asked Michael if he thought about keeping the money.

"Yes, just for a second, but the Bible says, 'Thou shalt not steal' (Exodus 20:15 KJV), and the Holy Spirit reminded me of that verse when I thought about keeping the money, so I told you about it."

"I'm so proud of you!"

The Holy Spirt guided my son that day. I guess he listened when I told him that we need the Spirit and the Word to make good decisions, just like a lamp needs electricity.

O—Observe the situation. **"Everyone should be quick to listen, slow to speak and slow to become angry" (James 1:19 NIV).**

The minute my son encounters a problem, I feel the need to interfere. I do not want to see him hurt or confused. I get angry with myself if he fails. *Maybe I didn't teach him correctly.* Then I remember my leadership training. When teaching a task, there are three steps.

1. Demonstrate the task.
2. Have the onlooker do the task with you and verbally repeat the steps.
3. Observe (not hover) as the student does the task alone.

I follow these steps when teaching my son. Sometimes it takes him a few attempts, but this hover mom needs to allow her son to figure it out.

Oh, no! I just did it again! (Yes, while in the middle of writing this). I lifted off my hover pad and violated my son's learning space.

My son is working on his hand-eye coordination. While teaching him to pour liquid into a container, we've cleaned up many spills. He was pouring juice into a cup and almost dropped the pitcher (I thought). I ran over, "NO, NO, NO, NO! Grab the bottom of the pitcher!"

He jumped, causing a little bit of juice to miss the glass. "You're being a hover mom, again!"

"But the last time you spilled it," I said.

"How am I going to learn anything if you don't give me a chance?"

"I'm sorry, Michael, will you forgive me?"

"Yes, Mom, but please ask me if I need help first. Remember we talked about this and you said you would ask."

Ouch. I did not "Observe" that he had the pitcher by the handle.

I wiped up the juice from the counter. After all, it was my fault it spilled.

I am back at my launch pad. I think that I will power down this hover craft, relax, and allow my son to breathe.

V—Valuable lessons. "Fathers, do not exasperate your children" (Ephesians 6:4 NIV).

Moms can exasperate their children too. My son woke up one morning and wanted to surprise me by making coffee in the Keurig.® I stopped him. He said, "Mom, how can I learn to do anything if you don't trust me?" I watched as he poured water into the machine and it overflowed onto the floor. He looked at me with fear. My heart was crushed. I said, "You tried, and that is what matters." I proceeded to teach him how to do it properly. He had a difficult time pouring the water into the reservoir, but did not give up.

The next time he made coffee (yes, I actually allowed him to do it again), it was perfect. I reaped the benefit of a yummy cup of Java because I took the time to teach him and he persevered. When a child fails, he learns a valuable lesson. He learns persistence and how to solve problems. He becomes a better decision maker.

E—Examine yourself. "Let us examine our ways and test them, and let us return to the LORD" (Lamentations 3:40 NIV).

I asked myself and other parents, "What are the reasons why we hover?" Fear, perfectionism, controlling, and pride were just some of the reasons.

Pride was and still can be my problem. If my son can't ride a bike, cook for himself at age fifteen, or be left alone for one hour so I can go get some groceries, I look like a failure as a parent. I realize I can care more about what others think than my son's well-being. I'm right there when he makes himself a sandwich. Especially when we have company. I don't want him getting peanut butter all over the counter. It will look like I did not teach him well. Yes, I can be selfish and prideful. I hate that about myself. I asked God for help. The Spirit reminded me that love is patient and thinks more highly of others. I apologized to my son, once again. I continue to examine my motive behind my hovering so I can be a better parent.

R—Relax. "Cease striving and know that I am God" (Psalm 46:10 NASB).

Being a hover parent is exhausting. The continual motor revving, waiting for lift off to intervene, takes a toll on me and my son.

"You are hard on your son." My younger sister expressed her concern during a phone conversation. "I felt bad for him today at breakfast. You didn't allow him to do the things he already knows how to do. You need to relax." I felt horrible. My sister only gives her opinion after much thought. We celebrated my older sister's birthday at Newport Creamery. That morning at breakfast, I was hovering again. "Michael, put your napkin in your lap please" (I did say please). "You are using too much ketchup." "Watch out you are going to spill your juice!" My hands were all over the table trying to help him. I was horrible and this time my entire family witnessed it. I thanked my sister and apologized to my son for embarrassing him. I promised my son that I will relax and not help unless he asks. I also asked him to tell me, respectfully, when I'm a hover mom.

I love my son and desire to see him succeed. My son is becoming a godly man. His respectful way of showing me my fault has given me a closer relationship with him and with God. I will make mistakes. That is inevitable. I don't want him to learn to hover over his children so I am relying on the Holy Spirit for guidance, observing the situation before I take off, letting my son learn from his mistakes, examining my motives before I engage in lift off, and I'm learning to relax.

I want my child to grow wings and fly. I want him to learn that God can change a person, even his mom. The only time this helicopter is going to take off from the launch pad is if my child is in immediate danger. Otherwise, I am grounding myself.

Prayer:

Lord, You are the perfect parent. You are patient, kind, trustworthy, and the best teacher. Help me to be more like You when I parent the child You entrusted to me. Show me where I am a hover parent. Help me to teach my child and trust him to learn and grow. Give me patience when my child makes a mistake because You are patient with me. Thank You that You never leave us nor forsake us. In Jesus' Name.

Questions:

1. Do you see any helicopter traits in your behavior toward your kids? Explain.

2. What point resonated with you the most? Why?

3. How can we stay grounded and let our children take flight?

The Legacy of Kindness
by Evelyn Wells

*Thus says the LORD of hosts, "Render true judgments,
show kindness and mercy to one another."
Zechariah 7:9 ESV*

My grandfather's farm was located on a dusty, rural road. During those years, many people walked wherever they went, since they didn't own a vehicle. Some strangers who were traveling by foot, stopped by their farm to ask for a drink of water. They were welcomed and offered not only water, but iced tea and lemonade as well. They were also given food. They sat in the shade of a big elm tree and ate their refreshments, then rested for a bit before resuming their journey.

When they left, they didn't leave empty-handed. My grandmother sent them on their way with a container of cool water and the remainder of the sandwiches, so they could be refreshed as they traveled. Who knows the eternal consequences of this kind act? Hebrews 13:2 says not to neglect showing hospitality to strangers, for by doing so some have entertained angels unawares.

What if my grandmother had looked at the travelers and decided not to offer refreshments to them? Proverbs 31:20 says, *She opens her hand to the poor and reaches out her hands to the needy.* Grandmother didn't turn these strangers away, and in the process, showed her children and grandchildren what a Proverbs 31 woman looked like.

Character Lived Out

Children occupy a front row seat in their family theater. They watch our truth, integrity, and love, or lack of them. They watch as we play out the scenes of our lives. They see our behavior at home in front of them, and they watch our behavior in front of others. Are these two scenes consistent with each other? Do we live differently away from home than we do at home?

In order to build character in our children, we need to intentionally live out godly attributes not only in front of our children, but in every aspect of our lives. We have been entrusted with a great responsibility to pattern good habits and truth, so they will copy those as they grow into adulthood.

> *Be kind to one another, tenderhearted, forgiving one another, as God in Christ forgave you.* (Ephesians 4:32)

Sometimes those we love hurt us, and we find it hard to readily forgive them. We tend to hold on to our hurt by holding grudges. But we're called to forgive, and the only way we can do that is through demonstrating the love of Jesus to those who have hurt us and to tenderly treat them with kindness.

Kindness Goes a Long Way

When I was a child, my siblings and I were encouraged by our parents and teachers to be kind in whatever situation we found ourselves. The days of my grandparents' welcome invitation to strangers appears to be long gone. In today's society, we're not likely to invite perfect strangers into our backyards and serve them refreshments. But we can be kind to those we encounter daily. Kindness reveals character. When our children live in a home where kindness is displayed in their daily lives, they will be more likely to treat others in the same way.

> Kindness reveals character.

Proverbs 31:26 says, *She opens her mouth with wisdom, and the teaching of kindness is on her tongue.* Parents can encourage kindness in their children by speaking positively of others. Do we build others up, or do we bring them down with the words we speak? Since children easily pick up on what they hear, we may hear our own unkind words echoed from little mouths. As we speak kindly of others, we are teaching our children a valuable lesson. Our goal should be to teach them to speak words of hope and encouragement.

Proactive Ways to Teach Kindness

As our children watch the way we live, we have many opportunities to display kindness. At the grocery store, at church, on the telephone, and in traffic are a few of the daily situations that we can use as life lessons.

Grocery store checkout lines are frustrating to me, because I usually get in the line that have price checks and other delays. This could be my opportunity to let everyone around me know just how busy I am and that I absolutely don't have time for this. On the other hand, I could use this opportunity to notice the people in front of me and behind me and offer them a smile or a kind word.

At church, we have many opportunities to welcome visitors. For instance, when someone is sitting alone, we can introduce ourselves and sit with them during the service. A number of years ago I had accepted a position in a church where I knew no one. The Pastor had asked that I attend church the Sunday before I was to begin working there. He wanted to introduce me to the congregation. Almost as soon as I got there, a lady sat down on the pew beside me and introduced herself. I'll never forget the kindness she showed me that day.

When we're caught in heavy traffic, we can make a difference in a fellow commuter's day. Enabling them to merge more easily is a blessing we can bestow on them. Sometimes we're in such a hurry to reach our destination, we fail to remember that others are feeling the same way. Remember, it only takes a few seconds to be kind to other drivers.

The lessons learned by our children in these scenes are priceless. When they see kindness displayed without comment, they learn to regard this type of behavior as normal and the right thing to do. As we're working to build good character and integrity into our children, speaking to them about godliness and living it out go hand in hand. Proverbs 22:6 tells us that when we train up children in the way they should go, even when they are old they won't depart from it. These lessons have eternal consequences, and kindness is a legacy that will stay with our children as long as they live.

Prayer:

Heavenly Father,
Thank You for showing us how to be people of character and how to teach our children to be kind to others. Guide us in our journey of bringing up children of godly character. Give us wisdom as You direct our path. We glorify You in the name of Jesus. Amen.

Questions:

1. What are some ways we can show kindness to strangers?

2. Would you change your methods of parenting if you remember how closely your children watch your behavior? If so, how?

3. What are your goals in modeling integrity before your children?

4. What are some different ways that we can show kindness to strangers today? To those in need?

5. Can you think of ways you can be a better neighbor?

*All Scripture verses are taken from the ESV.

God's Pattern
for Intentional Parenting
by Jenifer Kitchens

The statistics are alarming concerning how many young people turn away from the church.

> "61 percent of today's young adults who were regular church attendees are now 'spiritually disengaged.' They are not actively attending church, praying, or reading their Bibles."[1]

> "Despite strong levels of spiritual activity during the teen years, most 20-somethings disengage from active participation in the Christian faith during their young adult years—and often beyond that."[2]

But statistics also show that children who grow up in households where God is a part of their home life, are less likely to leave the church than those who attend church but had no spiritual instruction at home.[3]

What can we do to make faith as a way of daily life, real for our kids? How can we create an environment that prioritizes their spiritual development? How can we partner with God in the lives of our children so that they don't become "disengaged"?

In Deuteronomy 6, God laid out His pattern for parents to intentionally invest in their children. Through Moses, He gives instructions for how Israel should live as His people. God's desire is that His people will be blessed for generations though obedience, and these instructions begin with the family.

1. Love God. The passage begins, *The LORD is our God, the LORD is one. You shall love the LORD your God with all your heart and with all your soul and with all your might* (Deuteronomy 6:4-5 NASB'). As Christians, we serve the triune God and love Him with every element of our lives. There is no one like God and nothing can compete with Him. Loving God with all our heart, soul, and might encompasses every area of our lives.

As parents who desire that our children have a relationship with God, we have the first opportunity to introduce our children to Him through our family life. Our choices, demonstrated through our actions, communicate more than our words. This causes me to consider what my children are seeing in me. Do I model reverence? Do they see love for God reflected in every area of my life?

2. Keep God's Word on your heart. Moses continued, *These words, which I am commanding you today, shall be on your heart* (Deuteronomy 6:6). Just as we would re-read a precious letter from a loved one until its message is ingrained in our hearts and minds, we have God's Word available for us to pour over until it becomes a part of our spiritual DNA.

As we absorb God's Word, it guides our thinking and we realize how great a treasure is at our disposal. Oh, how often we need the comfort and direction it gives! When our children see us seeking guidance from God's Word, they learn its value in their own lives. Our children are strengthened when we share passages with them that encourage us. In addition, the humility and wisdom created by sharing Scripture that has convicted us, are unparalleled. When God is revealing Himself to us through His Word, it will splash out of us onto our children.

3. Teach God's Word to your children. Not only are we to commit God's Word to our hearts but, *You shall teach them diligently to your sons and shall talk of them when you sit in your house and when you walk by the way and when you lie down and when you rise up* (Deuteronomy 6:7). We are directly commanded to teach God's Word to our children. I don't see this as limited to family Bible study. Whether we are sitting at home or on our way somewhere, if we are going to bed or waking up, we can seize and even create teachable moments with our children.

Intentional, frequent conversation with our children about God's Word is counter-cultural. How easy is it to put in a movie or hand them an electronic device instead of having conversations in the van on the way to practice? How often are we distracted by our smart phones rather than sharing God's Word with our children? I know I am guilty of checking social media at breakfast when I could be hearing the hearts of my children and equipping them spiritually for the day ahead. We might have young children in this season of life, but we have to connect with our kids around God's Word while they are young to lay a framework for this kind of relationship when they are older.

I want to encourage you. We don't have to have everything figured out. Kids don't need an expert, they need a humble example of someone who is learning and excited about God's Word. So often we want to let the professionals handle the spiritual training of our children. The responsibility to pour God's Word into our children is given to parents, not to churches, ministers, or schools. God has equipped you in His Word with everything you need to teach your children about Him.

4. Make the influence of God and His Word obvious in your daily walk. As Moses is giving instructions on how to live like God's people, he then gives instructions about God's Word that might seem unusual to us. *You shall bind them as a sign on your hand and they shall be as frontals on your forehead* (Deuteronomy 6:8). Jewish men took this literally and tied small boxes, called phylacteries, containing Scripture to their head and hands.

Just as phylacteries were obvious to those encountering Jewish men, God's Word can be obvious to those we encounter. The words we choose, our actions, and our reactions are all ways that God's Word is written on us. Do we show grace and forgive as Christ has forgiven us? Are we moved with compassion and respond when we see need or pain? Our kids should be able to "read us" and learn about God's nature and His plan for our lives by what they see.

5. Give God's Word a prominent place in your home. God's Word doesn't only have a place on us, but also in our home. Deuteronomy 6:9 says, *You shall write them on the doorposts of your house and on your gates.* Having Scripture both inside and outside our home creates an environment rich with God's Word. It is in front of us as we seek to soak His Word into our hearts. It is in front of our kids as we look for opportunities to teach them. It is also in front of our neighbors as we seek to share God's love with them. Our home can and should bear witness to what God has done and is doing in our lives.

Christian bookstores and select home decor and craft stores carry beautiful items bearing Scripture for our home and garden, making it easy to fill our home with God's Word. Handwritten verses on the refrigerator or taped to the bathroom mirror allow us to frequently personalize what we see. If we want to surround ourselves with Scripture, we will find a way to make it happen.

God has given us His plan for how we can live as His people and intentionally share Him with our children. What a joy we have in being able to follow the design of our Creator to bless our children by raising them His way! Our home can become a place where our children meet God and then cultivate a relationship with Him.

Prayer:

Lord,
You created families with the purpose of passing on to the next generation Your Word, Your love, Your nature, and Your story. It's time for me to do my part. I pray for forgiveness for missed

opportunities and eyes to see them in the future. Please give me the words to say to my children and, Lord, may they have soft, receptive hearts. I know the Enemy fights against families. Please strengthen and empower me as I fight to keep our Christian family from becoming a statistic.

Questions:

1. The first step to taking action is seeing a need. How do you see the culture becoming disengaged from God, His Word, and the Church?

2. What do your children, or children in your life, see that reflects God's place of authority and priority in your life?

3. Are you leaving the spiritual training of your children to the professionals (ministers, Sunday school teachers, and school teachers) or are you trusting that God, through His Spirit and His Word, has equipped you with everything you need to invest in your children's spiritual lives?

4. What habit can you begin today to move toward the goal of intentionally parenting your children's hearts?

*All Scripture verses are taken from the NASB.

1. Ken Ham, Britt Beemer, and Todd Hillard. Already Gone: Why Your Kids Will Quit Church and What You Can Do to Stop It. (Green Forest, Ark.: Master Books), 2009. www.answersingenesis.org. October 20, 2011.
2. Ibid.
3. Ibid.

Begin at Number One
by Rick Kauffman

Raising kids is not rocket science. I've done that, and this is much harder. When the little bundles of joy arrive, they don't come with a set of instructions. We need help to know how to raise our children to be godly people. So we turn to the only Expert that I know of—God. We can follow His Instruction Book for Life, and when life takes us off grid, we don't have to panic. We can pray and ask our heavenly Father what to do next. He'll know, because He's had lots of experience at this.

Four instructions will get us started.

Instruction #1: Love your kids.

Everything that breathes wants to be loved. I do. For as long as I can remember, I have wanted love and acceptance, not that I understood it in those terms. Everyone does. Test the theory. Direct an act of loving kindness toward an unsuspecting victim and see how they respond. If they light up, you have proved the point. If not, see if there was some distraction or hindrance, something that got in the way. People love to be loved.

> Everything that breathes wants to be loved.

Jesus' example shows us that sometimes loving people requires a sacrifice. Scripture says, "By this we know love, because He laid down His life for us. And we also ought to lay down our lives for the brethren" (1 John 3:16 NKJV). It says, "We love Him because He first loved us" (1 John 4:19). I don't think that dying is the only way to show love, but it is the ultimate way. Jesus' example shows us that loving someone can take some serious effort and self-sacrifice. Even for kids. But our children are worth it. After all, we brought them here.

Loving our kids includes praying for them. We can't always be there for them, but God can. As we learn to trust Him to look after them, we discover just how good He is at it.

Instruction #2: Train your kids.

Start when your kids are young, because their little minds are constantly in learn mode. And yes, no bad habit goes unnoticed.

Read them Bible stories, the ones where the main character is a godly role model who will motivate them to do good. You can't go wrong with stories about Jesus—how He loves children, how He helps those who are hurting, how He welcomes those who are lonely. Your kids will get to know Him and treasure Him. Feed their minds with good things like you feed their bodies with good food. Guard what influences them. If they watch TV, monitor their programs. Cut out those that are full of negative attitudes and violence, because kids usually mimic what they see and hear.

Teach your children what is right and motivate them to choose it. You may have noticed that most children already know how to be selfish, even yours, but selfless is the goal. Build on those stories about Jesus. In the 1990s, a ministry to teenagers was based on the theme, WWJD, What would Jesus do? The goal was to get teens to reason through a decision they faced and to address it as best they knew how as Jesus would. Another goal was to get them to consider the consequences of their actions.

Again, start when they are young. When your kids learn to read, buy them a Children's Bible with pictures. Get them on a daily reading routine. This works best if you do it with them. God can use this time in their lives and work wonders with it. As they approach their teenage years, encourage them to have a quiet time with God the first thing every morning, just as Jesus did. Remember to ask them about what they are studying and how they plan to apply it.

Instruction #3: Build memories with your children that nurture their creativity and imagination.

Most kids love to pretend and role play. How often do you see little girls playing house with their "kids" (dolls and stuffed animals) all lined up. Now they get to be the Mommy and teach something. Everything you do gets passed on. Little boys like to pretend and role play as well. When I was young, cowboys and soldiers were popular. Now I think it's Power Rangers from the costumes we see at Halloween.

Kids also love special places—a tent made of sheets in the living room, or a fort made of cardboard boxes in the den. Dress them up as their favorite Bible character. If you don't like making costumes, you can usually find them at Party City or seasonally at stores like Target. Help them to act out the stories that you have been reading to them. Be sure to include a demonstration of the character quality that you are trying to build in them— courage, kindness, endurance. The effort you put into the script, set, costumes, and dress rehearsals will be rewarded with their excitement and joy. Long after the event is over, your kids will keep the memories of doing it together, the fun you had, and what they learned.

Instruction #4: Set boundaries, and enforce them.

We all need boundaries. Believe it or not, boundaries give us security. In His word, God has given us boundaries for daily life that keep us from hurting ourselves and others. When God says "do" something, He is saying "Enjoy this." And when He says "don't do this," He is saying "Don't hurt yourself." Games are a good example of this for kids. To play the games they love, they have to follow the rules and stay clear of any out of bounds areas.

It takes self-discipline to observe the rules, and intervention when that fails. Remember to discipline fairly and let the consequences suit the violation of the boundaries. Never discipline your kids when you're angry, but follow God's example and do it lovingly. "Whom the LORD loves He chastens" (Hebrews 12:6).

Make a list of household rules similar to the Ten Commandments, with the penalties for not keeping them. Write them on a poster and hang it in a good spot. That way there can be no dispute when it's time for discipline. Let your kids help determine the penalties. You may be surprised at how tough they are on themselves. Several forms of discipline may prove effective: restriction of privileges, extra chores, the extreme—no cell phone, and so forth.

Doing well with the first three instructions may make the discipline of #4 less frequent. However, if all else fails, begin again at number one.

Prayer:

Dear Father,
Show us how to love our children so that they know it's real and they feel loved. Help us to be mindful of them and understand how to teach and train them to be prepared for life and to have godly character. Show us ways to be creative with them and to help develop their creativity. Please help us to discipline them fairly and teach them to be respectful of others and not to be selfish. Help them to be kind and gentle like You. I ask this in Jesus' name, Amen.

Questions:

1. Have you noticed how children respond to love? What is your favorite way to express your love to your kids?

2. What training techniques have you observed that work well with children?

3. Does your favorite childhood memory involve an activity with a parent or older sibling?

4. What family activity do you think would be special and memorable to a child?

5. What method of discipline worked well on you as a child? What didn't work well, or you liked it the least?

6. Do you have any games or activities that could teach a child to play by the rules or to observe set boundaries?

*All Scripture verses are taken from the NKJV.

Laying the Foundation
for Good Character in Our Kids

by Jenifer Kitchens

When I was a little girl, I would play with my dolls in their dollhouse, dreaming of one day having my own house. I would rearrange furniture, and the area that was the bedroom suddenly became the kitchen. I didn't have to worry about the details of drywall, plumbing, or electrical. Completely remodeling my house was as simple as changing my mind.

Years later when my parents built a house, I saw the stages involved. The foundation was established, the house was framed, then paint, carpet, and tile were added. I realized just how little I knew about construction as a child.

My parents recently remodeled parts of that house, and as walls were rearranged, the established house changed. Adults are like houses that have been around a while. As our hearts are renovated, elements of our lifestyles have to change; they require remodeling!

As parents, we want our children to develop good patterns for life so that heart renovations are easier for them as adults. We want our kids to be smart and have good character demonstrated through solid morals and ethics. As Christian parents, we also want them to have faith in God, to worship, and to grow in the faith, while passing the Christian faith on to their children. We want so many things for them, but how do we start?

Peter's second letter gives a list that is a blueprint for developing godly character. The first three items in the list revolutionized my priorities in parenting. Second Peter 1:5 (ESV) says, "For this very reason, make every effort to supplement your faith with virtue, and virtue with knowledge."

Faith

A foundation has to be level and square because it sets the pattern for everything that is built on it. A crooked or uneven foundation will result in a house lacking structural integrity, one plagued with structural flaws. Faith in God is the foundation for our lives. Peter, in his letter, said to supplement faith with virtue. Intelligence and good character are built on the foundation of a solid relationship with God.

How can I make the development of my child's faith a priority? Taking them to church is a start, but it's definitely not the end of the list! Are church functions the first thing to be sacrificed for school projects or sports teams? Spiritual formation doesn't only happen at church, though. Are you spending time in God's Word with your kids? Do they catch you pouring over your Bible? I try to memorize Scripture with our kids, and I'm thrilled that they are better at learning verses than I am! As we observe the world around us and seek to live our faith, I want the words of Scripture to permeate our family.

Proverbs 3:5-6 (NASB) teaches us, "Trust in the LORD with all your heart and do not lean on your own understanding. In all your ways acknowledge him and he will make straight your paths." This is what making faith a daily priority in our lives looks like— actively trusting God in our daily lives, seeking His guidance, and desiring to give Him glory in everything we do. This gives the sure foundation we want for our children! Oh, but if we want to see that happening in our children, they need to see it happening in us!

Virtue (Moral Excellence)

We also want our kids to have character. Peter calls it *virtue*. Godly character is like the framing of the house. Just as framing is supported by the foundation and a house would collapse without it, godly character is built on faith.

We try to instill godly character in the lives of our children in many ways. We warn them, count to five, and punish bad behavior with time outs, grounding, or spanks. We set up sticker charts, reward with smiley faces, and even bribe them! But even with all the options we have in training our children, attempting to develop character in our children without developing their relationship with God as the guide for their actions, is just behavior modification. Proverbs 4:23 (NIV) tells us, "Above all else, guard your heart, for everything you do flows from it." Behavior is a reflection of what is going on in the heart. If we want to change behavior, we first have to change the heart.

We can start by evaluating what is going into our children. What they see and hear takes up residence in their heart and makes its way out through their actions and attitudes. We can't guard their hearts from everything, but we can dialogue with them about whether something is good to imitate or not.

When our child displays ungodly character, we need to evaluate what is happening in our child's heart. Too often behaviors we see mask deeper issues that need to be addressed. As I seek to raise our children with godly character, I am learning to find the root of their actions. When our four-year-old doesn't want to pick up her toys, I need discernment to know whether this is an issue of laziness, not honoring her parents, or lack of gratitude for what she has. When our eight-year-old has an ugly attitude toward her sister, is jealousy the root, or could she have some pride issues that are showing up in this way?

Knowing our child's heart takes time, such as creating time to really listen to her. Sometimes we have to listen to lots of incidental dialogue that doesn't flow from their hearts, to earn their trust and really hear what's inside.

Also, I have to remember that I can't expect my child to act like a mature Christian when she is not yet mature. After becoming a Christian, our children begin to learn to be led by the Holy Spirit and to fight their flesh, and as parents, we are still learning the same.

Knowledge

How often do we see bumper stickers that brag about honor student status? We want our kids to learn and be intelligent. We grow concerned when they aren't accomplishing what we believe they are capable of. It's easy to place top priority on our child's education. Knowledge in our child's life, though, is like the finishes of a house. It is the drywall, tiles, and flooring; while these are essential for living in a home, without a foundation and framing, there is nothing for them to rest on.

Peter challenges us to focus on knowledge after faith and character development. This is backwards to our culture, but think of how faith and virtue pave the way for education. When our children are growing in faith, we are able to guide hearts and build character. When hearts have good character, distractions from learning are diminished. When my daughter knows that diligence honors God, and she works on that trait, her math lessons are positively affected. How many teachers struggle because virtues like respect for authority, self-control, and kindness are lacking in class. This shows us new ways to apply, "The fear of the LORD is the beginning of wisdom" (Proverbs 9:10 NASB).

We cannot buy into secular society's lie that faith, character, and knowledge are independent of one another. When we have all the right structures in place in our children, the trajectory is set for good things to come into their lives, including the character traits Peter listed in the subsequent verses: self-control, steadfastness, godliness, brotherly affection, and love. By starting with the foundation of faith, building virtue on top, and following that with knowledge, our children can become effective, fruitful parts of the kingdom of God.

Prayer:

Father,

Thank You for my children. Thank You for giving wisdom from Your Word to know how to raise them. Please help our family to prioritize faith, character, and knowledge correctly according to Your plan. Please forgive me when I fall short as an example for my children and give me wisdom to lead them. I pray this seeking Your glory, Lord. Amen.

Questions:

1. Are your priorities for your child Biblically aligned?

2. It's easy for other things to sneak into the foundational faith we seek to lay for our children. What do you have to be vigilant for in your family?

3. How can you be more intentional in the spiritual development of your children?

4. What behaviors are masking deeper issues in your children? What steps are needed to address these deeper concerns?

5. When can you do an activity with your child with the goal of listening to his or her heart?

6. Are character concerns hindering your child?

Helping Our Children to Grow in Humility

by Jennifer DeFrates

The closer I draw to Christ, the more I realize my immense need for humility, but it's challenging to teach humility in a culture so focused on self. Where do I begin?

When I was younger, I loved logic puzzles—the more challenging the better. Large grids helped me solve the mystery from a few given facts. Lying on the rough shag carpeting of my lilac bedroom, I would spend hours with my sharp Number 2 pencil filling in the little boxes, working towards the solution. I found the best way to solve the puzzles was to focus on one known detail and work backwards.

Parenting is so much like those old logic puzzles. I have some basic information. Some answers I can work out, but others will take lots of working backwards from the one thing I know is true. Sometimes I don't know the right choices when it comes to day-to-day parenting. Is organic really better or just more expensive? Should we homeschool? Which activities are best?

I won't ever have all the answers, but there is a solution when I start from the right place, God's word. The daily decisions lose their weight in the face of eternity. And I know my hope is for my child to become an authentic servant of God.

So how do I help her get there? More is caught than taught.

When I watch my daughter play, I'm always surprised to see just how many of my mannerisms she has adopted. She imitates my gentle snuggles with her baby dolls and my irritated tone of voice when our pets are acting up. I didn't set out to teach her either of those things, but she learned them through imitating me, which is terribly convicting.

If marriage is an iron sharpening iron, parenting is a very clear mirror of who I really am. I've had to work on my own walk with the Lord so I can see Him reflected in that mirror more than my sinful nature.

How can we help our children to grow in humility?

1. Be imitators of me, as I am of Christ (1 Corinthians 11:1 ESV*).

I know my daughter is going to imitate me, so my first calling is to be the best imitator of Christ I can be. Starting each day with prayer and time in the Word helps me focus and gives me peace for whatever the day brings, whether it's grumpy attitudes, stomach bugs, or just the typical, unglamorous mom jobs.

The best way I can teach her to be a humble servant is by humbly serving. When I pull out the vacuum or wash my husband's dirty uniforms, I get to choose my attitude. Having a servant's heart and a joyful attitude about the tasks that we don't always enjoy, like dishes or laundry, will go much further than a thousand book lessons about service.

I love to include my daughter in our daily tasks. We sing praise songs while folding laundry. We talk about why we serve. One afternoon, she really wanted to play a card game, but the floor was really messy. I asked her to imagine how coming home to a dirty house might make Daddy feel. I explained how taking a few minutes to vacuum and put his feelings first is one way I love him. She understood, we saved the game for later, and she saw a concrete example of humble service.

2. Let the greatest among you become as the youngest, and the leader as one who serves (Luke 22:26).

Culturally, service is often seen as lowly, but real leadership is born of service, even when those we serve don't even see much of what we do for them.

> Real leadership is born of service.

In Luke 22, Jesus was eating with the disciples and they began to argue over which of them would be the greatest. Jesus immediately chastised them, contrasting how differently leaders of the world and leaders in His kingdom would behave.

Sometimes as parents we get caught up in our own authority, hung up on our position and the respect we think we deserve. I know I've stood over my child talking back to me and started to get angry. *How dare she? She can't talk to me that way!*

But in my anger, I forget God didn't call parents to exalt our position. It's not about my deserving her respect as much as her learning to respect authorities that God places in her life. Honoring her parents is part of submitting to God. I demonstrate my own submission to God in respecting my husband, following the law, and how I obey His Word.

3. Do nothing from selfish ambition or conceit, but in humility count others more significant than yourselves (Philippians 2:3).

This verse really shifted my attitude towards parenting. I have read it many times, but never considered it in light of parenting. Was how I treated my daughter really demonstrating I thought more of her than I did of myself? I don't think so. Being exasperated when she struggles with her behavior says my agenda is more important. I needed to change my attitude about my role in this season of motherhood.

Instead of getting frustrated, I try to remember to seek the cause of inappropriate behavior, not just treat the symptoms. One afternoon, she was getting really bogged down over directions for a math worksheet. As frustration began to build, I took a deep breath, and considered what she might be feeling.

Her distress was over a fear of making mistakes. I encouraged her to do her best and reminded her that mistakes are how we learn. She learned a new perspective on learning through mistakes. Humility used that moment to build character in us both, instead of tearing us apart and creating a foothold for Satan to exploit.

Thinking back to those logic puzzles, I remember when I used to get really frustrated, I'd peek at the answers in the back of the book. Technically, the only person I was cheating was myself, but aren't we glad that in parenting we have a book full of answers that God wants us to use? I love how His word influences my parenting more each day as I allow it to transform and renovate my heart.

Prayer:

Dear Heavenly Father,
Help me focus first on being obedient to Your calling in my life as Your child. Guide me in being humble and demonstrating grace so I reflect those values for my children. Help me seek forgiveness when I have wronged my family. May I always demonstrate grace as I discipline and guide my child to become Your fervent and humble disciple. In Christ's name, Amen.

Questions:

1. Do you think any areas of your parenting are negatively affected by pride? If so, how can you change your ways to reflect humility?

2. Have you ever been convicted by watching your child(ren) imitate you? How did (can) you grow from that experience?

3. Who has had the greatest impact on your life as a godly example? What character traits of theirs would you most like to emulate?

4. Look up Ephesians 4:1-3 and 1 Peter 5:5. How do they add to the messages of Luke 22:26 and Philippians 2:3?

5. Look up Galatians 5:22-23. How could these verses transform our parenting as Christians?

6. How can you incorporate humble service into your family life?

*All Scripture verses are taken from the ESV.

Sowing and Reaping Godly Character in Your Children

by Barb Syvertson

Whatever a man sows, that he will also reap.
Galatians 6:7 NKJV

When we first moved from New York City to rural Pennsylvania, we were excited to have a small plot in a community garden. We love corn from roadside stands so we bought a pack of corn seeds to plant. Having no experience with gardens, farms, plants, vegetables, or growing anything, we figured you just put seeds in the dirt and corn eventually grows. How hard can it be?

We dug a little trench in the soil and poured in our seeds, covered it with dirt and sprinkled some water on it. We felt like real farmers. Now all we had to do was wait until the day we could pick all our corn and serve it with butter and salt. It rained a lot that summer so we didn't even see the need to go and water our plot. When we started to see fresh corn in the supermarket, we realized that it must be time to harvest our crop of corn. Imagine our surprise when all we found was one scrawny emaciated stalk with one miniature ear of corn on it, surrounded by dead seedlings. We calculated later that for our $20 investment, we netted approximately two teaspoonfuls of corn.

We knew the expression, "You reap what you sow," but this was our first experience with that principle in the actual agrarian setting. In our case, we sowed enough seeds but not in the correct way, and we also neglected the care of our plot yet we expected plentiful and delicious corn.

Sowing and reaping is a law of nature, a law of God, and a very important principle in raising children.

One of the few things that we did right in our first garden experience was that we at least planted corn seeds. We didn't plant watermelon seeds in hopes of getting corn. Sounds like an elementary principle when we think about gardens but it is also true in developing godly character in our children. We need to plant seeds of love, respect, boundaries, laughter, sympathy, God's word, prayer, and compassion to see those things bloom as our children grow. If we plant criticism and anger and unforgiveness into their lives, it makes sense that we will reap those qualities in our children as well.

Another aspect of growing is that each seed has its own requirements for proper growth. Some plants need lots of sun, some need shade. Some need to be planted close together, others need lots of room to grow. We need to know these differences before we try to plan our garden. Likewise, our children are each unique with their own needs to thrive. Each child receives encouragement in different ways.

Introverted children need more time alone to recharge. Active children might need more bonding play time. Study your children and learn what their unique personalities require.

All gardening takes time. It is not a hobby for the impatient. I remember when our young sons were learning to fish, they didn't actually fish but they *hunted* for fish. They ran around the pond looking for a fish and threw in their fishing line and hook near it. When it swam away, they reeled in their line and ran after it to try again. Gardening, like fishing, is not for the impatient. It takes time, lots of time to develop a beautiful garden. In the same way it takes time to develop godly character. It doesn't happen after one nice conversation or after one great vacation together.

Watering a plant is essential to its success. Water is not only refreshing but we cannot live without it. Likewise, we must refresh our children with the water of encouragement, of soothing and refreshing words, hugs and kisses, kindness and love. These all refresh our children and keep them growing.

Another essential in growing a beautiful garden is to fertilize it. Manure is used to enrich the soil, creating the perfect environment for growth. There are valuable minerals in the muck that help the plant become hardy and beautiful. This is the hardest for some parents to grasp in relation to their family "garden." We want life to be easy for our children. We don't want them to suffer or go through hard times especially in the teenage years when life can be so difficult for both parents and children. But just like our gardens, we don't want to remove all the yucky things in our kids' lives. It helps to develop godly character. During those times when people, things, and situations are adding "fertilizer" to their lives, we need to saturate them with the water of encouragement.

In many aspects of gardening, pruning is needed. This is when the plant is cut back to allow the other branches to grow better and bigger. God prunes us (John 15) and our children so delicately and precisely that it allows for more power and growth in our lives. Some of the pruning involves allowing our children to live with the consequences of their sins. If we always rescue our children from the natural consequences of their actions, we delay their maturity and enable them to be irresponsible.

Thinking back to our corn-planting story, let's suppose that our well-meaning friends realized how terrible we were at planting. So they snuck up to the plot and dug up the seeds and planted them according to the instructions. Then they went each day and watered and weeded the plot, and even added fertilizer. When the big reveal happened we would have gotten great corn. But we would have incorrectly thought that we knew how to grow corn. This is what we are tempted to do in the lives of our children. Dealing with the natural consequences teaches our children and helps to develop godly character.

Farmers cannot grow produce without the ultimate input from God, the Creator of sunlight, rain, and dirt. Likewise, we as parents can sow into, weed, prune, water, and fertilize our children's little hearts, but it still takes a miracle of God and the working of His Spirit to produce godly character. As parents we are dependent on the Holy Spirit to take our humble efforts and to make good things happen. The family is the framework that God created for children to mature. He could have created infants with all the godly character that they need for life. But He didn't. Infants are totally dependent on parents. And growing children need parents too. It is a great responsibility, especially since parents are still maturing themselves.

Lastly, remember that corn has no choice but to grow if the conditions are perfect. But children, unlike vegetables, have been given a free will. They are not robots or puppets. Even our best efforts cannot guarantee that children will choose to love the Lord or follow our guidance. But the "ground work" that we have done as parents will help to cultivate a heart that God can speak to. Maybe growth won't happen exactly when we want it, or in the way that we want it, but remember that farmers are patient. And the Son is shining even on cloudy days.

Prayer:

God, Creator of all things,
Please help me learn how to be a gardener in my children's lives. When I sow toxic things into their lives, please reveal them to me so I can ask for Your forgiveness and their forgiveness as well. I am grateful that You are slow to anger and full of compassion and You don't treat us as our sins deserve. Give me the courage to accept Your grace in my life and Your loving pruning too. Forgive me of my desire to be the perfect parent because that just causes high expectations from my children and disappointment in me. Speak to me, Lord, as I am quiet before You. In Jesus' name, Amen.

Questions:

1. Look at 2 Corinthians 9:6 and list some of the ways that you sow generously and sparingly into your children's lives.

2. First Corinthians 3:5-9 reminds us that we each have a job to do but that God makes things grow. What are you praying for in the lives of your children that you know only God can make happen?

3. I memorized Galatians 6:9 as a teenager, and it helped me when I was knee deep in childrearing. Read through that verse and think about some ways that you might be "fainting" in your work as a parent. Is there a promise here?

4. What specific things can you do for each child individually to "water" them with refreshing encouragement?

Not Boring
by Beebe Kauffman

As the evangelist told each Bible story, the children in the Vacation Bible School leaned forward in interest and anticipation. He related a portion of the story, then stopped and said, "Interesting," or "Amazing," to emphasize some part of it. The tone in his voice convinced us that he thought it was interesting or amazing. It was almost like confiding his thoughts to the group in a half-whisper. He was using the words of Scripture to tell the story, but he brought its meaning to life for the kids with the WAY that he told it. Their expressions reacted to the events and to the words spoken by the people in the Bible story. It was like listening to a master storyteller.

"Boring" is not what Scripture is, nor should it be the way that we teach it to our children. I once had a fourth grade VBS that tested me on this point. We were having a good time getting to know each other on the first day, and I said, "Now it's time to talk about God." A boy sitting directly across from me said, "God is boring." I wasn't ready for that reaction, and before I thought, I responded, "God is the least boring person through all eternity." He asked humbly and quietly, "Why?" That took all of the wind out of my sails. I told him we were going to spend the rest of the week talking about God as our Father, Savior, Lord, and Friend; and I would ask him at

> God is the least boring person through all eternity.

the end of the week if he had changed his mind. A few days later, he said he had.

How can we teach the Bible to our little ones so that they understand it and appreciate God? What can we do to give our children the best chance of having their young characters affected by God's great wisdom, His overwhelming love, and the record of conversations and interactions between God and real people?

We can start by finding a great children's Bible. The one my family used had wonderful illustrations that captured my daughter's attention. We set a regular time aside for reading the stories and discussing them. Sometimes we had snacks ready. We ended with prayer that applied some part of the passage to our lives.

Here are nine more suggestions that may help you to make reading Scripture a blessing to your children.

1. Tell the story in a way that helps your kids step into the moment, into the action. Make the most of the details that are given in the story.

For example, when Scripture calls Goliath a giant, get your kids' ideas on just how tall that is. As tall as their dad, or the ceiling? Ask them why Israel's army was scared of Goliath. Then when David comes into the story, compare him to Goliath. Was he as tall as Goliath? Was he scared of Goliath? Why not? Let them tell the part of the story that they understand, and help them to see how to apply it to themselves, such as "Do you think God will help you to defeat some big problems in your life?"

2. Help your kids to "see" God—to know Him, love Him, and trust Him.

For instance, when you're talking about the disciples following Jesus, ask your children what kinds of things they might have done together. How did they get from place to place? Would your kids have liked to see Jesus do His miracles? Were they glad to see Him be kind to that person? Do you think Jesus wants you to be kind to the people in your life? What are some ways that you can do that?

3. Take different passages from 1 and 2 Corinthians, Ephesians, and other books, and talk to your children about God's family—the way He wants us to get along well and help take care of each other. Let them read the verses that encourage the members of God's family to also be a team, doing what God wants done to bless people.

4. As your kids grow up, adjust the topics of your reading to address issues they are facing. Early on, it might be getting along well with siblings or friends. Later it may be preparing your kids to make honorable choices that are consistent with good character and conduct. Read with them what Scripture says about the blessings of doing good, and the difficulties and struggles that come from selfishness, anger, and so on.

5. Find passages to read together that connect "sin"—doing what God says is wrong—with its effects. Show them in Scripture that sin messes things up and makes people sad. Sin keeps us from being and doing something better.

6. Teach them to appreciate God. Explain the roles He will take in their lives with the stories that illustrate them. Get them to memorize verses about these roles.

7. Use Scripture to build a respect for people in their hearts. Show them what God did for people, and what He said about them in His word. He called Abraham His friend, and David a man after His own heart. Find the passages in the Bible that discuss the building of those good relationships. Ask them how we can follow that example. Prepare them to respond to friends or classmates who don't practice the best manners yet. Show them the examples of Joseph, Paul, and Jesus in difficult situations.

8. Make the most of how Scripture characterizes who God wants us to be—a farmer, a soldier, a runner, and so forth. For little ones, let them act out that part while they say the verse with you. For older children, discuss why that picture is used for a Christian. Ask them how they can apply those principles in their lives now.

9. If the songs your children are learning in Sunday School come from the Bible, show them where they are in Scripture. Talk about what was happening at the time. Or look for lyrics for children's songs that come from the Bible, and see if anyone sings it on YouTube. If so, play it for them. For little ones, if there are no hand motions to go with the song, make some up.

Scripture is God's amazing and powerful resource to build and refine Godly character. He wants parents and others to use this resource to nurture in our children a love for Him and His ways of life. Seeing who God is, how much He cares, and the investment that He makes daily in our well-being, may inspire our children to place their trust in Him, and to want to grow up to be just like their heavenly Father and His loving and courageous Son.

Scripture is anything BUT boring because "God is the least boring person through all eternity." May He guide you and help you to make your time with your children in His word memorable, joyful, and character-building.

And these words which I command
you today shall be in your heart.
You shall teach them diligently to your children,
and shall talk of them when you sit in your house,
when you walk by the way, when you lie down,
and when you rise up.
Deuteronomy 6:6-7 NKJV

Prayer:

Heavenly Father,
Please guide us when we teach the Bible to our children. Help them to see who You are, what Jesus has done for us, and what kind of life You make possible for those who place their faith in Him. Help them to live out the great good that Your word teaches and to apply Scripture to the situations of their lives. Let them live in this world as Your dear children and as fitting ambassadors of Your kingdom of love. In Jesus' name, Amen.

Questions:

1. If you were taught the Bible as a child, can you remember your favorite Bible teacher? If so, what did you like best about how he or she taught the Bible?

2. If you read the Bible with your children, what parts of it do they like best? Are those the same as your favorites?

3. If your children are little, what is their favorite Bible song? If they are older, have any of the Bible songs they learned early on, stuck with them?

4. What does the Bible say about the issues facing our children today? If your children are old enough, do they know how to find those passages in Scripture?

5. What do these verses say about children?

    a. Matthew 19:14
    b. Ephesians 6:4
    c. Psalm 127:3
    d. Psalm 127:4
    e. Proverbs 22:6

Craftsman at Work:
The Fruit of the Spirit

Weeks 9-10

Cooperating with the Cultivator of Our Souls

by Lauren Craft and Beebe Kauffman

Many apple orchards are tucked into the countryside of Virginia. The trees tower on the rolling hills, opening their leafy branches wide, as if wanting to embrace. In the springtime, baby apples sprout from the ends of the branches. When ripe, the red and green creations hang heavy, asking to be picked.

Apple trees don't produce fruit alone, though. The rains keep the leaves lush and trickle down to the apple, infusing it with juice. Sunshine strengthens saplings into trees and keeps the leaves alive and green. The soil keeps the tree anchored to the ground over its lifespan and provides it with nutrients. Without these means of support, seedlings would wither away, never to thrive and grow.

Christians are called to bear "fruit" in our souls. This fruit is the result or effect that is produced as the Holy Spirit cultivates, crafts, and refines our character. He works to produce nine excellent and beneficial qualities—"love, joy, peace, patience, kindness, goodness, faithfulness, gentleness, and self-control" (Galatians 5:22-23 NLT). These qualities mirror God's character, and they fit us for a productive, healthy, and satisfying life. The Holy Spirit is a Master Cultivator who skillfully transforms our willing and cooperative souls unto godliness.

Like a Master Gardener, the Holy Spirit breaks up the hard soil of our hearts and plants the seeds of mercy, compassion, and generosity. He develops an understanding of God and His ways that bears the fruit of obedience and wisdom. He carefully and conscientiously trains our minds to apply God's word and His ways to the circumstances of life before us. He nurtures a growing dependence on God that produces a quality of life that we can't attain on our own. The Holy Spirit faithfully teaches, guides, comforts, and helps us.

Fortunately, we can taste the results of the Spirit's hard work. Although difficulties will come, living for Christ and cooperating with the Spirit produce a great harvest, a life of abundance (John 10:10). If we use self-control, our lives will be more stable and secure. Gentleness and love will heal our relationships. Joy and peace will give us the energy to continue improving, even if we stumble.

Bearing the fruit of the Spirit also guards us from producing rotten fruit, "the works of the flesh" (Galatians 5:19 HCSB). Scripture has a long list of this bad fruit, which includes: sexual immorality, idolatry, hatred, strife, jealousy, outbursts of anger, selfish ambition, dissension, envy, drunkenness, and carousing (Galatians 5:19-21). How miserable. Such a life would surely be filled with heartache, emptiness, and loneliness.

As believers, how well are we cooperating on a daily basis with the work of the Holy Spirit? Are we taking good advantage of His willingness to invest in the quality of our character? Take an honest look at how you're faring with each fruit of the Spirit. Make a list of one to three concrete steps that you could take this week to cooperate with the Spirit as He cultivates your soul. Here's what my (Lauren's) list looks like:

1. To be more gentle, I'll pause before I speak so I don't react in anger.

2. I'll use better self-control in spending money.

3. To show more love, I will share in others' grief and rejoice in their blessings.

Just like trees that take months to produce fruit, spiritual fruit comes slowly, step by step. But the surpassing quality of this fruit makes it well worth the wait.

Prayer:

Father,

Thank You for the cultivating work of the Holy Spirit in my soul. Help me to cooperate with that work by keeping my mind and heart in Your Word and by staying close to You in fellowship and obedience. Help me to walk in the Spirit so that I do not fulfill the lust of the flesh. Let me draw from You what I need to live the new way of life that You make possible and to serve Your good purposes in the world. Give me the courage to address the areas where I fall short, and help me to grow in all of the fruits of the Spirit. Thank You for tending to the cultivation of my heart and my character. In Jesus' name, Amen.

Questions:

1. What are some of the practical steps that you could take to cooperate with the Holy Spirit's cultivating work of your character?

2. Which of the nine fruits are the most appealing to you, and which ones seem like they would take the most time and cooperation? Which one do you think would make the greatest change in you unto godliness?

3. Think back to the last trial that you went through and how God related to you. Which of these nine qualities did you experience from Him, and which one meant the most to you at the time?

4. Has God ever used a milestone event in your life to show you the need for change?

5. If you grow flowers, plants, or crops, what are some of the problems that you face? Do any of those problems correspond with the difficulties of transforming our character unto godliness?

6. What does the Holy Spirit do in our lives according to the following verses?

   a. John 14:26
   b. Acts 1:8
   c. Romans 5:5
   d. 1 Thessalonians 1:6
   e. Titus 3:5
   f. John 15:26
   g. Romans 8:13-14
   h. Romans 8:26

What's Missing?

by Beebe Kauffman

I couldn't find my husband. We were in Brazil on a mission trip with our church team, building a neighborhood church there. I looked behind the concrete blocks waiting to be stacked into walls, behind the roof panels waiting to be hoisted into place, and around the windows waiting to be installed. Then I looked up. I mean UP. And there he was, walking across a roof truss. No ropes, no failsafe. Only concrete below him.

My instinct was to call out and tell him to be careful, but I didn't want to surprise him and cause him to lose his balance. So I watched, stressed, until he made it to the scaffolding on the other side of the church.

Our goal was to build a church in a week. Before the American team arrived, the foundation was poured and a bathroom was built. Then, in usually five days, Americans and Brazilians worked together to construct a meeting place for the Christians in the area. They had outgrown meeting in homes and other nearby places. They needed a church home of their own.

This was a recurring project for our church, and it required many materials. Concrete, pipes, windows, wood for furniture, and so on. Sometimes the Brazilians had the supplies waiting on us when we came; sometimes our foreman and others went shopping once we arrived. But there was one material that was essential for every project. One ingredient in the whole process that was indispensable—love.

Sometimes the women on our team helped stack the blocks to build walls or painted the interior or exterior walls once they were ready. But other times we got to meet the children of the neighborhood and put on a Backyard Bible School for them. We could speak a little Portuguese, and they could speak a little English. When we exhausted that line of communication, we had smiles, hugs, games, and food. For the more important parts of our time with them, we also had an interpreter.

A week went by too quickly. On the last day, at the dedication of the new church, the children would bring us little handwritten cards with hearts, or "I love you" written in Portuguese or English. They posed with us to have their pictures taken so we wouldn't forget them. Sometimes a group of them prepared a special song for us, such as "Friends."[1] But singing the songs usually made them cry because the lyrics were about friends far away from each other. Some of the children even wrote to us for a while after our trip.

When our goal is to construct godly character, love is the essential building material. The project can't go on without it. When it's missing, something fills its place that is joyless, burdensome, or damaging. Like a cold and empty feeling of loneliness, instead of the warmth of fellowship with family and friends. Like the burden of isolation, instead of the joy of closeness and feeling like we belong. Hatred and grudges can reign in our hearts instead of the freeing power of forgiveness. Selfishness that is indifferent to other people's needs may govern our lives, instead of the loving heart and helping hands of selflessness.

Love is an indispensable ingredient to building godly character because it's so versatile and adaptable. It helps us to see other people with understanding and goodwill. Love equips us to build up our relationships rather than damage them. Sometimes this is difficult, depending on the person, the circumstances, or the past history of either party. But God has designed love to value every person and to be versatile and adaptable to accommodate any need at hand.

In 1 Corinthians 13:4-8a (ESV), Scripture describes the amazing nature of godly love.

v.4: *Love is patient and kind; love does not envy or boast; it is not arrogant.*

Love receives injuries from others patiently.

Love is good-natured and does good to others.

Love rejoices over others' success and welfare.

Love doesn't desire to be noticed above others.

Love is not proud or arrogant.[2]

v.5: *[Love is not] rude. It does not insist on its own way; it is not irritable or resentful.*

Love doesn't behave disrespectfully or indecently.

Love is not selfish.

Love is not easily provoked to anger.

Love is not suspicious of others.

v.6: *It does not rejoice at wrongdoing, but rejoices with the truth.*

Love doesn't rejoice when others commit sin or are accused of it.

Love rejoices not in error, falsehood, or deception, but in the truth being accepted, valued, and embraced for eternal and daily life.

v.7: *Love bears all things, believes all things, hopes all things, endures all things.*

Love doesn't broadcast someone else's faults or shortcomings.

Love believes the best about people.

Love hopes that other people want the best for one another, or will come to that mindset.

Love takes all difficulties and hardships in stride, and keeps going.

v.8a: *Love never ends.*

The reality of love and its insights will never fail.

When love fills its rightful place in the hearts of believers, its value and benefits are beyond price. Even though we can't buy it, we can't get it in any department store, and we can't order it online and have it delivered to our homes, there are no worries. God has an inexhaustible supply, and He delights in sharing.

> *The love of God has been poured out in our hearts by the Holy Spirit.* (Romans 5:5 NKJV)

The construction project that God had in mind from the foundation of the world, was to build a "Forever Us," and its essential element is, and always has been, love.

Prayer:

Father,
Love is how You describe Your own character (1 John 4:8, 16). Thank You for relating to us with such grace and forbearance. Thank You for working within us to conform us to a reality of heart and character that is so delightful, satisfying, and unifying. Help us to draw from You what we need to walk in love in our relationships and daily lives, so that what we do and say may please Your heart. Help us to grow more and more into Your loving likeness. In Jesus' name, Amen.

Questions:

1. Besides loneliness, isolation, hatred, and selfishness, what other negative qualities plague people when love is missing?

2. Which statement about love under each verse of 1 Corinthians 13:4-8a, is the most meaningful to you?

3. Verse 8 (NKJV) says, *Love never fails*. Does that have any different connotation to you than the ESV, *Love never ends*? Why are both translations helpful?

4. For each verse, which description as applied to the way that God loves us, is the most meaningful to you?

1. Michael W. Smith, "Friends," 1983.

2. All of the application statements for 1 Corinthians 13:4-8a are taken from: Beebe Kauffman, *A Whole Lot of Wonderful—Application of the New Testament for Today*, (Buford, Georgia: Lighthouse Bible Studies, 2018), 346-347.

The Joy Giver
by Adria Wilkins

I had to get away. I had all I could take of the tension and stress. My son, Blake, was in the pediatric intensive care unit at the hospital. Tears began to well up in my eyes. I left his room and found a bathroom as far away as possible. I closed the door and began to weep and beat on the concrete walls.

I spoke out loud to God. "This hurts so bad! No one should ever have to feel the pain of losing a child." I cried and tears ran down the wall as if it were raining. Fortunately, this was a bathroom for only one person. I decided this was my bathroom for as long as I needed it. I leaned against the wall as if it were my only support.

This was the most painful situation I had ever been in. Yet, deep inside I had joy. I knew I was going to be just fine. God had been with me all my life and I knew He was not going to forsake me.

At the age of nine in a small Kentucky town, I asked Jesus to be the Lord and Savior of my life. That is when my true joy began. True joy is different. It comes from Christ, from within. The peace and contentment that comes from this joy are unaffected by my circumstances.

We all have tough days. Our family has lived through being laid off from work, several car wrecks, and two years of a long adoption process. But we've strived to keep our focus on Jesus. He has sustained us with joy no matter the situation.

In the book of Philippians, Paul wrote a letter of joy while in the midst of tough circumstances. He was in prison! The prison was probably cold, smelly, and dark. Still, Paul made a choice to be thankful and joyful. Philippians 1:3-4 (NIV) says, "I thank my God every time I remember you. In all my prayers for all of you, I always pray with joy."

Joy is mentioned sixteen times in the book of Philippians.

All of us have prisons in our lives such as depression, anxiety, greed, or anger, to name a few. We can combat these prisons by focusing on things that are true, lovely, and praiseworthy. Philippians 4:8 says, "Finally, brothers and sisters, whatever is true, whatever is noble, whatever is right, whatever is pure, whatever is lovely, whatever is admirable—if anything is excellent or praiseworthy—think about such things."

I have several techniques to help me change my perspective and stay focused on the joy that Jesus gives:

- Make a list of things that are lovely.
- Pray and name things that are true about Jesus.
- Meet with a friend and share concerns, while asking her to help me stay centered on God.
- Listen and sing hymns or worship music.

Paul could have grumbled at his circumstances, but he stayed fixed on his mission. Philippians 2:14-15 says, "Do everything without grumbling or arguing, so that you may become blameless and pure, 'children of God without fault in a warped and crooked generation.' Then you will shine among them like stars in the sky."

During our son's life, people often told us that we were so positive and upbeat. They would ask, "How do you do it?" I would tell them we were leaning on Jesus. We were just living day to day. We were doing what we had to do to survive. We wanted Jesus to be honored and glorified in our lives, no matter what was going on.

Paul wrote from experience and shared his struggles so that the church—including you and me—can be encouraged to continue. Philippians 1:29-30 says, "For it has been granted to you on behalf of Christ not only to believe in him, but also to suffer for him, since you are going through the same struggle you saw I had, and now hear that I still have."

Philippians 4 is one of my favorite chapters in the Bible. It is encouraging and gives me hope. In verses 4-9, Paul encourages us to:

- Be full of joy in the Lord always.
- Ask God for everything you need by praying.
- Give thanks.
- Think about God's peace and His goodness.

Our goal during our son's life was to help him live as "normal" a life as possible. We stayed close to God and relied heavily on Him. Our hope was in Jesus. We knew we couldn't make it without His strength and power. The verse I relied on during our son's life was Philippians 4:6, "Do not be anxious about anything, but in every situation, by prayer and petition, with thanksgiving, present your requests to God."

> No matter what situation we find ourselves in, God is there.

No matter what situation we find ourselves in, God is there. He is waiting to be our companion. He will be there with us during the good and bad times.

I often look back on the day we had to take our son off life support and think, "How did I make it through that day?" The only thing that comes to mind is, it was God who got me through. As I walked out of his hospital room, I didn't have tears. I had joy and peace. I was rejoicing that all the burdens I carried were now in Jesus' care.

Prayer:

God,

There are days I feel sad or discouraged. Help me to seek You in those moments and remember You are my friend and companion. Thank You for being the Joy Giver! You are my joy! You are my peace! You are my contentment!

Questions:

1. What is a memory that brings you joy? Look back and see God's goodness in it all over again.

2. How did Paul find joy even in prison?

3. List some things that Paul encouraged us to be and to do in Philippians 2:12-18.

4. What was Paul's secret to being content and happy in Philippians 4:12-13?

*All Scripture verses are taken from the NIV.

How Do You Find Peace?

by Ginger Harrington

The sun sets, painting the sky vivid with colors. Sitting on a dock, I dangle my feet in the water. My gentle movements disturb the glass-like surface, which echoes the wonder of the sky. For the first time all day, this is a moment to savor solitude.

A moment to be still and to sink into peace.

To be honest, this has been a day wound tight with tension, setting my nerves on edge. Sprinting through the hours, "get it done, get it done" is the rant of my racing thoughts. Commitments, schedules, and assignments pile high with the pressure of too many unfinished tasks. The beauty of the evening cannot completely squelch the nagging worry and frustration of troubling situations.

Serene surroundings are not the same as truly experiencing the fruit of peace. And though I relish tranquility as the sun lingers near the water's edge, I know there is only one genuine source of peace. Still, there's a part of me that searches for peace in the sunsets and calm waters of life, but this moment is for remembering peace isn't something to find.

"Peace I leave with you; My peace I give to you" (John 14:27 NASB*). In this verse we discover peace is a gift rather than an achievement. *My peace* (the peace of God) *I give to you.* Wrapped up tight in this Christ-peace is His power. His trustworthiness.

Because Christ is peace and He is with us, our hearts can rest from efforts to create a fleeting version of harmony. Trusting Christ within, we can experience the peace He gives, this sweet fruit of His Spirit dwelling within. Dangling my toes in the water, I set aside all my efforts of the day. Breathing deeply, I remind myself peace is a fruit of His present Spirit, not the result of my trying to do it all right and get it all done. Silently, I count the treasures of His presence: "The fruit of the Spirit is love, joy, peace, patience, kindness, goodness, faithfulness, gentleness, self-control" (Galatians 5:22-23).

In today's world, stress has become our normal condition. Our culture has many formulas for peace, or at least lots of ways to make us feel better. *Try this, do that, buy this,* entice advertisements. The world's false peace shimmers on the horizon, visible, but always out of reach.

"The steadfast of mind You will keep in perfect peace, because he trusts in You" (Isaiah 26:3). Perfect peace has everything to do with what's going on in our minds. Isn't it interesting that the content of our thoughts relates to the condition of our peace? Too often, we fall into that old habit of equating peace with sunsets and the absence of problems.

The steadfast mind–this is the condition, the mental posture that enables us to receive the peace of Christ. We often think of steadfast as meaning strong and steady, but surprisingly, the Hebrew meaning of this word means to "lean upon" or "take hold of."[1] On days marked by stress, conflict, or fear, it is tempting to pursue peace through our own efforts. Gritting our teeth, we strive to calm the nerves, settle the argument, or solve the problem.

> The steadfast mind–this is the condition, the mental posture that enables us to receive the peace of Christ.

Leaning on God, we can depend on Him to provide the mental focus we so often lack. It is the turning, the depending on God that opens the door to receive the soul peace He offers.

This is the soul-habit I long to nourish.

The keeping of God.

When God keeps our minds in perfect peace, He guards, protects, and maintains. He does the keeping and we do the trusting.

- The steadfast of mind—our part is to lean our thoughts on God.

- He will keep in perfect peace—God's part is to bring on the peace!

God's recipe for perfect peace begins and ends with our participation of bringing our thoughts to Him in faith, yet He is the one who provides and keeps.

For me, a key factor in trusting God is letting go of my desire to control life. Unsteady, I want to know the answers, finish the work, and forge my desired path. I want to find peace in performing well and pleasing others. Maybe this is your challenge as well. Most of our stress and problems can be reduced to this common denominator of seeking control versus trusting God.

When we choose to turn our thoughts to God's faithfulness, we can let go of the mental and physical striving to fix, solve, or force things to turn out. Trusting God, relying on Him, we can set down our heavy load, burdens we were never meant to carry alone. Resting against the unwavering strength of His presence, we take hold of what He offers: the complete peace of His presence and provision.

The sun slips out of sight as smoky blue clouds drift by. I'm grateful for the fruit of peace in my heart that comes with releasing my worries and leaning on Christ. The sun will rise and set, evening and morning will dance, and time will pass. Walking home, I steady my mind with this truth: peace is God's gift to receive rather than a goal to achieve.

Prayer:

Dear Father,
Calm my heart with thoughts of You. I cease my striving and instead rest in faith that You will provide for me and protect me. I also trust You to take care of the ones I love. Transform me from restless to steadfast. My heart is willing and open for You to do Your peace-giving work. In Jesus' name, Amen.

Questions:

1. With life's hectic schedule, challenges, and emergencies, how we can we keep our minds steadfastly fixed on God?

2. Which character qualities of God's heart bring you peace?

3. Write down the truth, promise, instruction statement, or testimony captured in these verses that replace anxiety with peace.

   a. Deuteronomy 31:8
   b. Psalm 145:18
   c. Psalm 147:5
   d. Proverbs 3:5-6
   e. Proverbs 3:25-26
   f. John 16:33
   g. Psalm 55:18

4. To prevent anxiety from stealing your peace, create a reminder to keep your mind fixed on God. Pick one of the creative ways below, or think of your own. Have the reminder ready when stress or demands threaten your peace.

   a. Which praise song calms your heart the most? Insert that song into your playlist.

   b. Do you like to draw or paint? Use paint pens to draw your favorite verse or promise from the Bible on a canvas, and then set the canvas where you will see it all the time.

c.   Write a prayer on an index card, and stick it in your purse or wallet. Focus on God's greatness, goodness, and love in the prayer, and ask Him to help you to keep your focus on Him. Pull out the card and read it when anxious thoughts dart across your mind.

d.   Unplug from social media and television, and read your favorite go-to passage in the Bible for encouragement. Let its truth soak into your heart, and meditate on practical ways to live out its message.

*All Scripture verses are taken from the NASB.
1. https://www.blueletterbible.org/lang/lexicon/lexicon.cfm?Strongs =H5564&t=KJV.

Cultivating a Beautiful Garden
by Denise Roberts

Hey honey, do you think this is a weed?

My husband and I were working in our flower beds this past spring, cleaning up, pulling weeds, and preparing the beds to be mulched.

I came across a plant that I wasn't sure about. He wasn't sure either. So we decided to leave it alone to see what it did. That was in April.

Letting that plant grow took a good amount of patience. Since it looked like a weed I wanted to pull it out. But every time, I'd make myself wait, refraining from doing what I wanted to in the moment.

In late June that plant bloomed bright pink flowers. Phlox. I planted it there years before but had never seen it bloom. Probably because every year, I'd pull it up thinking it was a weed. Never before had I exhibited the patience to wait and see what might happen.

In its essence, this is what the fruit of patience looks like when it manifests itself in our lives. In his letter to the Galatians, Paul puts forth quite the list of what the desires of our sinful nature look like. Sexual immorality, impurity, lustful pleasures, quarreling, jealousy, anger, division, and envy to name just a few. Paul is pretty clear that these are weeds in our lives and need to be pulled out.

But he goes on to say that when the Holy Spirit tends the garden of our lives, He will produce fruit in keeping with the character of Christ. *Fruit that includes the patience not to do something. Fruit that includes the patience to let beauty bloom.*

> Christlike patience means exhibiting internal and external control that manifests itself by delaying an action.

Christlike patience means exhibiting internal and external control that manifests itself by delaying an action. Some translations will render this particular word as long-suffering. And I do like that because it conveys a sense of something that takes work. Something that takes time, conscious thought, and a yielding of our will to that of Jesus.

What does this look like?

As we work to weed out anger in our lives, choosing to not respond in anger is patience. This takes work. It goes against our worldly natural instincts. But when we refrain from letting this weed grow in the first place, peace will bloom.

Patience is deciding to be thankful for the blessings we already have instead of giving action to jealousy and envy. In a culture that elevates wealth and glamorizes beauty, not succumbing to a keeping-up-with-the-Jones mentality takes work. Contentment and joy will bloom.

Refraining from clicking that website to indulge our impure or lustful pleasures is patience. This takes work as we consciously determine that satisfying our flesh in the moment falls short of the delight and pleasure of honoring God with our hearts and minds. Freedom will bloom.

Christ-like patience is not passive. It is very actively choosing to abstain, refrain, or not do something so that something else much better can happen. Just like I had to actively choose not to pull that flower out of the ground in order for it to bloom.

That sounds funny doesn't it? But it's true.

And it is a reflection of God Himself. He longs for all of His creation to be restored to Him, and the Bible teaches that there is judgment ahead for all those who stubbornly persist in living with rampant weeds in their lives. But God, in His patience, actively refrains from meting out that punishment.

Why? Because He wants to see our lives bloom. God's desire is that our lives reflect His character, and long-suffering patience is one of God's characteristics.

> *But you must not forget this one thing, dear friends: A day is like a thousand years to the Lord, and a thousand years is like a day. The Lord isn't really being slow about his promise, as some people think. No, he is being patient for your sake. He does not want anyone to be destroyed, but wants everyone to repent ... And remember, our Lord's patience gives people time to be saved.* (2 Peter 3:8-9, 15 NLT)

Patience—yours, mine, and God's—cultivates a beautiful garden out of our lives.

Prayer:

Holy God,
Thank You for the promised Holy Spirit who shows us the weeds in our lives and tends the gardens of our hearts to produce Your beautiful blooms. Lord, grant me Your patience to do the hard work of not feeding the weeds. Instill in me the same character of long-suffering that You have for Your people as I grow into who You desire me to be.

Questions:

1. Look up Galatians 5:19-21, Ephesians 4:31, and Colossians 3:8. Make a list of the various "weeds" Paul identifies. Circle

or underline the ones that you recognize as weeds in your own heart.

2. Now look up Galatians 5:22-23, Ephesians 4:32, and Colossians 3:12-14 and list all of the beautiful blooms that can grow in our lives. Which of these are the ones missing that need to grow?

3. What is one thing you can do today to exhibit the patience to NOT feed a weed?

4. Look up Colossians 3:17 and write it out. If you can memorize, do that too. How does growing in the patience to NOT do something honor this verse?

One Light
by Rosemarie Fitzsimmons

The young woman stood at the top of a stairwell clutching a single, tapered candle and peering into the depths of the cavernous opening. The stairs disappeared into the nothingness below, and although she couldn't see signs of life, a cacophony of growls and snarls mingled with foul odors rose to greet her. She squared her shoulders and tucked her scarf into place; she'd let neither sound nor stench change her mind.

Shaking, she lit the candle with her only match and ventured into the abyss, keeping to the center of the stairwell to avoid touching the graffiti- and filth-covered walls on either side.

She stepped cautiously, scrutinizing the ground around her feet as best she could in the dim glow cast by the flame. Roaches, spiders, and centipedes scattered ahead of each footfall, but she refused to turn around. She felt, more than saw, the myriad cobwebs in her path. Those that didn't shrink back as the candle passed, she brushed away from her face with her free hand.

At last she reached the bottom step and saw the quiet form crouched to one side. As she raised the candle, its light fell across the boy's eyes, wide and white, and stark against the darkness. He couldn't have been more than ten years old, yet his cold and expressionless face told her he'd seen too much. She noticed the unlit candle in his hands and yearned to address it, but his hunger wasn't for light.

The young woman dug into her pocket and pulled out a small pack of crackers, which she held out to him. The wide-eyed boy accepted her offering with a solemn nod and a slight smile. He ate two crackers slowly, as if relishing each bite, and then he held out his candle.

She rested her burning wick against it until the light sputtered forth, pleased to see the boy's eyes shine against the flame. In the now brighter glow, she could make out a woman's hands, worn and scarred, resting on the boy's shoulders. The boy turned toward his mother, illuminating what must have once been a lovely face, now tired and wary. As the young woman reached out, she noticed a string of faded bruises that ran across the older woman's arms and up her shoulders. Then she raised her own sleeve, and the two women shared a knowing look.

The boy reached into his mother's apron pocket and pulled out a candle. Not much of a candle—a stub, really—coated with hardened wax drippings. The boy labored to rekindle the black remnant of wick which kept sizzling as his mother's tears fell upon it, but, at last, it sparked and sputtered to life.

As the flame strengthened, the woman turned to the man beside her, who held a large, solid candle that had never been lit. As her flickering light set his ablaze, the man took his wife's hands and they kissed, really kissed, for the first time in many years. Watching such tenderness unfold before her, the young woman could barely contain her joy, but she had to move on. She hugged the family tightly before turning back toward the darkness.

She hadn't gone far before she nearly tripped over a pair of large, rag-covered legs and lowered her candle to investigate. An elderly man lay face-down on the cold ground, groaning in his sleep. A haze of stale alcohol hung over him like a cloud, and she pulled the candle back, lest the cloud ignite. She roused the man gently, sat him up, and poured some water from her flask down his parched throat. His candle, which had been crushed beneath him, was in pieces on the ground. She salvaged a sturdy looking stub and lit it, placing it in his shaking hands before leading him across the alley to the family she'd just left. They greeted him with smiles and open arms, and they found him a new, whole candle.

On it went, as the woman passed through the dark tunnel, lighting first one candle and then the next, watching in wonder as each torch light strengthened and cast its glow further into the abyss. At one point she removed her scarf to wrap it around the neck of a small, coughing girl; at another, she sat quietly by a grieving man as he talked about the cancer that had taken his wife. While holding a restless infant so his mother could nap, she sang to him about the candle and the source of its light until the child drifted off peacefully as well.

With each encounter, another wick flared to life.

The walkway widened, and the young woman's candle began to flicker. A soft breeze brushed her cheek, and she looked up to see a beautiful, star-filled sky. This hadn't been an underground alley at all, but a simple city street, forgotten and swept aside into darkness.

She turned to look back, and had to gasp at the scene in her wake.

A row of brightly painted homes lined both sides of a delightfully vibrant cobblestone street, and a chain of lanterns had been strung from home to home, casting their radiant light along the route. Beneath them, people danced, children raced about, and laughter rang forth. She could see no darkness. The earlier groans had been replaced with singing, and the air smelled of gardenia blossoms and lilacs.

Turning back around, the young woman noticed two dark alleyways leading from the village square. She was far from finished. She stopped to rest at the well, accepting some cool, clean water from a grinning little boy, and the villagers refilled her pockets to brimming with crackers and treats. Some even offered to accompany her on the remainder of her journey.

They set off together toward the darkest alley, candles ablaze. She smiled to note that somehow, her still-burning taper hadn't diminished in size. In fact, now that she took a good look, it actually seemed a bit taller.

> *For you were once darkness, but now you are light in the Lord.*
> *Walk as children of light.*
> Ephesians 5:8 NKJV

Prayer:

Father,
Help us to show Your kindness to others as we go about our daily lives. May we take every opportunity to let our light shine. In Jesus' name, Amen.

Discussion:

1. Why does the young woman in this story not have a name? While we're at it, why are none of the characters named?

2. Each of these characters either has or doesn't have light. Some have never even seen light, while others have given up on the little light they once had. Why would that be?

3. As Christians, we all have light within us, because we recognize the work of Jesus in our lives. However, that light wasn't created to shine inward, but to flood into the darkness around us. Our lights shine in different ways, through gifts we've received from the Holy Spirit. Some of us might notice when others are hurting, others might love to write letters and cards, while still others enjoy calling friends just to offer encouragement. I know a retired woman who loves to shop but lives on a fixed income, so one day a week she offers to shop and run errands for some of the elderly in her neighborhood. What are some of the gifts you have? How can you imagine them blessing another person?

4. Try reading this story from the perspective of those living in the darkness. Have you ever experienced a moment when a simple kindness drew you out of the shadows? Many people have described being at the point of near suicide when a smile, a batch of cookies, or even a note from a friend arrived at just the right moment. Your subconscious "impulse" to reach out to someone may just be the Holy Spirit working in *that person's* life. How exciting to think you might be able to partake in a holy U-turn that brings someone out of this impulse.

5. The darkness into which our main character must descend represents our fears, selfishness, and the excuses we give for *not* going out of our way to help others. What we see as "our" spare time, or "our" resources can often be used against us at these times, as we subconsciously listen to the wrong voices. What sort of barriers or words from the enemy keep you from carrying your candle into dark areas?

Using our light to shine like Jesus is not a suggestion. Proverbs 19:22 (NASB) tells us that, "What is desirable in a man is his kindness." Since light is our greatest weapon against the darkness, kindness, which essentially is love, is the brightest form of light we can wield.

Jesus left us with only two commandments: to love God and to love each other. If we seek to be like Him, we must carry this torch of kindness wherever we go. This week, as you go about your daily routine, ask the Lord to show you opportunities to shine your light.

For we are His workmanship, created in Christ Jesus for good works, which God prepared beforehand that we should walk in them. (Ephesians 2:10 NKJV)

Goodness Is a Team Player

by Beebe Kauffman

On a dark, moonless night, the test started after a game of pinochle. My future husband and I had been playing cards with his parents at their home until it was quite late. It was pitch black when I went outside to my car. Since there were no streetlights on the cove, I could barely see past the reach of the front porch light. Then it happened. When I backed out of the driveway, I heard a metal-crunching sound. I had hit the neighbor's car that was parked on the street.

In that split second, it occurred to me that I could drive on and no one would ever know that it was me who had hit the car. (Not likely.) I wouldn't get in trouble with my parents, my insurance wouldn't go up, and the neighbors wouldn't complain about me to my sweetheart's parents. Tempting. But on the other hand, I knew someone needed to let the neighbor know what had happened, and somebody needed to pay to get it fixed. *Me.*

I got out of the car and started walking up the street to the neighbor's house. Immediately I saw someone fly out of the front door and head down the driveway. He had heard the crunch, and he was angry. Looking past me, he said, "You come back here. Don't you dare drive off!" It was so dark he hadn't seen me approaching. I was close to him when I said, "I'm right here." That knocked all of the wind out of his sails. He said calmly, "Oh, I didn't see you," and apologized for yelling.

Goodness is rewarding. We looked for the damage, as best we could. His bumper had a small dent for such a big crunch, and there was no damage on my car that we could find. So we exchanged names and telephone numbers. I gave him my insurance information and told him one of my parents would call him in the morning, and I drove home. I didn't have to feel guilty for not stopping, and I didn't have to worry about someone discovering the truth.

Goodness that the Holy Spirit cultivates into our souls is not a finite commodity. It takes different forms at different times. Yesterday it may have taken the form of courage, and today it may be forgiveness or friendliness. Goodness is expressed in words, attitudes, and actions that are "morally right, honorable, desirable, beneficial, or satisfying,"[1] those which are "pleasant, agreeable, appropriate, or excellent."[2]

Goodness is versatile and useful, like a team player who can play first base, bat, or pitch and do an excellent job at any position. It's like a quarterback who is also a phenomenal blocker and running back. As one of nine fruits of the Spirit, goodness can team up with any of the other eight to make life more enjoyable and rewarding. Goodness can be an expression of love, a cause for joy, and a sustainer of peace. It motivates patience, finds opportunities for kindness, and steels faithfulness when it's tempted to slip. Goodness empowers gentleness to respond in tough situations in place of destructive tendencies, and it encourages the grace and dignity of self-control.

> Goodness is versatile and useful, like a team player who can play all positions.

Goodness can become a way of life that blesses people until it finally becomes a legacy of a life well spent. That's how Scripture summarizes the lives of King Hezekiah and King Josiah of Judah.

> *Now the rest of the acts of Hezekiah, and his goodness, indeed they are written in the vision of Isaiah the prophet, the son of Amoz,*

and in the book of the kings of Judah and Israel. (2 Chronicles 32:32 NKJV)

Now the rest of the acts of Josiah and his goodness, according to what was written in the Law of the LORD, and his deeds from first to last, indeed they are written in the book of the kings of Israel and Judah. (2 Chronicles 35:26-27 NKJV)

In order for goodness to become the legacy of our lives, we need the Holy Spirit to cultivate it within our souls. He is busy crafting and conforming them to all the aspects of Christlikeness, including goodness. Scripture tells us that goodness is God's nature (Exodus 34:6, Psalm 107:8-9, Matthew 19:17), and by the enriching work of the Holy Spirit, it can be ours too.

Prayer:

Father,
Thank You for Your goodness to Your children. Thank You for sending a Savior, for sending messengers to tell us about Him, and for keeping Your word to redeem us from sin and death when we believe in Him. Thank You for the richness of life with You. Help us to be good stewards of the understanding that You have given us, to share it and to live it out, that we might be a blessing to the people around us. In Jesus' name, Amen.

Questions:

1. When no one was looking, have you ever had a test of goodness? If so, did it turn out well?

2. According to Psalm 107:9, what amazing kindness does God do?

3. What does the work of the Holy Spirit produce in our hearts and lives, according to Ephesians 5:9?

4. Can you remember a time when you received extraordinary goodness from someone? Did that motivate you to be and to do good to others?

5.   How does God's goodness affect the quality of your daily life?

1. *Webster's New World College Dictionary*, 4th ed. (Cleveland, Ohio: Wiley Publishing, Inc., 2008), "good," 611.
2. Larry Pierce, *The Online Bible*, CD-ROM (Winterbourne, Ontario: Larry Pierce, 2007), Strong's #02896.

Faithfulness in the Midst of Storms
by Rick Kauffman

The Destructive Potential of Storms

In 2005, after Hurricane Katrina ravaged New Orleans, the storm hit our state with tornadoes, strong winds, and rain. Some houses were destroyed. Others were damaged when the winds knocked down nearby trees. Many people barely escaped serious injury.

Peter's Reactions to Storms

Another kind of storm hit Peter on the night that Christ was arrested. Jesus warned Peter it was coming. When Peter told Jesus that he would never stumble in faith or allegiance to Him, Jesus said, *The spirit indeed is willing, but the flesh is weak* (Matthew 26:41 NKJV). Peter's zeal blinded him to his own vulnerabilities.

But the flesh is weak. Weakness was not just a problem for Peter. Jesus said that all the disciples would all be made to stumble, and they reacted to that news like Peter—they would not leave Him. But when Jesus was arrested in the garden, they fled. As Scripture says, *I will strike the Shepherd, and the sheep of the flock will be scattered* (Matthew 26:31). Our natural instinct in times of danger is self-preservation. Peter loved Jesus very much, but he got cornered in a weak moment.

Peter had grappled with fear in a storm before. He had walked on water with Jesus, then he took his eyes off Jesus and focused on the storm that was raging around him. He began to sink. But even then he knew the Source of his help. He had the presence of mind to cry out to Jesus to rescue him.

We can always count on God's faithfulness—in storms and out. He will always be there for us because of who He is and because He loves us.

If we are faithless, He remains faithful; He cannot deny Himself. (2 Timothy 2:13)

You in Your mercy have led forth the people whom You have redeemed; You have guided them in Your strength to Your holy habitation. (Exodus 15:13)

On the night of His arrest, Jesus told Peter, *I have prayed for you, that your faith should not fail; and when you have returned to Me, strengthen your brethren* (Luke 22:32). Even though Peter denied Jesus, Jesus still loved him and valued him. Jesus understood Peter's weakness even if Peter did not yet understand it himself.

When we placed our faith and trust in Jesus, when we committed ourselves to Him, then He committed Himself to us. Jesus knew that the disciples were not yet ready to take on the world before Acts 1:8, not before they received the Holy Spirit and His power to proclaim the gospel. What a difference before that day and after. After they received the Holy Spirit, fear had no stranglehold on their lives or ministries.

But you shall receive power when the Holy Spirit has come upon you; and you shall be witnesses to Me in Jerusalem, and in all Judea and Samaria, and to the end of the earth. (Acts 1:8)

Calming the Rise of Panic

I took a course in lifesaving in college. I enjoyed swimming, but this was a bit extreme. We had to swim a 40-lap (1¼ mile) warm-up at the beginning of each class. Fortunately we only met two days a week. We learned and practiced methods of rescuing people from drowning.

There were two major life lessons that I learned in that course. First, training for effectiveness in life and death situations involves a lot of hard work and discipline. All of the conditioning that we did built our strength for the final exam—rescue our ex-marine instructor from the diving well when he was fighting us, as a drowning person might. Bet you can't guess who got to go first.

The second lesson was this: When you're in water over your head, or in a life-threatening situation, if you panic, you will probably die. This is difficult to imagine if you haven't witnessed it before. Our instructor showed us newspaper clippings of double drownings in which the person being rescued grabbed the rescuer so tightly in a panic, that both of them drowned. Certified lifesavers are trained how to escape this, unless they themselves panic.

There are times when like Peter, the world or the enemy seeks to overwhelm us with danger, confusion, isolation, weariness, or doubt. We must recognize our weakness and our need for God's strength. We must act on what we know and enlist His help to have strength to stand strong in the face of adversity. To survive and thrive in the storm. As Paul commended the Ephesians, *Finally, my brethren, be strong in the Lord and in the power of His might* (Ephesians 6:10). Building our faithfulness to God requires building our faith in Him, and depending on Him for the strength and the calm that we need.

We need an understanding of how God works, of how to draw on His strength, and of how to discern when temptation or the enemy is sneaking up on us. Three ways that we can learn these lessons are by seeing, hearing, and experiencing.

God is a willing Instructor. He can teach us what we need to know, and condition and train us not to panic when the storms of life assail us. His Word is a favorite teaching tool. We can see in Scripture important principles played out in real life that forearm us for times of trial or danger. Bible study is foundational to faithfulness to God in adverse times. Regular Bible study that is insightful and application-oriented helps us to be prepared. We can usually find a good Bible study group at church or in the community where we live. If not, we could invite others to join us and do a study together.

Pastors and teachers help us to be prepared and faithful in the storms of life. As they explain the Bible and how it applies to our lives today, the Holy Spirit bears witness to the truth and helps us to understand the meaning and see the relevance of it to our lives and choices. I don't know how many times my pastor seemed to have prepared his sermon with me in mind. I listened to him in person three times a week, and then each day on the radio during the morning commute to work.

Serving others is another opportunity that God uses to instruct us about life and to prepare us for difficulties. God loves to help people, and He loves it when His children do too. When we serve others, God works with us and we gain practical experience of His working in our lives.

Our church always had a need for volunteers for various ministries. They organized everything, and we showed up. I liked the Community Missions Ministry that took on various projects in the inner city to help make life better there. I think the widow's ministries or ministries to single parents are a great way to serve people who could use a little help now and then. Raising children with two parents can be challenging; I can't imagine how difficult it would be with only one. I always loved seeing how God put volunteers and resources together to bless people.

How do we build faithfulness to God? We can start by knowing our own vulnerabilities and training to move past them. We can study God's word and apply it in our daily lives, and we can count on God to be to us and to do in our lives, what He promises in His Word. We

> We can build faithfulness to God by knowing our own vulnerabilities and training to move past them.

can learn God's ways, adopt them as our own, and by faith count on His strength and graces to live them out.

The storms of life come. They affect us all, and there are no exceptions. Some are more severe, some less, but they still come. When they come, may God find us faithful. May we have learned not to panic and apply the strategies and solutions to overcoming the problem at hand. May we keep our heads and cry out to Jesus for strength to endure or to overcome. But remember, if we stumble, Jesus has the will, the power, and the faithfulness to restore us.

Prayer:

Dear Father,
Help us to be faithful to You in the midst of storms. Help us to prepare beforehand, so that we are trained to look to You and practice what You have taught us. When trials come, help us to remember to call on You to withstand them, because we know You will be with us and act on our behalf. Help us also to "strengthen [our] brethren," to be there for them, and to encourage them. Thank You for Your love and faithfulness. In Jesus' name, Amen.

Questions:

1. Have you ever had a life-threatening experience or been in a major storm? How did you handle it? How did things turn out?

2. In the midst of a "storm," have you ever cried out to Jesus for help? What happened?

3. Do you have a plan for your family in case of an emergency?

4. Have you established a spiritual plan for your family to deal with trials? If you have children, have you trained them in good principles?

5. Our first response in a crisis reveals our preparedness. What should it be?

6. Of what benefit in the storm, is great faith as opposed to little faith?

7. Sometimes storms make us feel helpless. What is the power of faith according to Matthew 21:21? In Luke 17:5-6?

8. What is the power of faith against the enemy, according to Ephesians 6:16?

*All Scripture verses are taken from the NKJV.

Gentleness

by Trina Dofflemyer

You must worship Christ as Lord of your life. And if someone asks about your hope as a believer, always be ready to explain it. But do this in a gentle and respectful way. Keep your conscience clear. Then if people speak against you, they will be ashamed when they see what a good life you live because you belong to Christ. (1 Peter 3:15-16 NLT)

I was about to experience one of my most vivid memories as a little girl. I ran through the front yard of the farmhouse and into the flower garden. My grandmother sat on her bench in front of the pine tree with a patch of yellow snapdragons behind her. The faint smell of roses was in the air.

A Swallowtail butterfly lighted on the bush next to her. Slowly … slowly … slowly … she gently moved her hand up against the branch where the butterfly sat, as if her finger was an extension of the twig. Astonished, I watched as the butterfly tiptoed onto her finger. The yellow wings waved softly as it sat there for a few moments. Whenever the word *gentleness* is mentioned, this memory comes to mind.

A contemporary English dictionary doesn't capture the full concept of gentleness as used in the Bible. In Scripture, gentleness means meekness from a position of strength, not only in a person's outward behavior, but with an inward grace of the soul as well.[1] It was a sign of wisdom and was associated with peace, mercy, and righteousness (James 3:13, 17-18). Jesus described Himself as gentle and humble in heart (Matthew 11:28-29).

In John Chapter Four, Jesus was weary from a long journey. The Jews held great animosity towards the Samaritans, and yet Jesus was sitting by Jacob's well outside the Samaritan city of Sychar.

"Please give me a drink" (John 4:7 NLT), He asked of a woman who had come to draw water.

She was startled. She asked Jesus, "Why are you asking me for a drink (v.9) when your people have nothing to do with my people?"

Jesus answered, "If you only knew who you are speaking to! If you only knew the gift God has for you! Then, you would ask me to give you living water, and I would give it to you.

"Those who drink the water I give will never be thirsty again. It becomes a fresh, bubbling spring within them, giving them eternal life" (v.14).

"Please, sir," the woman said, "give me this water! Then I'll never be thirsty again" (v.15).

Then Jesus tested her, "Go and get your husband" (v.16).

"I don't have one," she replied.

Jesus said, "You spoke the truth. Although you have had five husbands, you aren't married to the man you're living with now."

The woman had just heard her entire history with men related by a stranger. She assumed He must be a prophet of God. She said, "So tell me, why is it that you Jews insist that Jerusalem is the only place of worship, while we Samaritans claim it is here at Mount Gerizim, where our ancestors worshiped?" (20). Maybe this spiritual man could give her the answers to the religious questions that had been bothering her.

Jesus responded, "What you're worried about isn't going to be relevant for much longer. It's not about *where* the Father is worshiped, but *how* he is worshiped; he must be worshiped in spirit and in truth."

Jesus acknowledged her question, but exposed the deeper issue. He didn't argue with her; He just stated the facts. At other times during His ministry, He did have harsh words for the haughty Pharisees, whom He said were whitewashed tombs of legalism. But the woman at the well? He spoke gently, "Believe me, dear woman ..." (v.21).

She responded, "I know the Messiah is coming. ... When he comes, he will explain everything to us" (v.25).

Jesus told her, "I AM the Messiah!" (v.26).

When Jesus interacted with the Samaritan woman at the well in a nonjudgmental way, she opened her heart to His words. Her acceptance of the truth then encouraged her entire community to listen to Jesus' message. The woman and many in her entire network came to believe Jesus was the Messiah and received the gift of eternal life.

People in present-day society are listening to the debates regarding spiritual issues the media are raising, but which perspective is right? Jesus' followers, motivated by love, will need to engage in conversations. Anger and self-righteousness will repel. Gentleness and humility will open hearts.

My grandmother's gentleness made a fragile butterfly feel safe. Jesus entered the neighborhood of the woman at the well and interacted with her in a nonthreatening way. While others saw a sinful Samaritan woman, Jesus saw someone outside of faith for whom He would soon gently surrender His life by way of a cruel death on a cross.

"Now we know that he is indeed the Savior of the world" (v.42), the villagers said. In this same passage Jesus told his disciples, both first-century and present-day, "My nourishment comes from doing the will of God, who sent me, and from finishing his work.... Wake up and look around. The fields are already ripe for harvest" (v.34-35).

Prayer:

Heavenly Father,
You are my Strength and my Rock. Thank You for your tenderness and compassion towards me. Forgive me for my self-righteousness that spills out in anger towards others who see things differently than I do. In my interactions with other people, may I reflect the gentleness of Jesus Christ, an inward grace of the soul and an outward strength of wisdom. May I see others through the eyes of Jesus Christ, seeing each person as someone He died to save. Amen.

Questions:

1. When you hear the word *gentleness,* what memory from your own life comes to mind? Describe it.

2. Biblical gentleness was described as outward meekness from a position of strength with an inward grace of the soul. What other stories about Jesus in the gospels illustrate this aspect of His character?

3. When are you most tempted to *not* respond to others in a gentle way?

4. Read Galatians 5:22-23 and Ephesians 4:1-3. What further insights do these verses give us about gentleness?

5. Is there a certain situation in your life in which you feel the Holy Spirit wants you to reflect more of Jesus' gentleness?

*All Scripture verses are taken from the NLT. Direct quotations from Scripture are cited by verse numbers; paraphrases are not.

1. Spiros Zodhiates, *The Complete Word Study Dictionary: New Testament,* electronic ed. (Chattanooga, Tenn.: AMG Publishers, 2000).

The Secret to Self-Control
by Ron Gallagher

Al was a friend I always looked up to. Actually, looking "up" to him was mandatory for most of us, because Al was a really big guy. Whatever internal device it is that lets our bodies know when it's time to stop growing evidently malfunctioned in Al's case. I could reach 6´ if I wore thick-soled boots, but Al was far beyond that. Making eye contact with him in close proximity hurt my neck.

Al had a grandson who was about three years old at the time, and I happened upon a captivating exchange between the two of them. They were standing toe-to-toe in the church foyer, frowning intently at each other. The boy's head didn't even reach his grandpa's knees, lending a kind of comedy skit character to the scene. Big Al had delivered some kind of directive to the child, and apparently it didn't sit well with him. The little guy spread his feet apart, placed clenched fists firmly on his hips, and glared up at the towering figure before him. Then, with an exhibition of bravado that would make TV wrestlers envious, shouted, "NO, ... I'm not gonna, and you can't make me!"

"Fascinating," I thought. "Another dramatic revelation of the human condition—determination to control running headlong into defiant resistance." The laughable imbalance of power and the hopelessness of winning the battle was no deterrent to the boy's insubordination. "How often," I thought, "has that same scene played out between God and me."

Every parent soon learns that their little "bundle of joy" came equipped with another bundle that is not so joyful—inexplicable, unreasonable, often unexpected, and sometimes heartbreaking opposition. The trail of bloody conflict and misery that marks our path through history chronicles our tragic failure to effectively deal with the issue of control. Since Adam's initial rebellion plunged us into sin, all of humanity has been crippled by a congenital compulsion to oppose restrictions and violate boundaries, even those that are designed for our protection and devoted to our welfare. We live out the sad paradox of inverted perceptions. Those things we tend to see as acts of freedom and self-indulgence so often result in bondage and self-destruction. We are born with an oppositional nature that is built-in, and fully functional, and the impact can be awful.

God warns us repeatedly about the behavioral implications of our fallen nature. Paul specified at least nineteen examples in a single passage. In warning Timothy about the prominent behavioral characteristics of the "last days," he said people would be, *lovers of themselves, lovers of money, boasters, proud, blasphemers, disobedient to parents, unthankful, unholy, unloving, unforgiving, slanderers, without self-control, brutal, despisers of good, traitors, headstrong, haughty, lovers of pleasure rather than lovers of God, having a form of godliness but denying its power* (2 Timothy 3:2-5 NKJV). He added even more in his letters to the Romans (Rom 1:21-32) and the Galatians (Gal 5:19-21).

We recoil from the sobering realization that every one of those repugnant traits and practices are perfectly natural. We fallen human beings are born with these tendencies, and some even worse. Charles Haddon Spurgeon said, "You cannot slander human nature. It is worse than words can paint it."[1] News reports are filled with evidence supporting Spurgeon's conclusion every day, providing frightening illustrations of the impact of uncontrolled human nature.

Since the beginning, controlling His creation has been an issue for God. His first test was a simple verbal command. Violating that command showed man's rebellious nature. Later, God articulated ten foundational principles, clearly defining what was acceptable, and what was not. Again, man failed the test. Men resisted every restriction, violated every boundary, and ignored every limit. Laws and rules, whether God's or man's, failed at every point. It became clear that the only absolute, sure-fire mechanism for ending any and all errant behavior in human beings is death. Small wonder, then, that God declared it to be the end result and final payoff for sin.

> The Master Creator introduced a controlling mechanism even more powerful than death. He introduced the incredible power of love.

But pronouncing death on the entire out-of-control race, would cost God everything He wanted to achieve in union with His beloved creation. So, the Master Creator introduced a controlling mechanism even more powerful than death. He introduced the incredible power of love.

Jesus Christ, born sinless, lived out that love, and rebelled only against the evil that confronted Him. Then He subjected Himself to the rage of a rebellious race, and they nailed Him to a cross in their final, desperate act of defiance. Three days later, their control mechanism failed, and the grave was left empty.

But how does that solve our control problems? Becoming one "of" us enabled Jesus to become one "with" us through His indwelling Spirit. Achieving total self-control through our own efforts is impossible, but the Spirit of Jesus Christ brings two things we cannot have without Him. He makes us one with a death that ends our rebellion, and establishes a whole new beginning. Then He adds the capstone—a love capable of overcoming the temptations that plague us.

We're obsessed these days with the issue of control. Libraries and bookstores are filled with volumes promising to reveal the "secrets" of self-control, and every generation produces new ones. God only published one, and the secret really isn't a secret at all.

"Self-control" is available to anyone, if the One with the power to control inhabits the "self."

Prayer:

Father,
My nature is to rebel against Your boundaries, and then to try to fix the resulting problems through my own efforts. Please help me always to remember that unconditional surrender is the only path to real victory and the freedom that comes with it. Thank You for providing a spiritual "death to self" and a corresponding resurrection that provides the most effective control mechanism ever.

Questions:

1. Consider the sins listed above in 2 Timothy 3:2-5. How would the incredible power of love counter and overcome them? (Contrast each sin with the good that might take its place.)

    "lovers of themselves, lovers of money, boasters, proud, blasphemers, disobedient to parents, unthankful, unholy, unloving, unforgiving, slanderers, without self-control, brutal, despisers of good, traitors, headstrong, haughty, lovers of pleasure rather than lovers of God, having a form of godliness but denying its power"

2. Does a sense of guilt for failing to control certain behaviors plague you? What Scripture verses give us wisdom for overcoming guilt?

3. Does the seductive hope of accomplishing victory by your own efforts include the illusion that God will love you more if you're successful? Does attempting to earn His affection seem more enticing than the full surrender Jesus calls for? Whose approach is really the most trustworthy? What Scripture verse supports your answer?

1. http://www.quotationspage.com/quote/26249.html.

Building in Blessing:
The Beatitudes

Weeks 11-12

Blessed

by Beebe Kauffman

When have you felt "blessed" in your life?

For me, one special time was a Christmas Eve long ago. The church was filled with flowers and candles. The guests at our wedding were smiling. The parents of the bride and groom had been seated, and waiting beside the pastor, was a young man who was beaming at me.

Several years later, I felt especially blessed at sunrise on a Thursday morning. Our daughter decided she wanted to be born two weeks before her due date, so we had quite an adventure the night before—first questioning if the symptoms were a false alarm, then rushing to the hospital and calling our families. Four other children decided early that morning to say hello to the world in person. So my doctor and another one were expressing some stress about needing to be in more than one place at a time. Later in the peace and quiet of our hospital room, I remember the joy that I felt as the sun gradually brightened the room while my husband slept on a cot on my right, and our brand new baby girl slept in her hospital bassinet on my left.

"Happy"[1] is my Bible dictionary's definition of *blessed*. I felt happy, or blessed, on those two occasions. Webster's definition adds a little more. *Blessed* means "enjoying great happiness, ... [or] bringing comfort or joy."[2] To bless means to "make happy or prosperous,"[3] and it also has a definition I haven't seen before—"to keep or protect from harm."[4] The definition of the word *blessing* is similar: "anything that gives happiness or prevents misfortune."[5]

The people who know Jesus are blessed.

Among God's people, the teaching of His word had been a way of life for generations that spanned more than a millennium. Then, at the right time, Jesus appeared on the scene, as the Son of a carpenter, a Builder. He taught the ancient Scriptures, and the crowds were blessed to hear God's heart and will in terms they could understand. The sick and diseased were blessed as the mighty Healer took compassion on them. Believers of that day and for two millennia since, have been blessed by the price that the Son of God paid to redeem us from sin and death.

When we listen to Jesus' teaching and allow it to affect our hearts, we are also blessed. In Matthew 5:3-12, in the Sermon on the Mount, the Master Teacher builds our understanding with this truth—traits of godly character become blessings in our lives.

> *Blessed are the poor in spirit, for theirs is the kingdom of heaven.*
> *Blessed are those who mourn, for they shall be comforted.*
> *Blessed are the meek, for they shall inherit the earth.*
> *Blessed are those who hunger and thirst for righteousness, for they*
> *   shall be filled.*
> *Blessed are the merciful, for they shall obtain mercy.*
> *Blessed are the pure in heart, for they shall see God.*
> *Blessed are the peacemakers, for they shall be called sons of God.*
> *Blessed are those who are persecuted for righteousness' sake, for*
> *   theirs is the kingdom of heaven.*
> *Blessed are you when they revile and persecute you, and say all*
> *   kinds of evil against you falsely for My sake.*
> *Rejoice and be exceedingly glad, for great is your reward in heaven,*
> *   for so they persecuted the prophets who were before you.*
> (NKJV)

These character qualities are essential materials for a successful heart renovation. They are keys to happiness, keys to being comforted in the trials and challenges of life, and keys to being protected from harm and for preventing misfortune.

When we are poor in spirit, we are protected from the harm of pride. When we mourn over sin and the damage that it causes, we are motivated to walk in God's ways. When we practice the trust and gentleness of meekness, we prevent angry attitudes and endless quarrels. When we hunger and thirst for righteousness, we lose our appetite for sin. The more we practice the lovingkindness and helpfulness of mercy, the more we will receive them from God. The more we are conformed to purity of heart, the more we will understand and appreciate Him. When we choose to sow peace rather than strife, we will be like our heavenly Father. When we are persecuted for righteousness' sake, we will gain a reward in heaven.

Christ teaches us that these godly character qualities will bless our lives. When we cooperate with God to make them a part of who we are, and when we practice them in the daily ups and downs of life, happiness will be unleashed in our lives and we will find comfort in adverse circumstances. With God's help, incorporating these godly qualities into the DNA of our own character, will prove a blessing to ourselves and others.

By God's grace and with His help, *blessed* can become more and more who we are, and *blessing* will characterize more of what we do.

Prayer:

Father,
Thank You for working in our hearts to bless us with the character qualities of the Beatitudes, and thank You for the benefits and privileges that accompany them. Help us to cooperate with Your loving work of heart renovation that we may grow more into Your likeness every day. In Jesus' name, Amen.

Questions:

1. When have you felt "blessed" in your life? Did anyone in the situation exhibit any of the Beatitude qualities?

2. Which of these character qualities is the most meaningful to you?

3. Which benefit or privilege do you cherish the most?

4. Scripture names other conditions for being blessed. What is the condition in the following verses, and is any specific benefit mentioned?

    a. Matthew 24:46
    b. Luke 1:45
    c. Luke 11:28
    d. John 13:17
    e. Ephesians 1:3
    f. James 1:12
    g. James 1:25

1. Pierce, Matthew 5:3.
2. *Webster's New World College Dictionary*, 155.
3. Ibid.
4. Ibid.
5. Ibid.

God, I Need You
by Katy Kauffman

I usually want to do it myself. I have a smart, resourceful, loving man for a father, and I know he knows how to do a lot. But often I want to be able to handle something on my own. I feel like doing something myself is an accomplishment, a rite of passage. Something important like putting air in my tires.

I couldn't do that by myself. On my way to a Bible study one night, my car indicated that my tire pressure was low. Great. I was already running late. I pulled into a gas station and parked in front of the air machine. Like I knew what I was doing, I pulled the tire pressure gauge out of the glove compartment, unscrewed the plastic cap on the tire that looked the lowest, and tested the pressure (like I've seen my dad do). Bingo. It was low. I tested all of the other tires, but only the front right one needed air. So I whipped out my wallet and inserted my credit card into the air machine. It roared to life, and I quickly put air in my tire. I used the gauge on the air hose to test the pressure, and found out that it was now lower than when I first checked it. *Where's my dad?!*

A kind-looking man was waiting behind me in a black pickup truck. I normally don't approach strangers at gas stations, but at this point I was desperate for help. I walked to his window with a tiny smile and asked him if he could help me. Like a gentle dad, he tested the tire pressure and put air in the stubborn tire. He told me that the gauges on gas station hoses are tricky, so you have to use your own gauge to make sure the numbers are correct. When he finished checking the tire, I thanked him for helping me and hopped into my car. Relief and calm overtook my heart, and I was grateful for the dads of the world.

I drove away knowing that it's not bad to need help. After all, God places us in families, and He has placed His own children in the body of Christ. We need each other. More than anything, we need God.

"Poor in Spirit" Makes Us Rich

We are stubborn creatures. We want to know enough, do enough, be enough. Yet our "enough" fades when we look at the reality of our sin in light of God's pure holiness. Then our "enough" to get into heaven or know God at all, is like an ant on a concrete sidewalk trying to jump onto the top of the Empire State Building. Not going to happen.

When we come to the end of our own ability, we discover the life-changing power of God's ability. His power is enough every single time it's needed. Enough to save a soul, transform a heart, heal old wounds, ease painful memories, and restore relationships. He is enough to provide and protect. To guide us and instruct us. To satisfy our longing hearts and fill them with His goodness (Psalm 107:9). Being "poor in spirit" means that we have a keen sense of our need for God[1] and we are OK with that. We embrace it. We long for Him to help us like only He can. When we are "governed by humility"[2] instead of pride, we open the door for God to act in our hearts and lives. We gain all of the glories of what He can do, the miracles He can work. Why then would we ever resist becoming poor so we can become rich?

> We long for Him to help us like only He can.

Blessed are the poor in spirit,
for theirs is the kingdom of heaven.
Matthew 5:3 NKJV

Recognizing our need for God unleashes heaven's blessings in our lives. First, we become a part of His kingdom when we believe in His Son and ask Him to forgive us of our sins. We realize we can't fix our sin problem on our own. Then we spend the rest of our journeys on earth following a new King—not ourselves anymore, but God Himself. His rule increases in our hearts when we empty ourselves of our own desires, agendas, and methods, and instead want what He wants for us and depend on His way to achieve it. The kingdom of heaven lives in our hearts and will be seen in our words and actions as we maintain a "poor in spirit" mindset. Then we will exit this life and step into heaven, fully understanding the great power of God and living as citizens of heaven for eternity.

I Am Not Going without You

When times are hard, we tend to desperately seek God's help, but when times are good, do we still remember that we need Him?

Moses didn't want God's promise without God's presence. He had seen God's people suffer in Egypt as oppressed slaves, and he understood what a land of their own would mean to them. God had promised that they would have one. But Moses also had seen the people, recently freed from Egypt, singing and dancing around an idol—a golden calf they had created while Moses was receiving the ten commandments from God. Since Moses was taking too long on the mountain, they made their own god to celebrate and to follow into the promised land (Exodus 32:1). The one true God didn't take too well to that. He told Moses that His Angel would go with him and the people to the land He had promised to give their forefathers, but He Himself wouldn't go lest He consume His rebellious people on the way.

Moses wouldn't let go of God. He pleaded with God to go with them, and pledged that Israel would be different from other peoples, meaning that they would worship God alone. He stood in the gap between the people and God, asking Him to remember that he had found grace in God's sight (even if the people hadn't). Moses' mindset was "I'm not going without You."

Is that our mindset today? Do we look at our schedules, our adventures, and even our challenges, and tell God, "I'm not going without You today, Lord"? Do we orient ourselves in heaven's direction before we take a step forward?

Maintaining a "poor in spirit" mindset in everyday life means that we do life with God. We recognize our need for Him, and we *want* to depend on Him. We want to see what He can make of our lives, not what we can make of it in our own strength. We want Him to infuse His love, grace, power, and creativity into every day that we face, and we want to share life's adventure with Him. If we look at what our lives would be like apart from God, we say, "I'm not going." If we hold on to all of God's promises, practice the truth He's given us, and depend on Him more than ourselves, then we say, "I'm all in! God, I need You. Wherever You want to go, take me with You. Let it be Your wisdom, Your power, and Your love that see me through."

Prayer:

O great and awesome God, the God of limitless power and matchless love, we choose You for our lives. Help us to depend on You for every situation we face, and when we try to do something on our own apart from You, pull us back into a heart connection with You that sustains us for the road ahead. We don't want to go anywhere without You, and if You're calling us to a life of adventure, we don't want to be left behind. In Jesus' name, Amen.

Questions:

1. Besides Moses, which person in the Bible greatly depended on God and remembered his or her need for Him?

2. What blinds most people from realizing their need for God?

3. What situations or events can remove their "blinders"?

4. What are the advantages of depending on God more than ourselves for life's problems and victories?

5. What are the blessings of depending on Him when times are good?

6.   In what one area of your life would you like to depend on God more?

7.   What steps can you take to make that happen?

1. Kauffman, 43.
2. Ibid.

Heed the Ding
by Katy Kauffman

My "smart" car has kept me out of trouble more than once. For one thing, I can't lock my keys in the car anymore. It senses when the key is hiding somewhere inside, and it won't lock me out. Another benefit is the little "ding" I hear when my tire pressure is low. Although this noise scares me at first because I wonder what's wrong, I am grateful for it. My friend and I avoided getting stuck in the middle of an intersection one day because of that ding. We were able to pull into a gas station and call for help.

Our consciences act like that little ding. When we run low on closeness to God or get too close to sin, an alarm sounds inside our minds and hearts. Sometimes we ignore the alarm and keep a "too busy to spend time with God" schedule or run headlong into sin, crashing a relationship or opportunity in the process. Other times we choose to slow down and steer ourselves onto God's path, avoiding a collision course with sin.

When we heed the "ding," we are able to practice what Jesus blessed in Matthew 5:4 (NKJV"):

Blessed are those who mourn, for they shall be comforted.

Keeping a heart that is sensitive to our conscience and broken over sin, paves the way for God's forgiveness. For His comfort. Wrecking our lives with sin is not a problem with no solution.

God's manual for safe "driving," or wise living, urges us to repent of sin—to mourn over what we have wrongly chosen and to steer ourselves in God's direction.

Maintain an Effective Alarm System

The first key to an effective alarm system is the quality of its programming. Regular maintenance is needed to protect our hearts, minds, and lives. Each of us is born with a God-given conscience that can discern between right and wrong to an extent (Romans 1:18-19), but if we neglect to program it with God's word, other sources may seek to shape its warning parameters.

The wrong programming can lead to head-on crashes in the immediate present and hurt our eternal futures. It can keep us from realizing our need for God and hinder us from accepting His remedy for sin. Some people may never realize that sin separates us from God unless they repent and believe in His Son. They may never "mourn" and find eternal salvation. Receiving the truth and heeding God's warning about sin alters our eternal destinies as well as our daily lives.

The second key to an effective alarm system is responding early to its warnings. It's easy to silence an inner alarm when we crave a sinful habit. But God knows that a sin, no matter how little, will harm us.

Little sins don't stay little, and they don't affect just one person. The apostle Paul warned the Corinthian church that they needed to handle a sin happening within their congregation. He asked them, *Do you not know that a little leaven leavens the whole lump?* (1 Corinthians 5:6). Just as leaven, or a piece of fermenting dough, can ferment a batch of "pure" dough, a small corrupting influence can spread to harm a whole group of people. If we allow sin to stay in our hearts or in the house of God—the Church—it will spread. But purging what harms makes room for what builds up, and cooperates with God's process of heart renovation.

Know When to Move On

Although we come with a built-in alarm system, it's important that we don't become paralyzed by its "dings." God wants us to listen to His warnings about sin, but He doesn't want to us to get stuck in regret. Like Ezra nearly did.

As the priest who oversaw the spiritual reconstruction of God's people after the Babylonian captivity, Ezra understood the damaging effects of sin. His people had just come home from being taken to a foreign land as judgment for their sin, and his job was to help them restore a close relationship with God (Ezra 7:9-10). So his initial reaction to the people's return to sin was a good one—he fell on his face before God and confessed their sin. His impassioned prayer begins with humility.

> *O my God, I am too ashamed and humiliated*
> *to lift up my face to You, my God;*
> *for our iniquities have risen higher than our heads,*
> *and our guilt has grown up to the heavens.*
> Ezra 9:6

When conscience triggers a warning about a sin we've committed, humility responds in repentance, but pride responds with either denial or apathy. Ezra's humble prayer shows that he was ashamed at what the people had chosen after God had graciously brought them back home. Their blatant sin, marrying people of the surrounding lands and most likely worshiping their gods (Ezra 9:1-2), warranted humble confession and brokenness over sin.

Yet God wanted them to move on. Yes, to confess and repent. But also, to get up and keep living. When Ezra heard about the people's intermarriage, he "sat astonished until the evening sacrifice" (Ezra 9:4). So God sent Ezra another ding.

Shechaniah told Ezra to get up. He called on him to lead the people to make a covenant with God to leave their sin behind.

His words to Ezra are an encouragement for us not to linger in crippling sorrow but to move forward into restoration.

Arise, for this matter is your responsibility.
We also are with you. Be of good courage, and do it.
Ezra 10:4

Confessing sin, turning from it, and moving past it is just as essential to our daily walk with God as realizing that we've sinned. When we mourn over sin, God comforts us with forgiveness and helps us to set things right. So what is the balance of being sorrowful over sin and moving past it?

Keep the Truth Close

Accepting the truth for ourselves not only tunes our alarm system to God's frequency, but it helps us to keep progressing in God's will for us. God's manual of truth details for us the proper sin-removing and sin-avoiding procedures.

If we confess our sins, He is faithful and just to forgive us our sins and to cleanse us from all unrighteousness. (1 John 1:9)

Your word I have hidden in my heart, that I might not sin against You. (Psalm 119:11)

Teach me Your way, O LORD; I will walk in Your truth; unite my heart to fear Your name. (Ps 86:11)

Therefore put to death your members which are on the earth: fornication, uncleanness, passion, evil desire, and covetousness, which is idolatry. (Colossians 3:5)

But now you yourselves are to put off all these: anger, wrath, malice, blasphemy, filthy language out of your mouth. (Col 3:8)

Let the word of Christ dwell in you richly in all wisdom. (Col 3:16)

When we heed what Scripture says—that God forgives us when we repent of our sins—we can confess our sin and then move forward in life. When we heed the ding of conscience and turn from sin to God, we can follow Him more fully. Veering out of lane can be temporary, and the journey God had in mind for us resumes. We just have to heed the ding.

Prayer:

Dear God,
Thank You for giving us an inner alarm system, one that warns of impending danger. Help us to regularly program it with Your word and to take action to avoid colliding with sin. When You get our attention about a sin we've already chosen, help us to see the harm and repent immediately. Help us to move forward and travel on Your path once again. You and Your ways are worth choosing. Every time. In Jesus' name, Amen.

Questions:

1. What can hinder us from immediately acting on a "ding" from our conscience?

2. What motivations help us to respond immediately?

3. God wants us to be broken over our sin, first to see our need for Jesus and accept Him as our Savior, and second to turn from sin as a habit of life. But He doesn't want us to wallow in guilt. Read Hebrews 10:19-25, and answer these questions.

    a. According to v.19, why can we enter "the Holiest" or God's presence?

    b. In v.21, what role of Jesus made closeness to God possible?

    c. Read Hebrews 9:11-12 to see what sacrifice Jesus offered as our High Priest, so we could draw close to God.

    d. In Hebrews 10:22, what does God want us to do?

    e.   What four things does He want us to do in v.23-25, indicating He doesn't want us to stay paralyzed in guilt?

4.   How do we sustain a change in our hearts once we have mourned over sin and moved forward?

    a.   What strategy does John 15:4 give?

    b.   What keys to walking in God's ways are given in John 15:9-12, and why are these helpful?

    c.   How else can we cooperate with God's renovation process in our hearts and not stall it?

*All Scripture verses are taken from NKJV.

Not Easily Yanked
by Katy Kauffman

My cat was an only child. Sam came into my life when I was nine years old. No collar, no known owner, no siblings. My family adopted him, and he was our kitty for eighteen years. Since he was the only pet in the house, you might think he was lonely or his play time was diminished. Not at all. I was there.

I could easily yank his chain. At almost any time of day (except when he was in a deep sleep), I could draw Sam into a game of cat-and-mouse. No, I wasn't the mouse. Well, only when we played hide-and-seek. With a feather, string, flash light, laser, hair, or other small apparatus, I could steal his attention and pull him into a chasing game. His green eyes grew intense, and he couldn't resist. His gray paws usually claimed their target, and whatever I was holding found its way between his teeth. Satisfied with his victory, Sam then returned to whatever sunbathing or explorative activity he had been doing.

Do You Have a Long "Chain" or a Short One?

Is your chain easily yanked? Not into a cat-and-mouse game of feathers and strings, but into a battle of words and egos? Into an enticing debate or challenge? My chain used to be too short, easily yanked. It can be hard to resist a good debate. But I discovered that instead of upholding the truth, I ended up arguing to prove I was right. We have a tendency to put up a fight when our "honor," rights, or egos are on the line. Maybe that's why Jesus included meekness in the Beatitudes.

> *Blessed are the meek, for they shall inherit the earth.*
> Matthew 5:5 NKJV*

I used to cringe when I remembered Jesus' blessing on the meek. I resisted giving up a "good" fight. I didn't understand that the meek don't give up their power to "win" in order to be godly—they give up using their power to harm. Sometimes that involves saying nothing or returning an insult with calm words. Their chain isn't easily "yanked by ego or temper into reacting with ungodliness."[1]

> The meek don't give up their power to "win" in order to be godly—they give up using their power to harm.

Why Is Having a "Long" Chain Worth It?

You would have to be almost super human not to ever let your chain be yanked into saying or doing something that would hurt God's reputation or your own. We need God's help to be meek. But when we do resist being yanked into an ungodly reaction, we gain *the earth* (Matt 5:5) or "the land."[2] Jesus' phrasing refers to how the Jews would express "any great blessing."[3] Their longed for promise of old was possessing the promised land. In the New Testament, such a reference can refer to great spiritual blessings.

Meekness keeps us in a right relationship with God. Since the land in the Old Testament often represented a relationship in good standing with God, we can reason that choosing to be meek reaps a right relationship with Him today, a longed for inheritance that is worth the self-restraint. When we let an opportunity pass by to get angry and react in ungodliness, we honor the One who has the most patience, grace, and endurance. We please His Father's heart, and we become more trustworthy in our relationships and God-given assignments. God can trust us to watch our words and actions and do what's right even when it takes some self-restraint. We don't interrupt our closeness to Him to "let someone have it."

We get our joy and sense of self-worth not in triumphing over others in our words and agendas, but in belonging to the great King whose agenda is always love.

How Do We Become a Master of Resistance?

There was no hope for my cat, Sam. He couldn't resist a yummy piece of string. But in our daily lives, the more we choose love over self, the more we will be able to resist a yummy argument or indulging in deceptively "joyful" revenge. When a situation warrants that someone do or say something and God gives us a green light, we keep ourselves under His leadership. Because He loves us, He will help us to know what to say or do, and He will fight on our behalf if need be. We can count on Him to set things right, either in our response or in the outcome of the situation. Nothing escapes His notice. God's love and help are our powerful allies when we choose meekness over ungodliness.

When we value God's purposes over selfish ones, it will help us win the inner battle and resist an outer one. When we remember that His mission is to save the world, we will value people as He does and be on guard not to hurt our testimony or His work in their lives. We will look for opportunities to say helpful words and not hurtful ones. We will take small offenses in stride or talk in private to the person causing the harm. We will appeal to our authority or leader when someone won't listen to our concerns or when a matter needs to be addressed, and we will depend on God to work what is right or fitting on our behalf.

We Have a Master Teacher

A major part of heart renovation is learning how to respond to people as Jesus does. When He was here on earth, Jesus knew when to say something to address an offense and when to take hurts in stride. He knew when action was warranted. He cleared the temple of those who were using it for monetary gain, and He exposed the hypocrisy of the religious leaders who were hurting the people instead of helping them. Yet He also bravely and quietly faced betrayal, ridicule, beatings, scourging, and the cross so He could die for our sin in our place. Jesus is the perfect combination of strength and meekness. Of zeal and restraint. Love for God and people governed everything He did, and does.

Since Jesus lives within us, never to leave, we can draw from His grace and wisdom every day to respond to difficult situations with godliness. Since Jesus spent three years in close company with the man who betrayed Him, we can learn from Him how to be meek. Since He overcame the temptation to get even with Judas or with the leaders who arrested Him, we can depend on Him to choose love and honor over revenge in our circumstances. Since He bore our sins on the cross, we can gratefully draw close to Him and find strength to forgive others when we are wronged. With Jesus' help, our chain becomes more locked into place by His wisdom, example, and leadership.

Prayer:

Dear Lord,
Thank You for bearing with me when I say hurtful words and do something that causes You or someone else pain. Please help me to depend on You to be meek when it's not easy and to take difficult situations in stride. Help me to be mindful of Your purposes and be a part of the good work You are doing in people's lives. Work in my heart to decrease the power of ego and temper, and to increase the power of love and self-restraint. In Your name I pray, Amen.

Questions:

1. When someone is trying to start a debate or an argument, what wisdom does Scripture give us?

2. How would the other character qualities found in the Beatitudes help us to restrain our words and actions to stay within godliness—humility (poor in spirit), mourning over sin, hungering and thirsting for righteousness, mercy, purity of heart, or peace-making?

3. Read Colossians 3:8-14, and answer the following questions.

    a. In verse 8, what are we supposed to "put off"? Which one might serve as the "first domino?"

    b. In verse 10, what helps us to put off the "old man" (v.9) and put on the "new man" (v.10)?

    c. In verse 12, what are we supposed to "put on"? What do these qualities have in common?

    d. In verse 13, what is a motivation for putting on these things?

    e. In verse 14, what is the crowning glory of how God wants us to relate to others?

    f. How much do you desire to have that crowning glory in your own life? How have you seen it change your life and others' lives?

*All Scripture verses are taken from the NKJV.

1. Kauffman, 43.

2. Albert Barnes, *Albert Barnes' New Testament Commentary*, quoted in Phil Linder, *Power Bible CD*, CD-ROM (Bronson, Mich.: Online Publishing, Inc., 2007), Matthew 5:5.

3. Ibid.

Yearning for More
by Connie Wohlford

I didn't realize I was in serious trouble until we consulted the ranger at the Indian Gardens ranger station. She instructed my husband, Guy, to have me immediately lie down on the ground under the water faucet and cool down my body.

As the cold, mountain spring water splashed onto my forehead, Guy repeatedly filled a container and soaked me from head to toe. This went on for several minutes—until the headache and dizziness subsided.

As instructed, I then lay on a picnic table to allow my body to rest and continue recovering from heat exhaustion. Guy and our sons, ages thirteen and fourteen, spent those two hours exploring the campground and relaxing in the shade. The small grove of cottonwoods and evergreens provided the only large trees we had seen since stepping onto the trailhead of Bright Angel Trail that morning at six o'clock.

The sun had pounded us all day as we made our way into the Grand Canyon, winding downward until we reached the swiftly flowing Colorado River. Though we each drank lots of water and ate proper trail food, it seemed that thirst never left me. My body yearned for life-giving water. I was thirsty.

We had passed through Indian Gardens on the way down and by the time we made it back there on our ascension, I knew I needed to rest a while. I was extremely tired and was suffering with a headache and lightheadedness.

As the ranger explained, I needed extra water to hydrate the cells of my body, regulate my body temperature, and rejuvenate my leg muscles, which felt as though they might give way. I had to recover before continuing the final three miles of the climb back up to the canyon rim.

I craved water. My body was crying out for rest, adequate food, and water.

In like manner, our spirits yearn for the life-giving meat and the living water of God's Word, and of Jesus Himself. When we hunger and thirst for the things of God, He abundantly provides.

Our spirit-man is like a dehydrated person, in need of life-giving—life-sustaining—water. We need living water to carry nourishment to our spiritual beings, just as we need water to lubricate our joints and bring health to our muscles and organs.

In our natural bodies, a drink of water quenches our thirst and a meal satisfies our hunger. But in a little while, we're thirsty again and hungry again. The same is true for our spirit-man. When we read and study God's Word, we are filled and satisfied, and our spiritual health is built up. But as time goes by, we want more—we need more. So again, we pick up our Bibles and drink the living water and feast on the meat of its truths. We talk to God through prayer and are refreshed by His presence.

Mary of Bethany was a woman who would hunger and thirst for the righteousness and the living water she found in Jesus. Along with her brother and sister, she was a friend and follower of Christ.

On one occasion when Jesus was visiting, she sat at His feet, gleaning all she could from Him—drinking in and feeding on every word He spoke. Mary had come to know that Jesus spoke words of life. She recognized the value of His presence as well as her own need for what He had to give His followers.

Meanwhile, her sister Martha became annoyed and complained to Jesus that Mary was not helping with the serving. She even asked Jesus to tell her to help out.

Jesus gently calmed Martha's frustration, saying,

Martha, Martha, you are worried and troubled about many things. But one thing is needed, and Mary has chosen that good part, which will not be taken away from her. (Luke 10:41-42 NKJV)

Jesus is love, peace, truth, and righteousness; and we see Mary's hunger and thirst for those things, yearning to be fulfilled. Her desire to be near Jesus and soak in His every word overruled everything else in her life that day. Her spirit was hungry and thirsty, and she knew Jesus was the only one who could satisfy her needs.

She was partaking of the abundance spoken of by the ancient prophet, when he said,

Why do you spend money for what is not bread, and your wages for what does not satisfy? Listen carefully to Me, and eat what is good, and let your soul delight itself in abundance. Incline your ear, and come to Me. Hear, and your soul shall live. (Isaiah 55:2-3)

Jesus said, *"If anyone thirsts, let him come to Me and drink. He who believes in Me, as the Scripture has said, out of his heart will flow rivers of living water"* (John 7:37-38). This is what Mary was after.

When we hunger and thirst for righteousness we're yearning for more—more of Jesus, more words of life, more of God's truth and wisdom, more peace and joy, more of the beauty of His holiness, more of pleasing God, and more of being like Jesus.

Prayer:

Oh Lord, I hunger and thirst for Your righteousness. I must have You in order to take hold of the life You have ordained for me. Just as a thirsty deer pants for water, I long for Your refreshing

(Psalm 42:1). And like Mary, I know You are the One who can satisfy. Oh God, thank You for abundant provision of living water and the bread of life, Jesus my Savior. Thank You that I can be so filled with Your righteousness that out of me will flow rivers of living water. I'm so grateful. In Jesus' name I pray—Amen.

Questions:

1. Can you recall a time when you were extremely hungry or thirsty? If so, what caused it?

2. Do you hunger and thirst for righteousness?

    a. If yes, how do you satisfy this yearning?
    b. If no, would you like to?

3. If your answer was yes, how would you encourage someone who answered no?

4. Besides Mary, who else in the Bible hungered and thirsted for the things of God?

5. When speaking of Mary, what do you think Jesus meant by saying, "that good part ... will not be taken away from her" (Luke 10:42)?

6. Write out the following verses:
    John 6:48
    Romans 5:19
    1 Peter 2:2

7. Write a prayer expressing to God your personal thoughts on this lesson.

*All Scripture verses are taken from the NKJV.

Mercy: The Power of a Clean Slate

by Lauren Craft

The road was slick with rain, and my wipers thrashed at full speed. I was in between errands and driving on a road humming with traffic. Up ahead was a winding, downhill stretch. I drove slowly, but I should have slowed down even more.

As I drove around one curve, my car started spinning. I tried to direct the steering wheel, but I was powerless. My vehicle swung into the lane on my left. Then right. Then left again. Cars screeched to avoid my vehicle. The view out my windshield was a blur of moving colors and my heart pounded against my ribcage.

Eventually, I regained control and came to a stop in a turn lane on the far right. It wasn't a busy lane like the others, so I was safe. But my pulse kept sprinting and I could barely breathe. I didn't know if my car was still drivable or not. I didn't even know whether I'd collided with another vehicle. It all happened so fast.

Then I spotted a car in the rearview mirror. A woman in her sixties hopped out and ran beside me. I rolled the window down.

"Are you okay, baby?" she asked. She reached for my hand. The warmth of her skin reminded me of my mother's touch. "I was praying for you the whole time!"

"I think I'm okay," I said, looking up into her brown eyes. "Did I hit anyone?"

"You didn't hit a single car. I couldn't believe it—you were swerving everywhere."

Another car drove around us, giving me a honk and a cold stare.

"Why isn't anyone else stopping?" The woman said as she wiped rain off her forehead.

"*You* stopped," I said.

The kind stranger stayed with me until a policeman arrived to help. I've never forgotten her. She didn't accuse me of going too fast, and she wasn't annoyed at me for disrupting traffic. Instead, she prayed for my safety and ran to me in the rain. It may have been a small thing, but it mattered so much. She showed true, genuine mercy.

In His Sermon on the Mount, Jesus told us to be generous with grace just like that woman—and in doing so, He reminds us of our *own* need: "Blessed are the merciful, for they will be shown mercy" (Matthew 5:7 NIV). Mercy is something we should give freely because we've all needed it ourselves, and we'll need it again.

Mercy can come in many forms, from the everyday to the unusual. If a new employee makes a mistake on the job, mercy speaks encouragement instead of rebuke. If a child breaks a family heirloom, mercy rushes to comfort the child instead of mourning the broken pieces. Instead of seeking an even score, mercy gives love whether it's deserved or not. Mercy says, "It doesn't matter what happened yesterday. Today is a fresh start."

Jesus modeled mercy again and again. One day as He passed through Jericho, He sought out Zacchaeus, a corrupt tax collector who had climbed a tree to see Jesus over the crowds. Jesus walked over to the tree and looked up at Zacchaeus, saying, "Come down immediately. I must stay at your house today" (Luke 19:5).

The townspeople were caught by surprise. "All the people saw this and began to mutter, 'He has gone to be the guest of a sinner'" (Luke 19:7). Mercy was unusual to witness in Jesus' day, and it's rare in our time as well. It's common for friends to avoid speaking for months, maybe years, after an argument. Those in prison are often forgotten by their families. Restaurant patrons speak harshly to servers for forgetting special requests.

Showing mercy isn't easy. We might equate it with being naïve—especially since many receive the gift of mercy only to abuse it. But mercy doesn't mean blindly setting ourselves up to be fooled. It's a posture of the heart. And if we hold back mercy, we hold back one of God's most powerful tools. When someone receives a clean slate, they can move on, not weighed down by their past. Gratitude overflows, and they look forward to doing better in the future. This is just what happened with Zacchaeus. During his visit with Jesus, Zacchaeus said, "Here and now I give half of my possessions to the poor, and if I have cheated anybody out of anything, I will pay back four times the amount" (Luke 19:8).

When we face the choice to show mercy or not, we can remember how life-altering it is. It's the opposite of what the world offers. I can think back to that day my car spun out of control, when one woman's actions stood out. She showed me mercy when others did the exact opposite.

Most importantly, we point others to Jesus when we give mercy. When our sins spin out of control, Jesus is the one that stops and intervenes. He stands by our side, watching over us despite our mistakes and weaknesses. In Him, our past is wiped away. The slate is clean for a new story to be written.

Prayer:

Father, You've given me so many things I never earned. You love me despite my past and give me purpose despite my weaknesses. Despite my sins, You prepare an eternal home for me. Place people in my path that need mercy so I may show them grace and point them to Your heart. Amen.

Questions:

1. Think back to Zacchaeus' change of heart. Has Jesus ever intervened in your life in a similar way?

2. Who's the most merciful person you've ever known? How can you follow his or her example?

3. Is there a right way and a wrong way to show mercy? How so?

4. When has someone given you mercy, and how did it influence you?

5. Who in your life needs mercy? How can you give them encouragement or love?

* All Scripture verses are taken from the NIV.

Soap Bubbles for the Soul
by Katy Kauffman

I walked onto the beach and stood in awe. It wasn't the white-capped waves that captured my attention or the small flock of pelicans that flew nearby. It was the soap bubbles.

The ocean was edged with soap bubbles, or what looked like them, as if God were cleansing the waters. White foam stood at attention along the beach, a reminder of what "clean" looks like. I played tag with the waves for a little bit, and then stepped into a foamy mound. My toes didn't feel it as much as my heart did. Clean. A sense of being made new, washed, set right. "Clean" is a refreshing word, and it is a reality usually achieved through hard work and care. It takes hard work to keep a house clean. How much more our hearts.

Is "Pure in Heart" Even Possible?

Just as it seems impossible to keep an entire ocean clean, it can seem impossible to keep our hearts pure all the time. Yet Jesus adds "pure in heart" as a condition for happiness and blessing.

Blessed are the pure in heart,
for they shall see God.
Matthew 5:8 NKJV

Blessed are those who are "free from wrong thinking, corrupt desires, and impure motives."[1] Happy are those who are free from the stain and misery of sin. The blessing that they receive is seeing God Himself—understanding more of who He is because they learn how to think as He does, in purity and holiness. Drawing close to Him without any sin or guilt reminding them that they can't. Knowing Him like never before and walking life's road with Him. "Pure in heart" is free from the gunk that makes us hesitant to draw close to God and serve Him, free from those ways of thinking, feeling, and acting that hurt our relationships. "Pure in heart" makes us clean lanterns through which God can shine His light of love and truth.

> "Pure in heart" makes us clean lanterns through which God can shine His light of love and truth.

While God's word makes it clear that purity of heart is a reality to strive for, it also clearly states that sin is an ever present reality, even in the believer's life. First John 1:8 testifies to the impure nature of the human heart—*If we say that we have no sin, we deceive ourselves, and the truth is not in us.* Even the apostle Paul, a champion of truth and righteousness, agonized at the war he felt in his heart between the law of God and the sinful ways of human nature. In Romans 7:24, he said, *O wretched man that I am! Who will deliver me from this body of death?* As long as we are attached to these human bodies, we will feel the pull of sin. When we depend on ourselves more than God and want our way instead of His, we will give in to it. So how can we stay pure?

Just as the waves continually lap onto shore and retreat into the ocean, bringing with it sand and shells, the word of God rushes into our hearts when we study it and pulls away the gunk and grime of everyday living. The Lord who spoke the sacred words of the Sermon on the Mount is the same Lord who today cleanses His church with the truth. "With the washing of water by the word" (Ephesians 5:26), Christ keeps His bride pure. When we obey the truth that we read, study, and hear, our souls are purified (1 Peter 1:22). Staying clean is no longer an improbability in a world filled with sin, guilt, and shame. It can be a reality as we stay close to the Cleanser of our souls and Renovator of our hearts. It can be a daily reality of continual cleansing and renewal.

How Does "Pure in Heart" Act in Everyday Life?

More of God and less of me. More of love and less of selfishness. As God renovates our hearts to be more like His, He not only cleanses away the bad, but He replaces it with the good. He instills in us the right way of thinking, feeling, and acting—His way, in His likeness—so that what we give out is not self-centered but God-centered. "Pure in heart" is a heart centered on God, fueled by His own character, mindful of His purposes in the world. Pure hearts are needed in our day to direct people's attention to the quality of God's love, to the strength of His character and goodness. When we say yes to a pure heart and choose love over selfishness, we will become better ambassadors for God and draw people to Him.

Have You Washed Your Soul Today?

Whatever deadlines and schedules call for our attention, whatever temptations pull at our hearts, let's take time each day to be in God's word and talk with Him. Let's allow His truth to wash over our souls and cleanse them from the dirt we've accumulated by walking in the world. Let's deliberately set our minds on things above, and allow the truth of God's word to transform us. Just like the waves that continually wash over the beach, God's "waves" of truth and lovingkindness cleanse us day by day. Then purity won't be an ideal that's out of reach, but a reality that we possess and treasure.

Prayer:

Dear Lord,
Cleanse our hearts from the gunk that clogs our relationships with You and others. Use Your truth to transform who we are so that more and more we choose Your way over sin. Build purity within us, and continually renew and strengthen it. May it become easier to refuse the sin that pollutes our hearts and to embrace Your way of thinking, feeling, and acting. In Your name, Amen.

Questions:

1. What kinds of distractions can keep us from being in God's word on a daily basis?

2. What motivations to be in His word are more powerful than those distractions?

3. In what environment does your heart feel the cleanest—at home, at church, on vacation, or somewhere else?

4. Besides taking in God's word, in what other ways can you cooperate with God to purify your heart?

5. If you were to pick the top three people in the Bible who had the purest hearts (besides the Father, Son, and Spirit), who would they be?

6. What can we admire about them?

7. How can we practice those character qualities in our daily lives?

*All Scripture verses are taken from the NKJV.

1. Kauffman, 43.

Avoid the Trap Stick
by Connie Wohlford

Avoid the "trap stick" if you want to be a peacemaker.

Picture this: A trap stick is the trigger—usually a wooden stick—of a trap used to catch an animal such as a raccoon. The raccoon touches the trap stick which sets the trap in motion to ensnare the unsuspecting animal.

Differing opinions, varying cultural backgrounds, a lack of understanding, selfishness, and being offended—these are just a few of the "trap sticks" waiting to ensnare us into conflict. If we give in to the triggers of anger, backbiting, and fighting, it will be harder for people to recognize us as God's children.

In His Sermon on the Mount, Jesus encouraged His followers saying, "Blessed are the peacemakers, for they shall be called sons of God" (Matthew 5:9 NKJV). If our desire is to be easily identified as members of God's own family, we must avoid the trap sticks which inevitably appear in our path.

Being offended is one of the easiest trap sticks to trigger and one of the hardest to resist. We become offended (resentful and sometimes vengeful) when someone insults us or treats us harshly. Perhaps someone cuts in front of us in the grocery store line or another adult scolds our child unfairly. A more enticing trap stick forms when our needs and expectations aren't met. When others' shortcomings disappoint us. Being offended can cause a rift between siblings and even the breakup of a marriage. It can be the catalyst to the ending of a friendship or the beginning of a major war between countries.

Minister and bestselling author, John Bevere, calls offense, "The Bait of Satan," in his book bearing that title. He cites the words of Jesus: *And then many will be offended, will betray one another, and will hate one another* (Matthew 24:10). He then cites the resulting progression. "An offense leads to betrayal, and betrayal leads to hatred."[1] He explains that offended people erect walls for protection to achieve self-preservation, even at the expense of others.

> "Christians are protecting their rights, making sure they are not mistreated or taken advantage of by other Christians. Have we forgotten the exhortation of the new covenant? ... Have we forgotten the words of Jesus?"[2]

> *But I say to you, love your enemies, bless those who curse you, do good to those who hate you, and pray for those who spitefully use you and persecute you.* (Matthew 5:44)

Mr. Bevere continues:

> "But now you see how serious the *sin* of offense is. If it is not dealt with, offense will eventually lead to death. But when you resist the temptation to be offended, God brings victory."[3]

As peacemakers, we can each determine in our hearts and minds not to take the bait, so when the trap stick is set, we will not be ensnared by an offense. Instead let's study the Prince of Peace and emulate His peacemaker qualities. In Ephesians, Paul describes how Jesus brought together two people groups, Jews and Gentiles, who had previously been separated.

> *Therefore, remember that you, once Gentiles in the flesh ... were without Christ, being aliens from the commonwealth of Israel and strangers from the covenants of promise, having no hope and without God in the world. But now in Christ Jesus you who once*

were far off have been brought near by the blood of Christ. For He Himself is our peace, who has made both one, and has broken down the middle wall of separation ... so as to create in Himself one new man from the two, thus making peace. (Ephesians 2:11-15)

Jesus brought peace in two significant ways—ceasing from separation and strife, as well as bringing unity through love and a common salvation through His own blood.

Consider these four strategies to help you resist the temptation to offend or to be offended, and instead, to be a peacemaker.

1. **Sow love.** "Above all, love each other deeply, because love covers over a multitude of sins" (1 Peter 4:8 NIV). Often we need to ask God to help us love others, and if we mean it, He'll really do it. I know that from personal experience. We can also resist the temptation to say and do things that will offend others. After all, why would we want to set a trap that would contribute to the downfall of another?

2. **Be a good example.** Others are always watching—whether it be children in our sphere of influence, other believers, or non-believers who need to see Christ in us. With Jesus as our example, we in turn become examples to others.

3. **Remember God is at work in situations.** God loves to work behind the scenes to bring His desired end. Be confident that God takes care of us and we don't have to demand our own rights or have our own way all the time. Not participating in heated discourse makes room for our Lord to step in and work things out. We might even be surprised by the positive outcome when issues are resolved His way.

4. **Study Jesus.** He is the ultimate Prince of Peace. He exemplified love and all of the other attributes of God the Father, including forgiveness. If Jesus could forgive those who crucified Him (Luke 23:34), and if He could forgive each of us of all our sins, then we can learn to forgive others. Forgiveness is an indispensable component in peacemaking.

In getting to know Jesus on a personal level and with the help of His indwelling Holy Spirit, we can exhibit the attributes of our Father and be called the sons and daughters of God. We can live out Hebrews 12:14 which says, "Pursue peace with all people, and holiness, without which no one will see the Lord."

I want to be blessed and I want to be known as God's child. Don't you?

Prayer:

Heavenly Father,
Thank You for calling me to be a peacemaker, and I praise You for sending Your dear Son, Jesus, the Prince of Peace, to be my example. Please help me to be mindful of ways I can be a better peacemaker, and help me recognize times when Your Shalom needs to be infused into a situation. I also ask that You help me avoid the snare of offense both as a receiver and a perpetrator. Through the power of Your Holy Spirit, I will seek to be the peacemaker You desire for me to be. In the name of the Prince of Peace I pray, Amen.

Questions:

1. Besides offense, what are other things that cause rifts between people?

2. In addition to sowing love and setting an example, list ways we can step into a situation and be a peacemaker.

3. Read 1 Peter 3:8-11, and answer these questions about the passage.

    a. In v. 8, what mindset are we to have toward other believers?

    b. In v. 9, what are we to return to others even if they do evil to us or revile us?

    c.   In v. 10-11, what should we turn away from, and what should we seek instead?

    d.   In v. 12, why?

4.   In Romans 12:18, what is the qualification for living peaceably with all people?

5.   When someone isn't willing to make peace with us, what should we do?

6.   Do you consider yourself a peacemaker? Explain your answer.

7.   Prayerfully list ways you can grow in your role as peacemaker.

*All Scripture verses are taken from the NKJV unless otherwise indicated.

1. John Bevere, *The Bait of Satan: Living Free from the Deadly Trap of Offense* (Lake Mary, Florida: Charisma House, Charisma Media/Charisma House Book Group, 2004), 19.
2. Ibid.
3. Ibid, 19-21.

Persecution in Modern Times

by Evelyn Wells

If the world hates you, keep in mind that it hated me first. If you belonged to the world, it would love you as its own. As it is, you do not belong to the world, but I have chosen you out of the world. That is why the world hates you. Remember what I told you: "A servant is not greater than his master." If they persecuted me, they will persecute you also. If they obeyed my teaching, they will obey yours also. They will treat you this way because of my name, for they do not know the one who sent me. (John 15:18-21 NIV)

Modern-Day Martyrs

If you try to hang on to your life, you will lose it. But if you give up your life for my sake, you will save it. (Luke 9:24 NLT)

Rachel Scott "was the first of 13 people—twelve students and one teacher—killed at Columbine on April 20, 1999, and was singled out because of her Christian faith. While she sat on a patch of grass, eating lunch with her friend, 18-year-old Eric Harris and 17-year-old Dylan Klebold approached her, shooting her three times. After realizing Rachel was still alive, the killers returned and asked her, 'Do you still believe in God?' She answered, 'You know I do,' whereupon he replied, 'Then go be with Him,' and shot her in the head."[1]

Rachel's brother, Craig Scott, hid under a table in the library after a teacher ran in and told everyone to get under their desks.

He was under the table with his best friend, Isaiah Shoels, who was singled out and fatally shot, leaving Craig unharmed underneath the table. Later, Craig learned Rachel was one of those killed that day.[2]

Craig finally was released from his anger toward the shooters during a trip to Africa and a chance meeting with a man who had lost seventeen members of his family during apartheid. Since that trip, the Scott family has begun a charity known as "Rachel's Challenge," which works toward reducing violence in schools around the world. This family chose to bring good out of the devastation of their tragedy.[3]

In an evening Bible study class on June 18, 2015, nine church members died a senseless death, as a young man who was visiting the class opened fire on them. The church's pastor was among those who were killed.[4] It was said that the shooter had sat with them for an hour before he began his shooting spree.

This is shocking to those of us who feel safe and secure in our churches. It is hard to grasp the fact of this happening in America. But it did. And it could happen again. Just as we have a God who loves us, we have an enemy who hates us.

What Is Christian Persecution?

According to Open Doors USA, Christian persecution is hostility experienced because of a person's identity as a Christian.[5] Persecution can take the form of verbal harassment as well as hostile action. They also reported that around the world every month, 255 Christians are killed, 66 churches are attacked, and 160 Christians are detained and imprisoned without trial.[6] We hear of children being prohibited from expressing "Merry Christmas" at school during the holidays, older adults in senior centers being prohibited from praying before a meal, and even religious symbols being removed, such as crosses and nativity scenes.

If we live godly lives, we can expect to be persecuted. *"Yes, and all who desire to live godly in Christ Jesus will suffer persecution"*

(2 Timothy 3:12 NKJV). Christians represent around one-third of the world's population. According to various news reports in the last few years, there is a "war on religion" in America. In our culture of political correctness, any mention of Jesus as the only way to heaven, is viewed as exclusivity. Our Biblical stance on subjects such as abortion, homosexuality, and even calling God "Father" often result in violent words or actions. Because we are believers in Jesus, we bear the brunt of extreme criticism. *"Blessed are you when people insult you, persecute you and falsely say all kinds of evil against you because of me"* (Matthew 5:11 NIV).

It is estimated that more Christians have lost their lives in the last one hundred years due to persecution than in all the centuries of church history combined—over 900,000.[7] A joint report by Texas-based Liberty Institute and Washington-based Family Research Council reports that "anti-Christian persecution is on the rise in America."[8] They say government agencies around the United States are "trying to push Christian expression out the door."[9]

How Are We to Respond?

Christians throughout the centuries have held to their faith in Jesus Christ. As believers who love Jesus and care about people's eternal well-being, we can hold fast to our faith and pray for all those in Christian service, including the members of our own church. Let's intercede for missionaries around the world who face danger and death every day, and take a stand in our daily lives for Jesus, the Savior of the world.

Those who have given their lives for the sake of Christ throughout the centuries have shown great character in the face of their persecution. They have counted the cost of suffering for Jesus and have not been found lacking in their faith. All of the original disciples were hunted down, beaten, and persecuted. Most of them lost their lives, as well. During the Middle Ages, many Christians were burned at the stake whose only crime was wanting the Bible to be available to all people, when only clergy had access to the Word and kept it under lock and key.

Of course, the real enemy isn't the terrorist with a weapon or the government official who wants to silence the voice of one proclaiming Christ. They have been deceived by our real enemy, Satan. Let us remember the merciful heart of Jesus who went to the cross to bear persecution for us.

We may never be asked to die for Jesus Christ, but if we love Him, we'll live for Him.

> We may never be asked to die for Jesus Christ, but if we love Him, we'll live for Him.

Prayer:

Dear Heavenly Father,
Teach us to pray effectively for persecuted believers, missionaries around the world, our churches, and the leaders in our city, state, and country. In the name of Jesus, Amen.

Questions:

1. Have you ever experienced persecution for your faith? If so, what was your reaction?

2. Are you more motivated to pray for persecuted Christians after reading this article? What specific things can we pray for them?

3. Would you like to be a member of a prayer group which focuses on praying for missionaries around the world?

4. "Prayer walking" is a great way to intercede for our churches, schools, and communities. Prayer walks are taken by individuals and prayer groups, who actually go to a site to intercede for the individuals who attend or work there. How important do you think prayer walking could be in a school zone?

5. If you could start a ministry in your church to help persecuted Christians, what would it involve?

6. Let's look at persecution through the lens of Scripture.

    a. What does Matthew 5:10 call those who are persecuted for righteousness' sake?

    b. What is theirs?

    c. What does Matthew 5:12 say that we should do when we are persecuted for Jesus' sake?

    d. Why?

1. Leah Marianne Klett, "I'm Not Ashamed" Movie Star, on Playing Rachel Scott, Her New Devotional, and Texting Sadie Robertson (Interview), https://www.christianpost.com/sponsored/im-not-ashamed-movie-star-on-playing-rachel-scott-her-new-devotional-and-texting-sadie-robertson-interview.html.
2. Stephanie March, US School Shooting: Legacy of Columbine High School Massacre 19 years Later, www.abc.net.au/news/2018-03-23/columbine-high-school-massacre-19-years-later/9577858.
3. Ibid.
4. "Charleston church shooting," Wikipedia, https://en.wikipedia.org/wiki/Charleston_church_shooting.
5. "Christian Persecution," https://www.opendoorsusa.org/Christian-persecution
6. Ibid.
7. ChristianPost.com, "Nearly 1 million Christians reportedly martyred for their faith in last decade," foxnews.com/world/2017/01/17/nearly-1-million-christians-reportedly-martyred-for-their-faith-in-last-decade.html) missing page 4/18/18
8. Michael Card, Persecution of Christians on Rise. www.wnd.com/2012/09/persecution-of-Christians-on-rise; Faith Under Fire, Persecution of Christians on Rise – in-u.s./
9. Ibid.

In Closing:

Building Now, Investing in a Legacy

In Closing: Building Now, Investing in a Legacy

by Katy Kauffman

I stepped into the ninety-year-old house, anxious to discover the beauty within. The biggest foyer I had ever seen in a "lived-in" home greeted me. (Only the Biltmore rivaled this house in my opinion.) Its grand staircase was crowned on the second floor by a wooden banister that went all the way around the two-story opening. I immediately thought this place could be a splendid bed and breakfast. Spacious rooms with high ceilings and beautiful windows flowed from the foyer. Their tall entryways beckoned me and my mom to enter. In the dining room I pictured Thanksgiving guests gathered around the table, feasting, laughing, and catching up on family news.

The kitchen looked too ordinary for a house of this age and splendor. Except for the carriage door. It was several times the width of a normal door and slid open to the side across a massive bar. It was large enough to allow horse-drawn carriages to unload passengers at the back entrance or to receive deliveries from wagons carrying milk, ice, and food.

Oh, the stories we could have written in such a setting. Perhaps the milkman fell in love with the homeowner's daughter. Each time he delivered milk, she heard his wagon and ran downstairs to see him. He left himself just enough room between his wagon and the door to jump through the opening and say good morning to her. It could have happened.

Our adventure of discovery continued. Gorgeous woodwork and slim pocket doors made me want to stay longer than our welcome. We found more sizable rooms upstairs, each large enough to serve as a bedroom and study.

Most likely lovers of history, the owners of this house had taken prestigious care to preserve its beauty. Since they had, it would be a treasure for future generations to come.

The godly character we build now is an investment in our legacy. Walking in godliness will bless not only those living around us now, but also generations to come. Those within our reach of influence—our children and grandchildren, those we teach or minister to, and others—will have reason to know more about God and how life with Him works.

> Every time we deal with hidden sin in our hearts, we become better able to live for God.

Every time we deal with hidden sin in our hearts, we become better able to live for God. The more we deal with our bad habits now, and the motivations, attitudes, or values that cause them, the less likely we'll have to deal with something similar in our children. Instead of passing along ways of thinking or acting that will harm them, we can pass along what flows from a renovated heart.

What kind of character do you want influencing the course of your life and affecting others? Until the day we step into heaven, God is building our characters to be like His, and we are building a legacy to leave behind. May we never stop the renovation process because it becomes too hard or it costs too much. May we remember that our godliness doesn't affect just ourselves, but it can bless others now and later.

Dr. David Jeremiah once shared a memorable epitaph[2] that summarizes what happens when believers go to heaven. It is also a fitting ending for this Bible study on constructing godly character:

End of Construction
Thanks for Your Patience

Prayer:

Dear God,
Thank You for being faithful to build godly character within us, and for giving us the strategies, principles, and motivation to cooperate with You. Thank You that Jesus left behind the perfect legacy of godliness, one that has been preserved in the words of Scripture and inscribed on the hearts of believers. Help us to pass along the truth we've been given and the love that we have been shown in a legacy that flows from a true heart renovation. In Jesus' name we pray, Amen.

Questions:

1. Which of the studies in this book have seemed like a special message of encouragement or hope to you?

2. In what ways may that message influence your character and the way you relate to the people around you?

3. Which of the studies have something in them that you would like to incorporate into the legacy that you leave behind for your kids, grandkids, or others?

4. Has God helped you to discover, or to deal with, any hidden problems that were lurking beneath the surface?

5. Have you tried any of the strategies in this book, and they worked for you?

6. What is one of your main takeaways from this study?

1. Dr. David Jeremiah, *Overcoming Confusion with Wisdom*, Shadow Mountain Community Church in El Cajon, California, March 25, 2018.

Contributing
Authors

Contributing Authors
In Alphabetical Order

Cherrilynn Bisbano is a speaker, teacher, and writer. She is a Volunteer Associate Editor at *Almost an Author*, and has written for several online magazines. Her ministry is to encourage her brothers and sisters in Christ to be all that God created them to be. She has been married for 18 years and has one son. You can connect with her at her blog: truthtoshine.blogspot. com.

Julie Coleman is a popular conference and retreat speaker. She holds an M.A. in biblical studies. Her award-winning book, *Unexpected Love: God's Heart Revealed through Jesus' Conversations with Women*, was published in 2013 by Thomas Nelson. Julie is the managing editor for *Arise Daily*. She is the mother of four and grandmother of six. More on Julie can be found at unexpectedgod.com.

Penny Cooke is a Certified Biblical Life Coach and writer. She has led in women's ministry and taught Bible studies for over 25 years. Penny is a contributor to *The Wonders of Nature* devotional (Worthy Inspired, 2016). She has written for CBN. com, Thoughts-About-God.com, and *Blessed Living Women's E-Magazine*. She also enjoys offering encouragement and hope through her blog, www. pennycookesblog.blogspot.com

Billie Corley, founder of Growing Girls, Gals, and Grannies, believes God's Word is the answer to life's challenges. She presents sound Biblical truths through her writing and speaking. Her passion can be summarized in her ministry's slogan, "Seeking to Teach, Inspire, and Encourage Women Everywhere for Jesus Christ." Billie resides in Georgia with her husband, Ben. For more information, visit www. billiecorley.com.

Lauren Craft loves writing about abundant life in Christ (John 10:10), filled with purpose, joy, and lasting hope. She has been blessed with opportunities to serve as a missions leader in her church, share the gospel around the world, aid in Bible translation, and work as a magazine and book editor. Connect with her at www.laurencraftauthor.com.

Jennifer DeFrates is a blogger and speaker who shares the inspirational lessons God teaches in the daily life of a military spouse, adoptive parent, homeschooling mom, and passionate follower of Christ. She writes about the power of seeing God in the mundane bits of her life and how He transforms her daily at *Heaven not Harvard* (http://heavennotharvard.com).

Trina Dofflemyer has served as an adjunct professor of Biblical studies, leadership mentor, retreat leader, and writer. She currently serves in an apologetic ministry and loves all things theology, hiking with family, reading, and drinking tea. Connect with her on Twitter at https://twitter.com/TrinaDofflemyer.

Rosemarie Fitzsimmons is a retired Marine Corps gunnery sergeant and displaced Rhode Island native living in Northern Virginia with her husband Jerry. As *The Portrait Writer*, she writes about God's touch through the lives of everyday heroes. She has ghostwritten two books, *Caged Sparrow*, and *From the Remnants*, true stories of the wonderful, yet unexpected ways God brings light from darkness. Connect with her at https://rosethestoryteller.com.

❀

Ron Gallagher, author of *Right Side Up Thinking in an Upside Down World*, is a gifted storyteller and humorist, church consultant, featured speaker, and columnist. His ministry includes weekly blog articles addressing relevant topics from a Biblical perspective, producing study materials for Bible classes, and contributing regularly to *Refresh Bible Study Magazine*. Connect with him at www. GallaghersPen.com.

Karen Griffin enjoys challenging women to be transformed by the living Word. Having successfully homeschooled three children, she now encourages other women through mentoring and conference speaking. Her greatest desire is to help the bride of Christ make herself ready for His return (Rev 19:7). Learn with Karen at www.karengriffin.blog.

Author of *Holy in the Moment: Simple Ways to Love God and Enjoy Your Life*, Ginger Harrington is an award-winning blogger, speaker, and ministry leader of *Planting Roots: Strength to Thrive in Military Life*. Enjoy Ginger's writing at www.GingerHarrington. com, *Planting Roots*, *LightWorkers*, *Guideposts*, *(in) courage*, *The Praying Woman*, and *For Every Mom*.

Beebe Kauffman is a co-founder of Lighthouse Bible Studies, LLC, the Chief Editor of *Refresh Bible Study Magazine*, and the award-winning author of *Isaiah: Setting Things Right*. Her latest Bible study (2018) is a book of application for every book, chapter, and paragraph of the New Testament called, *A Whole Lot of Wonderful—Application of the New Testament for Today*.

Katy Kauffman is a Bible teacher, an award-winning author, and a co-founder of Lighthouse Bible Studies. She is an editor and a designer of *Refresh Bible Study Magazine*. Her Bible studies for women focus on winning life's spiritual battles. She loves spending time with family and friends, making jewelry, and finding the best peanut butter cookies. Connect with her at www.lighthousebiblestudies.com.

Because Rick Kauffman is a lighting engineer, his boss told him to "go light the world." That's his mission in ministry, too. Rick is a co-founder of Lighthouse Bible Studies, which he started with his wife Beebe and daughter Katy. Visit www.lighthousebiblestudies.com/rickkauffman to see his speaking topics and teaching series. He is working on his first book, a Bible study for men on 1 Kings.

Lisa Kibler is a writer who lives with her God-sent kitty, Lewis, in Kent, Ohio. She is a member of the Jerry Jenkins Writers Guild and is president of the Kent chapter of Word Weavers International. She is a core team member of the new Tree City Church. Interact with her at www.lisakibler.com.

Jenifer Kitchens is a full time wife and homeschooling mother, and a passionate writer and teacher. She desires that every project glorifies her Lord and Savior Jesus Christ. A graduate of Union University, Jenifer now lives in Columbia, Tennessee with her husband Jacob and her two daughters (and son who is on the way). Follow Jenifer at www.dirtydishwaterholyhands.wordpress.com.

Julie Lavender and her husband David are parents of four and in-laws to one. Although she is a former teacher, Julie's favorite career was homeschooling mom. Julie writes for *Guideposts* and newspapers, authored *365 Days of Celebration and Praise* and *Creative Sleepovers for Kids,* and contributed to *Chicken Soup* and magazines like *Refresh, Clubhouse, Southern Writers, Focus on the Family,* and *Mature Living.* Follow at https://julielavender.blogspot.com.

Patricia Luellen Nicholas is a lover of God's word. After the death of her husband and her father, she sought God's comfort and grace. She found it in 2 Corinthians 12:9 (NASB)—"My grace is sufficient for you." She now writes Bible studies and contemporary romance. She loves to share God's grace with others. She lives in the mountains of North Carolina. Connect with her at http://www.hissufficientgraceministries.com.

Dawn Owens is an award-winning author, speaker, radio show host, and nonprofit executive who is passionate about helping people learn how to live worthy of the call they have been purposed to in Christ Jesus. Learn more about Dawn's ministry, books, and podcast at www.dawnmowens.com.

Katherine M. Pasour is an author, teacher, and speaker with a passion for wellness! She seeks to nurture others in their journey to achieve and maintain better health. Her Bible studies and blog focus on developing a closer relationship with Jesus and making lifestyle choices for a healthier and happier life in service to our Lord and Savior. Connect with her at https://www.katherinepasour.com.

Denise Roberts loves good food shared with friends at the kitchen table, slobbery dog kisses, doing life with her husband, being a mom to grown-up kids, and encouraging others to connect the life-giving and life-sustaining Word of God at that messy place where faith and life intersect. Connect with Denise at www.deniseroberts.org.

Patty Schell constantly looks for opportunities to show hospitality to others, loves serving her community, and enjoys getting to know new places and cultures. Through these activities, God reveals His stories of faith, hope, and love; and she means to tell others about them every chance she gets. You can see what she's up to at her award-winning blog *Girl on Adventure* at https://pattyschell.com.

Lyneta L. Smith is an award-winning author and freelance editor who regularly writes for inspirational and Christian publications. She and her husband live as happy empty nesters near Nashville, Tennessee. She blogs regularly at www.lynetasmith.com.

Barb Syvertson is passionate about God's Word, nature, art, and children. Her writing incorporates these themes into Bible studies and devotionals. She can be contacted at BarbSyvertson@gmail.com.

Jeannie Waters delights in offering encouragement through writing and speaking. She writes for *Refresh Bible Study Magazine,* and she has contributed to *Breaking the Chains* (Lighthouse Bible Studies) and devotional books. Jeannie teaches ESL and enjoys time with family and friends and just-for-fun hiking. Visit Jeannie at www.jeanniewaters.com for ideas on Brightening Someone's Day.

Laura W. Watts is a pastor's wife, speaker, Bible teacher, and writer who works full-time as the CFO for the SC Department of Revenue. A country girl at heart who loves coffee, the outdoors, and Jesus. She is co-founder of Full Course Ministries with a mission to help individuals connect with God in spirit, mind, and body. Follow Laura on www.fullcourseministries.com.

Evelyn Wells is passionate about glorifying God through her writing which includes devotions, short stories, articles, and creative nonfiction. She enjoys a good book, her two cats, traveling, and especially spending time with her children and grandson. She participates in short-term mission trips, both domestic and international. You can connect with Evelyn on Twitter (@venable_wells).

Adria Wilkins writes and speaks about how what's in our "box" called life is often unexpected. After suffering the unthinkable—death of three-year-old Blake—Adria found that Jesus sustains and even surprises His followers with joy. She is writing a book called *Joy Box Stories.* Connect with her at https://www.joyboxstories.com.

Jean Wilund is a writer, Bible teacher, and speaker, passionate about coffee, comedy, and Christ. She blogs at www.JeanWilund.com to encourage people to love God and His Word and laugh while doing it. She lives in Lexington, South Carolina with her husband, Larry. Their children live scattered across the country.

Encouraging individuals to deepen their intimacy with God is Connie Wohlford's passion. A former public-school teacher, she has written Bible studies and curriculum for adults and children, has published children's books and a devotional, and has had articles published. She edits for ministry publications and enjoys speaking for civic and church events. Connie and her husband, Guy, live in the mountains of Virginia. Connect with Connie at https://www.facebook.com/ConnieWohlfordAuthor/.

Leader Guide

Leader Guide

Heart Renovation is a compilation of short Bible studies about constructing godly character. They use stories, principles, strategies, and application of Scripture, all based on the analogy of house renovation. They help us to know what God's part is in this process and what our privilege and responsibility is. These studies provide a blueprint for what godly character looks like in daily life and an instruction guide for how to construct it.

Our authors are not only Bible study teachers, writers, and speakers, but believers who have discovered effective strategies for growing in Christlikeness and for overcoming the hidden problems of heart renovation.

A Flexible Study

This book can be adapted to fit any time frame. The whole study can be divided into thirteen weeks—a week of introduction and twelve weeks of Bible study.

If you don't have thirteen weeks available, you can decide which chapters to cover, or give your group members a survey (included at the end of this guide) to see what their topics of interest are.

The Thirteen-Week Plan

If you have a full thirteen weeks, use the schedule below. The studies usually take about five to ten minutes to read, which makes them great for part of a daily quiet time. Answering the questions will provide a good basis for discussion when you come together as a group.

> Session 1: Use this time to get to know each other, have someone read "Introduction: Renovation Needed," and discuss the questions at the end. Remember to give the reading assignment for the next session.

<u>Reading Assignments for</u>:

Session 2: Read Week 1 on Repairing the Hidden Problems of Character.

Session 3: Read Week 2 on Hidden Problems.
(Look for the following symbol to find where Week 2 starts: ⌒)

Session 4: Read Week 3 on Constructing Character that Overcomes Life Issues.

Session 5: Read Week 4 on Life Issues.

Session 6: Read Week 5 on Blueprints of Character: People in the Bible.

Session 7: Read Week 6 on Christ: The Model of Godly Character.

Session 8: Read Week 7 on Construction Zone: Helping Our Children to Grow in Godly Character.

Session 9: Read Week 8 on Our Children.

Session 10: Read Week 9 on Craftsman at Work: The Fruit of the Spirit.

Session 11: Read Week 10 on the Fruit of the Spirit.

Session 12: Read Week 11 on Building in Blessing: The Beatitudes.

Session 13: Read Week 12 on the Beatitudes and In Closing.

Discussion Questions for Session One

During the first session, discuss the questions at the end of the Introduction, plus any of the ones below. The following questions preview the book's sections. If you aren't going to cover the whole book, pick the appropriate questions for your teaching plan.

1. What do you think are some of the hidden problems of growing in godliness?

2. Of the issues that come up in life, such as money problems or difficult relationships, what are some of the most difficult to handle?

3. What aspects of godly character do we need in order to deal with them?

4. Which men and women in the Bible stand out to you as godly examples to follow, and why?

5. What reassures you about Jesus' character?

6. Part of this book discusses the Beatitudes and the Fruit of the Spirit. Let's see which of these character qualities you admire the most.

   a. Let's read Matthew 5:1-12.

   b. Based on what you know already about these characteristics, which one do you need the most right now, and why?

   c. Now let's read Galatians 5:22-23.

   d. Which one of these do you think Christians in America need the most?

   e. What about Christians around the world?

   f. Which one do *you* need the most?

   g. Which one can be the hardest to practice?

7. Let's close our time with two passages in 1 Corinthians Chapter 3.

   a. Could someone read verses 9-11?

      i. What, or Who, is the foundation of every believer's life?

      ii. Verse 10 (NKJV) calls Paul "a wise master builder." How was he building on the foundation of Christ in believers' lives?

   b. Verse 10 says we should be careful how we build, and verses 11-17 say why. Could someone read those verses for us?

      i. Why should we be careful how we build in others' lives and in our own?

      ii. What does verse 16 call God's people?

      iii. In verse 17, we see that God takes it very seriously when someone hurts His temple, or His people, the church. So we need to be careful and wise builders, and use only the best materials for building godly character in our lives. In addition to the qualities in the Beatitudes and the Fruit of the Spirit, can you think of any other character qualities that would help us to build wisely?

Discussion Questions for Every Article

Choose your group discussion questions from the ones at the end of the Bible studies, make up your own, or use some of the following questions on the topics of the week. Consider how long your group time is, and how well your group usually likes to discuss things.

1. Why is this character quality needed in everyday life?

2. Why is it sometimes hard to practice?

3. How have you seen God help you practice this character quality?

4. What practical help do you see in the article that makes this character quality easier to live out?

5. What instructions or insights does Scripture supply regarding this character quality?

Discussion Questions for the Last Session

Wrap up your last session with the questions at the end of the study called, "In Closing: Building Now, Investing in a Legacy." End your session with a group prayer. Ask your group members to pray one or two sentences based on what they learned from the study. If some group members prefer not to pray aloud, they can simply touch the elbow of the person sitting next to them to keep the prayer going. Pray for wisdom and strength to keep building godly character into your hearts, and thank God for the work He has already done. Thank you for being a part of this study.

We Want to Pray for You

If you use this book in a small group study, email us at lighthousebiblestudies@hotmail.com before your first session begins, and we will pray for your group.

If you are interested in using scrapbooked cards as an activity for your group, visit www.lighthousebiblestudies.com/scrapbooked-bible-study to see examples of the cards and instructions for how to make them.

Don't forget that the last page of this guide has a survey for your group, in case you need to create a lesson plan that is less than thirteen weeks long. God bless you as you participate in the adventure of heart renovation.

Grateful for our Master Builder and His character of love,
Katy Kauffman and the Lighthouse team

Heart Renovation Survey

Which topics are you interested in? Which would you like to hear your group discuss? Rate each topic below according to the scale.

3 – Very Interested

2 – Interested

1 – Somewhat Interested

0 – Not Now

Heart Renovation Section Topics:

_____ What are the hidden problems of heart renovation?

_____ How does godly character deal with common life issues?

_____ Which people in the Bible serve as parts of the blueprint for godly character?

_____ How does Christ model godly character for us?

_____ How can we help our children to grow in godly character?

_____ How does the Holy Spirit cultivate godly character in us, and what are its facets?

_____ What is it about the nature of the character traits in the Beatitudes, that constitutes a blessing?

Specific Topics:

_____ Two Powerful Tools for Heart Renovation

_____ Growing in Self-Control

_____ Dealing with Hidden Sin

_____ Conquering Perfectionism

_____ Learning to Accept Change Well

_____ Dealing with Loss

_____ Handling Money Wisely

_____ Overcoming Loneliness

_____ Finding Joy in Work

_____ Dealing with Difficult People

_____ Keeping a High Priority on God's Word

_____ Motivation to Forgive

_____ Becoming a Godly Leader

_____ Becoming More Like Jesus

_____ How to Teach Your Kids to Pray

_____ What to Do When Your Children Suffer

_____ How to Avoid the "Helicopter Parent" Syndrome

_____ How to Build Your Kids Up in Godly Character

_____ How to Teach the Bible to Your Kids

Bibliography

Barnes, Albert. *Albert Barnes' New Testament Commentary*, quoted in Phil Linder, *Power Bible CD*, CD-ROM. Bronson, Mich.: Online Publishing, Inc., 2007.

Bevere, John. *The Bait of Satan: Living Free from the Deadly Trap of Offense*. Lake Mary, Florida: Charisma House, Charisma Media/Charisma House Book Group, 2004.

Clarke, Adam. *Adam Clarke's Commentary*, quoted in Phil Lindner, *Power Bible CD*, CD-ROM. Bronson, Mich.: Online Publishing, Inc., 2007.

Family Bible Notes, quoted in Phil Lindner, *Power Bible CD*, CD-ROM. Bronson, Mich.: Online Publishing, Inc., 2007.

Kauffman, Beebe. *A Whole Lot of Wonderful—Application of the New Testament for Today*. Buford, Georgia: Lighthouse Bible Studies, 2018.

Newman, B.M and P. C. Stine, *A Handbook on the Gospel of Matthew*. New York: United Bible Societies, 1992.

Owens, Dawn. *Like Me or Not*. Nashville, Tenn.: Worthy Publishing, 2018.

Pierce, Larry. *The Online Bible*, CD-ROM. Winterbourne, Ontario: Larry Pierce, 2007.

Webster's New World College Dictionary, 4th ed. Cleveland, Ohio: Wiley Publishing, Inc., 2008.

Zodhiates, Spiros. *The Complete Word Study Dictionary: New Testament*, electronic ed. Chattanooga, Tenn.: AMG Publishers, 2000.

Connect with Us
We would love to hear from you!

The mission of Lighthouse Bible Studies
is to connect people to God
through His Word.

E-mail us at
lighthousebiblestudies@hotmail.com
to subscribe to our free online magazine,
Refresh Bible Study Magazine.

Visit us at
lighthousebiblestudies.com.

Find us on:
Facebook: Lighthouse Bible Studies
Facebook: Refresh Bible Study Magazine
Twitter: @KatyKauffman28

CPSIA information can be obtained
at www.ICGtesting.com
Printed in the USA
FFOW04n0540160518
46680094-48774FF